Snapshots of Great Leadership

LEADERSHIP: Research and Practice Series

A James MacGregor Burns Academy of Leadership Collaboration

SERIES EDITORS

Georgia Sorenson, Ph.D, Research Professor in Leadership Studies, University of Maryland and Founder of the James MacGregor Burns Academy of Leadership and the International Leadership Association

Ronald E. Riggio, Ph.D, is the Henry R. Kravis Professor of Leadership and Organizational Psychology and former Director of the Kravis Leadership Institute at Claremont McKenna College

---

Bligh-Riggio (Eds.), *Exploring Distance in Leader-Follower Relationships: When Near is Far and Far is Near*

Howell, J. P., *Snapshots of Great Leadership*

Snapshots of Great Leadership

Jon P. Howell

Professor Emeritus, New Mexico State University

College of Business

Routledge
Taylor & Francis Group

NEW YORK AND LONDON

First published 2013
by Routledge
711 Third Avenue, New York, NY 10017

Simultaneously published in the UK
by Routledge
27 Church Road, Hove, East Sussex BN3 2FA

Routledge is an imprint of the Taylor & Francis Group, an informa business

Library of Congress Cataloging in Publication Data
Howell, Jon P.
    Snapshots of great leadership / Jon P. Howell.
    p. cm — (Leadership: research and practice ; v. 2)
    1. Leadershi—Case studies. I. Title.
    HM1261.H69 2012
    303.3'4—dc23
    2012005619

ISBN: 978-0-415-62482-4 (hbk)
ISBN: 978-0-415-87217-1 (pbk)
ISBN: 978-0-203-10321-0 (ebk)

Typeset in Garamond and Optima
by EvS Communication Networx, Inc.

Printed and bound by CPI Group (UK) Ltd, Croydon, CR0 4YY

To my sweetheart, Julie.

Contents

Table

Series Foreword

Leadership is a very popular topic, with hundreds of research articles and dozens of scholarly books published each year. Much of this scholarship, however, is focused narrowly on business leadership. Our intent with this new book series, *Leadership: Research and Practice*, is to expand the boundaries and include scholarly work from the wide range of disciplines and professions that study and practice leadership. In addition to business leadership, you will see authored and edited books from political science, the humanities, psychology, sociology, the arts, and importantly, the professions. We will publish scholarly collections, but also practical guidebooks that are soundly based in research.

We are very pleased to present one of the first books of the series, Jon P. Howell's *Snapshots of Great Leadership*. There is a long history of presenting stories of leaders and their great challenges as a way of illustrating leadership theories and concepts, and it remains a favorite approach in teaching about leadership. In fact, this is the way that the study of leadership began many centuries ago, with stories of the exploits and qualities of mythic leaders from Greece and the Orient. Jon Howell continues this tradition, and updates it, with this exceptional collection of stories of great leaders, some well known, others less so. These cases of leaders and leadership are indeed brief snapshots, but each is clearly embedded within leadership theory, so this book is readable, practical, and scholarly.

While *Snapshots* contains stories of great historical leaders (e.g., Churchill, Gandhi, Lincoln), there are more contemporary leaders included such as Mary Kay Ash and Mark Zuckerberg, and some who are relatively unknown. In addition to the great leaders who championed positive social change and led nations to greatness, there are snapshots of bad leaders and leadership (e.g., Hitler, Idi Amin). This suggests that we can learn a great deal from the good and successful leaders, but also learn what we, as followers of leaders, and leaders ourselves, must avoid.

While we fully expect *Snapshots of Great Leadership* to appeal to scholars and to anyone interested in the serious study of leaders and leadership, we also anticipate that this book will make its way into many classrooms. It is an ideal reader or casebook for any course that touches on leadership, and students will find it an exciting way to learn about leadership theories and applications. The Editors would like to thank Jon Howell for being one of the first authors of our book series, starting it off in such fine fashion, and Anne Duffy, our Editor at Taylor & Francis, for her extraordinary efforts to bring this book series to fruition.

Georgia Sorenson
University of Maryland

Ronald E. Riggio
Claremont McKenna College

Preface

The idea for this book has a long history. I have taught leadership in university classes and conducted research on leadership for over 30 years and I have managed private business organizations for over 40 years. I used several different leadership textbooks in my teaching, including a book I coauthored with Dan Costley titled *Understanding Behaviors for Effective Leadership* (2nd ed., 2006, Pearson Prentice Hall). Most leadership textbooks focus on leadership theories and the research that supports them while our text addressed leadership behavior patterns—what leaders really do to influence followers toward effective performance. In our book and in several other texts, brief descriptions of real leaders in action were included to demonstrate how the leaders enacted the leader behaviors and theories. When using these textbooks in class, I noticed that most students remembered the real leader action descriptions more vividly and accurately than the leadership theories or behavior patterns. Students repeatedly mentioned the real leader examples in class discussions and when answering essay questions on examinations.

I finally realized that the majority of students were learning about leadership in a different manner than most leadership professors taught. Professors usually describe different leadership theories or behavior patterns and the research supporting them, occasionally followed by real life examples of leaders who exemplify the theories or behaviors. But most students learning about leadership seemed to begin with the stories of real leaders in action. These stories grabbed their attention and sparked their interest in learning about leadership behaviors or theories that help explain the real leaders' success. This realization, after many years of teaching leadership, resulted in this book with its focus on stories of great leadership.

This book may be most useful as a supplement to be used with other leadership textbooks in a college or university level leadership class. The main core of this book is contained in Chapters 2–26 that provide descriptions (Snapshots) of individuals who demonstrated great leadership. The Snapshots describe how the leaders influenced their followers to achieve amazing feats—such as building an international organization to successfully serve the poorest of the poor, or creating and running an incredibly successful high-tech business organization, or preserving a nation from being permanently split apart by a disastrous civil war, or developing and leading a long lasting organization to successfully help individuals overcome addiction. These Snapshots also include descriptions of the leaders' background, other life experiences, and the environmental context in which they worked. This contextual information often helps explain the leaders' behavior and why they had such amazing effects on followers and others.

This book also includes in Chapter 1 brief descriptions of major leadership theories that are described in detail in most leadership textbooks. A matrix (Table 1.1) is provided following the theory descriptions to indicate which theories address aspects of the leaders' behavior in each Snapshot. In addition, after each Snapshot is a brief description of how that leader's behavior and characteristics reflect the different leadership theories in Chapter 1. This is designed to help students connect the actions of real outstanding leaders with existing leadership theories. I expect that instructors will use the Snapshots as cases to introduce a specific leadership theory or behavior pattern. The cases may be discussed and analyzed by students in class with the instructor's guidance—explaining how the leaders enacted the leadership theories. This might be followed by a lecture or reading assignment with a more thorough explanation of the theory or behavior pattern the instructor prefers to emphasize. After several guided sessions, lectures and reading assignments, students should begin to connect the leaders' actions with leadership theories on their own. This will begin to make the theories "come alive" as real descriptions and prescriptions of outstanding leadership.

Also included in Chapters 27–31 are five Snapshots of bad leadership. These leaders are sometimes judged by scholars or historians as immoral or evil (examples are Adolf Hitler or Idi Amin) or simply incompetent (examples are Ken Lay or Al Dunlap). These bad leaders also had very strong influence on their followers, but the outcomes were disastrous for followers and many others. The Snapshots of bad leadership are also related to leadership theories and are useful for students to compare with great leaders to facilitate their understanding of how leaders can go wrong.

For leadership students who are using a separate leadership textbook, the theory descriptions may be repetitious and unnecessary. However, there may be theories described in this book that are not covered in some textbooks. For readers who are not reading this book for a college or university class and who have no interest in leadership theories, Chapter 1 can be skipped. Some readers may simply learn best about leadership from real life examples, rather than from abstract theories.

Jon P. Howell
New Mexico State University

Acknowledgments

Numerous individuals provided invaluable assistance in completing this book. First and foremost, my wife Julie was irreplaceable as an editor and advisor throughout the project. My colleague Peter Dorfman provided advice regarding my choice of leaders to be included. My editor at Taylor and Francis, Anne Duffy, was supportive throughout the project. And numerous experts gave valuable time and effort to reviewing earlier versions of the manuscript and providing important feedback for the book. These reviewers are listed below:

Ronald E. Riggio, Henry R. Kravis Professor of Leadership and Organizational Psychology, Claremont McKenna College

Sharon Clinebell, Assistant Dean, University of Northern Colorado

James Weber, College of Business, St. Cloud State University

Georgia J. Sorensen, James MacGregor Burns Academy of Leadership, University of Maryland

Don Jung, Yonsei University, Korea

Jagdeep Chhokar, formerly Indian Institute of Management

Leanne Atwater, University of Houston

References and Source Material for this Book

I used two types of source material for this book. For the leadership theories, I made extensive use of my class notes from over 30 years of teaching leadership. Of course, my teaching reflected a myriad of leadership books and journal articles I have read over the years, but the actual copy for this book was written from my own understanding and teaching of these theories over the years. No copy was taken from other sources.

For the descriptions of great leadership, I consulted biographies, journal articles, and web-based sources that addressed different aspects of the leaders' lives. My strategy in researching and writing the leadership descriptions was to first consult web-based sources to obtain general information about a leader. I then consulted what appeared to be the best sources cited in those web articles and followed the reference trail to find biographies that were widely cited as outstanding sources for each leader. Once I had read and made notes on each leader, I wrote the description reflecting my own interpretation of the leader's actions and how they related to theories of leadership. These leadership descriptions and interpretations are my own and are not taken directly from any single source. No authors' quotations or written copy was taken from any of the references used for this book. The only quotations used are brief sayings or statements by the leaders themselves or their followers. All sources used are cited in the references at the end of each chapter.

About the Author

Jon P. Howell is Professor Emeritus of management in the College of Business at New Mexico State University (NMSU). He received his MBA from the University of Chicago and his Ph.D. from the University of California at Irvine. He taught and conducted research on leadership for 31 years and was previously the Bank of America Distinguished Professor of Management. He received awards for excellence in teaching and research at NMSU. Professor Howell has published a leadership textbook titled *Understanding Behaviors for Effective Leadership* (2nd edition, 2006, Pearson Prentice Hall) as well as numerous book chapters and articles in the *Academy of Management Journal, Academy of Management Review, Leadership Quarterly, Organizational Dynamics, Journal of Management, Journal of International Business Studies, Journal of World Business,* and other journals. He has received awards for his research from the Society of Industrial and Organizational Psychology, Academy of Management, the Center for Creative Leadership, and the Global Leadership Advancement Center. He served on the editorial board for *Leadership Quarterly* and *Journal of World Busin*ess. He is a country co-investigator on the Global Leadership and Organizational Behavior Effectiveness (GLOBE) Project which was led by the late Robert House of the Wharton School, University of Pennsylvania. His primary research interests are leadership and followership, substitutes for leadership, and leadership across cultures.

Part I

Theoretical Basis of Leadership

Chapter 1

Theories of Leadership

This is a book of stories. Most of the stories describe great leaders who accomplished amazing feats such as creating, preserving, or changing a nation or industry, or saving a group of people from exploitation or annihilation. A few of these stories describe bad leaders who brought destruction or death to scores of people. In retrospect, the disastrous effects of these bad leaders are no less astounding than the incredible accomplishments of the great leaders. Although the goals of these individuals were often quite different, the leadership processes they used were frequently similar. In relating stories of these leaders, I have described who they were, what they accomplished, and how they did it. I have referred to existing leadership theories to help explain their leadership tactics and behavior as well as their effects on others. The use of these leadership theories will hopefully make the leaders' impressive effects more understandable and will clarify how the theories relate to leadership in action.

Scholars have developed theories of leadership to help understand and explain how leaders affect the organizations and people they lead. Organizations are simply groups of people working together in a cooperative and coordinated effort to achieve some goals. Based on research, leadership theories generally focus on specific leader characteristics and/or behavior patterns that are important in shaping societies and organizations over time. Different scholars have focused on separate leader characteristics and behaviors, resulting in numerous distinct leadership theories being proposed and researched. The most popular theories are described in well-accepted leadership textbooks, and these theories are briefly summarized in this chapter. For students of leadership, this chapter may repeat information they previously studied. For the reader without this background, this chapter may provide a framework to help the reader understand how the great and bad leaders described in this book shaped and changed the societies and organizations they led.

A definition of leadership seems appropriate at this point to give readers an idea of what is described in this book. Leadership is an influence process, usually (but not always) carried out by one person. The leader influences a group, who view the influence as legitimate, toward the achievement of some goal or goals. The leader may utilize many different strategies to influence followers' efforts toward goal achievement. She might describe a desirable vision of the future that includes a mission with inspirational goals to be achieved, she might offer rewards to followers when they achieve the goals, or she might encourage followers to participate with her in setting desirable goals and strategies as a means of gaining followers' ownership of the goals and their commitment to achieve them. These are all examples of leaders influencing followers to achieve goals, which is the essence of leadership. *Snapshots of Great Leadership* describes how different leaders used these and other strategies to lead their followers in achieving outstanding results.

Trait Theories

Through much of the 20th century, most people believed that great leaders were born, not made. We now know that leadership is complex and not simply the result of one or more personal characteristics of an individual. Over 100 years of research on personal characteristics of leaders (often called *leadership traits*) failed to demonstrate that any single trait or set of traits make a person a great leader. Leadership traits are characteristics of an individual that do not change from situation to situation, such as intelligence, assertiveness, or physical attractiveness. Literally hundreds of studies were carried out on scores of different traits and many traits were identified that *may help* an individual become an effective leader in *specific situations*. However, the key traits for one situation may be different for another situation. The following set of categories summarizes the mass of trait research and encompasses the most important leadership traits found in research.

Determination and *drive* encompass traits such as initiative, energy, assertiveness, perseverance, masculinity, and occasionally dominance. Individuals with these traits work long hours, pursue goals with a high degree of energy and perseverance, are often ambitious and competitive, and may dominate others. *Cognitive capacity* includes intelligence, analytical and verbal ability, behavioral flexibility, and good judgment. Individuals with strong cognitive capacity are able to integrate large amounts of information, formulate strategic plans, create solutions to complex problems and adapt to changing situations. Great leaders such as Steve Jobs and Abraham Lincoln clearly exhibited the determination and drive as well as the cognitive capacity to persevere and deal effectively with their complex changing environments.

Self-confidence includes the traits of high self-esteem, assertiveness, emotional stability, and self-assurance. Self-confident individuals believe in their own capabilities and judgments, they do not hesitate to act on their beliefs, and they project their self-confidence onto others to build trust, respect, and commitment among followers. *Integrity* describes individuals who are truthful, trustworthy, principled, consistent, dependable, loyal, and not deceptive. Leaders with integrity are honest and open, they keep their word, adhere to generally accepted principles of behavior, and share common values with followers. Winston Churchill and Nelson Mandela demonstrated self-confidence, integrity, and determination to persist with assertive and principled behavior in achieving their goals.

Sociability describes individuals who are friendly, extroverted, tactful, flexible, and interpersonally competent. Sociable leaders like to interact with followers and others, they adapt their behavior effectively in social situations, and they are diplomatic when solving problems and relating to other people. Mother Teresa and Laymah Gbowee were highly sociable, determined, and showed amazing integrity in their diplomatic dealings with influential individuals outside their organization.

Despite problems with the early trait research, these categories of leadership traits appear to be helpful for effectiveness in many situations. Few great leaders possessed all the important leader traits, but these leaders all demonstrated characteristics that were essential to succeed in their situation. Leadership traits themselves do not cause an individual to emerge as a leader or to become a great leader. The key traits for a specific leadership position make it more likely that a leader will take effective action by demonstrating needed leadership behaviors in the situation. A leader who is sociable and controls her emotions will likely be effective at providing needed encouragement and interpersonal support for followers during stressful, threatening episodes that sometimes occur in organizations. Leaders who are intelligent, original, and assertive are more likely to create and instill an inspiring vision and mission for the organization. Leaders who are self-confident, assertive, and energetic will be comfortable in providing directive leadership for followers in solving difficult job or organizational problems. Specific leadership traits can clearly be important preconditions for effective leadership behavior. When a leader possesses the traits needed for a specific position and reflects those traits in her behavior, she is more likely to obtain the trust, respect, and cooperation needed from others for effective group or organizational performance.

Early Behavioral and Contingency Theories

In the 1950s, several university based research programs began to focus on identifying the most effective behavior patterns of leaders. At first, these programs sought to identify one or two behavior patterns that characterized all effective leaders. This was later described as the "one best way" approach to leadership effectiveness. After numerous investigations, they identified two behavior patterns that seemed especially important. The different researchers used several labels for these two behaviors. One was called *consideration, relationship orientation, concern for people,* or *supportive leader behavior* and included showing a concerned and caring attitude toward followers, being friendly, encouraging followers' feelings of personal worth, and supporting efforts to develop their capabilities. The second leader behavior pattern was called *initiating structure, task orientation, concern for production,* or *directive leader behavior* and emphasized a focus on task accomplishment by clarifying followers' roles and the leader's expectations of followers. This often included goal setting or setting performance standards, assigning tasks, scheduling, and explaining rules and procedures. These two leadership behavior patterns became the basis of several leadership theories developed over the next 25 years.

The Leadership Grid

One such theory that became popular with consultants was the Managerial Grid, later renamed the Leadership Grid, which was developed by Robert Blake and Jane Mouton. This model includes the two leader behavior patterns described above in a two dimensional coordinate system that provides a grid-like representation of different levels of *concern for people* and *concern for production*. Concern for production is represented on the horizontal axis and concern for people is on the vertical axis. Five distinct leadership styles were described by Grid developers, depending on the amount of each leader behavior a leader demonstrates in her/his behavior.

Consultants who emphasize the Grid use questionnaires to obtain scores for each leader on the two behavior patterns, allowing leaders to plot their own position on the Grid. Working with the consultants, leaders presumably determine how they can adapt their style to improve their leadership effectiveness. Grid developers maintain that *Team Leadership,* which describes leaders who are high on both concern for people and concern for production, is the most effective style. Despite its popularity with consultants, research shows no single leadership style is best for all situations. Grid developers recently acknowledged this and describe some leaders as shifting styles over time, but maintain that most leaders have a single dominant style. The Grid developers do not describe different situations as requiring different leadership styles.

The Contingency Theory of Leadership

Another leadership theory that was developed about the same time emphasized the same two leader behavior patterns. The Contingency Theory of Leadership, developed by Fred Fiedler, labeled these two behaviors *task oriented* and *relationship oriented* leadership and included a unique questionnaire for measuring these behavior patterns. It was more complex and realistic than the Grid theory, in that it specified that the most effective combination of the two leader behavior patterns must fit the situation to be most effective. No single level of task and/or relationship oriented leadership was effective for all situations.

Fiedler described three important situational characteristics that determined which combination of the two behavior patterns was optimal. These situational characteristics were the *leader's power* to control rewards and punishments for followers, the *quality of the relationship* between the leader and her followers (that is, are followers friendly and cooperative with the leader), and the clarity of *task structure* for followers (that is, are the task goals, procedures, and measures of their performance clearly specified). Fiedler rated situations as high or low on each of these three factors. The three were then combined to classify a situation as favorable or unfavorable for the leader. If the situation reflected high leader power, good leader-member relations, and high task structure, then the situation was considered highly favorable to the leader. A moderately favorable situation might include a poor leader-member relationship, high position power, and high task structure or some other combination of high and low scores on the situational factors. A very unfavorable situation had a poor leader-member relationship, low leader power, and low task structure.

The Contingency Theory predicted that a leader's style was either task oriented or relationship oriented. A leader could not be both task and relationship oriented, although Fiedler later added a *socio-independent* leadership style that was apparently medium on both leader behaviors. Task oriented leaders were predicted to be most effective in highly favorable or highly unfavorable situations. Relationship oriented leaders were most effective in moderately favorable situations. Socio-independent leaders were predicted to be effective in very favorable situations.

Fiedler and his associates believe that leaders have a predominant style and attempts to change this style are unrealistic. They suggest that if a leader is ineffective, his style does not match the situation and he should be moved to another situation that is more appropriate. If this is not possible, the leader's situation could be modified to fit the leader's style. A training program was developed to teach leaders how to assess their own style and the situation, and to modify the situation to improve their effectiveness. The Contingency Theory has been researched extensively with conflicting results, but it has many advocates among practicing leaders.

The Situational Leadership Theory

The Situational Leadership Theory, developed by Paul Hersey and Ken Blanchard, also emphasized the same two leadership patterns which they recently renamed *directive* and *supportive* leadership. Their model is presented in a two dimensional coordinate system similar to the Leadership Grid. However, the Situational Leadership Theory asserts that the most effective leadership style must match the situation. In this sense, it is similar to the Contingency Theory, but Hersey and Blanchard describe a very different situational factor as important for the leader to consider. They point to the *followers' maturity and readiness to perform* as the key factor the leader must evaluate as she adjusts her leadership style. Followers with a low level of maturity and readiness are described as unable and unwilling to work on their own, requiring a *telling* leadership style that is highly directive with little supportiveness. Followers who are high in maturity and readiness are both willing and able to work on their own and require a *delegating* leadership style, with little direction or support by the leader. Followers who are in between low and high on maturity and readiness, require different combinations of directive and supportive leadership. Although the Situational Leadership Theory has been popular with consultants, perhaps because it is easy to understand, it has not received strong support from researchers.

Directive and supportive leadership are basic behaviors for leadership and most great leaders reflect one or both of these behaviors in some form. When the United Farm Workers Union members were threatened and exploited by growers, the great labor leader, Cesar Chavez, became highly directive with union members to organize a quick response. He also developed a credit union for union members, participated in picket lines and marches, and provided strike funding and other activities that reflected his supportive leadership. Steve Jobs was extremely directive with his employees as he demanded they produce ever smaller computers with additional features within unreasonable time constraints.

Fiedler's Contingency Theory and the Situational Leadership Theory are both considered contingency theories because they assert that the most effective style must fit (is contingent on) the situation. Fiedler's model is unique in assuming leaders cannot adapt their style to the situation. Although the three models described above all focus on leaders' behavior, today they are generally considered overly simplistic because they fail to consider other important leadership behaviors needed for effective group and organizational performance.

Advanced Behavioral/Contingency Theories

The Path-Goal Theory

The Path-Goal Theory was first developed by Bob House and his colleagues in the early 1970s as a contingency approach that included a more inclusive set of important leadership behaviors than earlier approaches. In addition to the traditional *directive* and *supportive* leadership behaviors, it included *participative* and *achievement oriented* leadership. Participative leader behavior involves encouraging followers' input for decision making with the leader concerning operations of the group, and consulting with followers by asking their opinions, and building consensus. Achievement oriented leader behavior involves encouraging followers to strive for excellence by setting high performance goals, continually seeking improvement, and showing confidence in followers. This behavior pattern formed a basis for later charismatic theories. Numerous situational factors were proposed in this theory to modify the effectiveness of specific leader behaviors. When followers' work tasks are not clear and the methods for successful performance are uncertain, then directive leadership is said to be especially effective. When organizational members are faced with deadlines, their organizations are threatened with intense competition or their tasks are dangerous then they generally appreciate and respond well to a supportive leader who sympathizes with their situation and shows a friendly caring attitude. When organizational members are highly competent and their work tasks require creativity and cooperation, then a participative approach by the leader encourages input from all members to develop the best solution to their demanding tasks. And when constant improvement and excellence in performance is critical to success, achievement oriented leadership behavior may be needed.

Path-Goal Theory is based on two major assumptions that may limit its effectiveness in some situations. It assumes that people are motivated to perform well because they expect some type of favorable reward. The outcome may be money, a promotion, an award or a positive feeling of accomplishment, but the favorable outcome is personal to the follower who experiences it. This theory also assumes that people are rational in their deliberations regarding how much effort they expend on a specific task. They will only perform well if the effort seems reasonable for the expected outcome. These assumptions of rationality and exclusive self-interest are limitations because people are sometimes motivated by emotional appeals, symbolic behaviors (such as self-sacrifice by the leader), or their own self-image.

In the 1990s, Bob House developed a Reformulated Path-Goal Theory that added several other leader behavior patterns to the model. The new leader behaviors included *work facilitation* (providing resources, developmental experiences, and mentoring), *interaction facilitation* (resolving conflicts, encouraging collaboration and teamwork, and facilitating communication), *representation* (advocating for the group, obtaining resources, and defending the group from criticism), *charismatic leader behavior* (inspiring followers, engaging their identities in the group effort, and increasing follower self-image through identification with an outstanding group), and *shared leadership* (developing followers' abilities to assume leadership roles within the group). Several of these leader behaviors address *group* performance, which was not specifically included in the original theory.

Path-Goal Theory has been researched with mixed results. For example, supportive leadership is often found to be effective under stressful conditions as predicted, but is also found effective under most other conditions. Directive leadership improves performance in many studies, but not always in the situations predicted by the theory. Research on participative and achievement oriented leadership in this model is very limited and inconclusive. The complexity of the *Reformulated Theory* makes it difficult to test its predictions but the new leadership behavior patterns it identifies are clearly important for individual and group performance.

The Multiple Linkage Model

The Multiple Linkage Model is another sophisticated contingency theory developed in the 1980s by Gary Yukl. This model describes how several leader behaviors affect intervening variables which are essential for group or organizational performance. Examples of these intervening variables include the degree of followers' understanding and commitment to their work tasks, their training, and ability to complete those tasks, the organization of the work, the adequacy of cooperation and team effort to complete the groups' tasks, availability of resources needed for the task, and degree of coordination with other groups needed for successful organizational performance.

The essential leader behavior patterns in the Multiple Linkage Model have been modified over the years, but an unusually complete list was provided in Yukl's excellent textbook. Leaders are described as *supporting and helping* with follower development, *consulting and delegating* tasks to followers, *recognizing and rewarding* followers, *clarifying and monitoring* task performance, *motivating and inspiring* followers, *planning and organizing* the work tasks, *problem solving and informing* followers of needed information, and *representing and networking* for the group with higher ups and other groups. This latter behavior is currently referred to as a type of *boundary spanning*.

This model also describes situational and follower characteristics that influence the leadership process. Some characteristics may *neutralize* a specific leadership behavior by making it ineffective. This can occur when a large spatial distance between leaders and followers can make leaders' efforts at clarifying and monitoring task performance ineffective. Other characteristics may *substitute* for particular leader behaviors, making that leadership pattern unnecessary. This occurs when a professional, trained and committed work force requires little or no clarification or motivational efforts by the leader. These employees are already motivated and capable of completing their tasks effectively without input from their leader. This aspect of the Multiple Linkage Model was adapted from Substitutes for Leadership Theory which is described later in this chapter.

This model suggests that the leader's primary role in the short run is to fill in for deficiencies in the intervening variables, and in the long run to modify situations to improve the intervening variables. Like other contingency models, the Multiple Linkage Model describes effective leadership as requiring a pattern of leader behaviors that fit the group or situation. Research findings on this model are sparse, but existing studies of individual elements in the model show that all the leader behavior patterns are important for group performance.

The Reformulated Path-Goal Theory and the Multiple Linkage Model present a more realistic picture of the activities of effective leaders than the theories described earlier in this chapter. While their complexity makes them difficult to test with empirical research, many great leaders have utilized numerous behaviors specified in these theories. Mother Teresa was a master at motivating and inspiring her followers, as well as boundary spanning with others outside her organization, the Sisters of Charity. Bill Wilson avoided making any major organizational decisions in leading Alcoholics Anonymous, without thorough participation and approval by his group of alcoholic members. And Pat Summitt inspired the Lady Vols basketball team of the University of Tennessee to achieve unprecedented success in women's college sports while supporting and clarifying to her players that hard work and dedication can produce amazing results in all aspects of life. Summitt's numerous boundary spanning activities on behalf of her university are unmatched.

Charismatic Theories

In the 1980s and 1990s the study of charismatic leaders became popular. Previously charisma had been viewed as a mysterious quality some people possessed and was not easily studied by behavioral scientists. Interest in charisma eventually led to new leadership theories being proposed with various labels including charismatic leadership, visionary leadership, value-based leadership, and transformational leadership. The most common versions today are charismatic and transformational leadership, which are very similar and are based on work by Bob House, James McGregor Burns, Bernard Bass, and Bruce Avolio. Charismatic leaders have exceptionally strong effects on followers by appealing to their individual emotions, aspirations, needs, and values. Followers attribute charisma (literally meaning "divine gift") to a leader because s/he seems extraordinary and followers become convinced the leader will help them achieve a noble goal or vision of the future that is more important and desirable than they had previously thought was possible.

Early leadership theories focused on directive and supportive leadership, sometimes supplemented with other task related leadership behaviors and the use of recognition and rewards for good performance. These theories were very rational and were labeled "transactional" by advocates of charismatic leadership. The transaction involves the leader providing guidance, support, and rewards in exchange for followers' efforts and good performance. This simplified description of transactional leadership is often presented in contrast to charismatic leadership. But charismatic leadership also involves a transaction that is more intense and emotional than transactional models. The leader is said to offer an inspiring *vision* or *mission* that transcends typical organizational and individual goals. Through *carefully crafted communications* the leader describes the vision and mission to achieve it and the *critical roles followers must play* to achieve it. The vision *appeals to followers' higher order needs and ideological values*, it "feels right." Followers respond by *identifying with the vision and the leader, believing that together they can achieve the vision*, they put forth *extra effort*, and the *collective goal takes precedence* over their own wants, needs and goals.

Charismatic leaders also act as *role models* for followers and thus embody the principles and ideals that are consistent with their vision and commitment to the vision. Examples are leading protest marches or soldiers into battle or accepting a salary of one dollar a year to save an organization in financial trouble. These leaders convey an *inspirational message* that arouses strong emotions and motivation in followers and increases their identification with the leader and the mission. Examples are Martin Luther King's "I Have a Dream" speech or John Kennedy's famous inaugural address. They *encourage innovative and creative behavior* that includes "thinking outside the box" to create novel solutions to problems. Examples are Steve Jobs of Apple Inc. challenging engineers to make "killer products" that change the world or Mohandas Gandhi advocating peaceful resistance against the British to attain Indian independence. They also exhibit *symbolic behaviors* that demonstrate dedication to the vision and mission and the ideological values they reflect. Examples are self-sacrifices by Mohandas Gandhi who lived under extremely ascetic conditions as he led the Indian movement for independence or Cesar Chavez who turned down well-paying jobs to earn $6,000 per year as leader of the struggling Farm Workers Union.

Charismatic leaders also possess certain personal traits such as a *high need for power* which is the desire to influence and control their environment, often including other people. Need for power may be expressed in two ways. Leaders may dominate others, allow followers little autonomy, and make all the decisions themselves—often called *personalized* need for power. Alternatively, they may build up and support followers to make them more capable and give them autonomy of action to create an organization that influences and controls its environment—often called *socialized* need for power. Although the socialized version of need for power is normally the best leadership strategy in the long run, charismatic leaders emerge with both types of need for power. These leaders also have a *strong belief in the correctness of their own values and motives* and are highly *self-confident*. These theories predict that the leader's vision and mission as well as their behaviors and traits build followers' self-confidence and infuse their tasks with a higher purpose, making their work tasks meaningful and personally satisfying rather than simply asking followers to perform for a specific material reward.

Transformational leadership has become very popular in recent years and includes three charismatic leader behavior patterns described earlier and one behavior pattern from earlier leadership theories. These patterns are labeled *charisma* which is displaying self-confidence and ideological arguments with dramatic emotional rhetoric; *inspirational motivation,* which involves communicating a noble vision and mission and exhibiting symbolic behaviors to model the leader's commitment to the vision; *intellectual stimulation* where leaders encourage followers to challenge the status quo and attack problems using creative and innovative approaches and perspectives; and *individualized consideration,* which includes showing concern and support for individual followers as needed and fostering their future development. Transformational leadership places a stronger emphasis on intellectual stimulation than other charismatic theories and its emphasis on individualized consideration is unique among charismatic theories. Transformational leaders appear to reflect the socialized need for power described earlier. The overall results predicted by this model are similar to other charismatic theories.

Charismatic and transformational theories have removed the mystique from charismatic leadership and identified specific behaviors and traits used by these leaders. Research on these theories often shows the strong effects that some leaders have on their followers. Followers usually like these leaders and identify with them, but the effects on follower performance are mixed when objective performance measures are used. The effects of these leaders on organizational performance are also mixed and uncertain at this time. These theories ignore other important leadership behavior patterns such as participative, directive, and boundary spanning leadership. They often ignore important risks such as the abuse of power by some charismatic leaders, and possible violations of societal expectations and environmental factors. These issues are shown later in this book in the descriptions of bad leaders such as David Koresh and Adolf Hitler. The emphasis in transformational leadership on individualized consideration and socialized need for power may prevent the abuse of power that occurs with some charismatic leaders. Advocates of these theories seem to believe charismatic/transformational leadership is appropriate for all situations—similar to the "one best way" approach of early leadership theorists. Others maintain it is most effective in crises or during times of environmental uncertainty or turbulence. More research is needed to identify conditions under which charismatic/transformational leadership is most effective.

Other Behavioral Theories

Other leadership theories have been developed that focus on specific aspects of the leadership process. Most are not intended to describe all aspects of effective leadership, but they often identify and clarify elements of leadership not addressed or emphasized by the more comprehensive contingency theories.

The Normative Decision Theory of Participation

The Normative Decision Theory of Participation was developed by Victor Vroom, Phillip Yetton, and Art Jago. This theory deals with the degree of involvement of followers in a leader's decision making process—often termed participative leadership. Numerous great leaders used participative leadership including Abraham Lincoln, George Washington, Bill Wilson, and Nelson Mandela. The Normative Decision Theory addresses the issue of *what process a leader should use to make a specific decision.* Should he make the decision on his own, relying on his own knowledge and expertise without input from followers? Should he gather information from individual followers about the decision before deciding himself? Should he hold a meeting with followers to get their help as a group in making a decision? This model identifies multiple ways a leader can involve followers in decision making and tries to identify which approach is best for a given decision situation.

Consistent with other contingency theories, Vroom pointed out that different decision situations facing a leader often require different degrees of follower involvement. This model has evolved over the years, and the following five categories—called *decision styles*—now represent these different degrees of involvement. *Decide*—The leader makes the decision himself, relying on his own expertise and any information he collects on his own. *Consult Individually*—The leader discusses the decision problem with individual followers to obtain their suggestions and makes the decision himself. *Consult Group*—The leader discusses the decision problem with followers as a group to obtain their suggestions, he then makes the decision himself. *Facilitate*—The leader presents the decision situation to the group and acts as a facilitator to obtain group consensus on a solution. He helps the group develop and analyze possible decision alternatives and may specify constraints on the alternative chosen. *Delegate*—The leader describes the decision situation to followers as a group and allows them to generate solutions and to make a decision. The leader provides encouragement, resources and information if requested, but the group makes the decision.

This theory identifies several *situational characteristics* that are used to determine which decision style is best for a given decision problem. These situational characteristics are described in a series of questions to be answered by the leader, using a computer program that allows for identification of the best decision style very quickly. The major situational questions are described here. *Decision Significance*—Is the decision of critical importance to the success of the group's project or organization? *Importance of Commitment*—Is group member commitment to the decision alternative chosen, essential for successful implementation? *Leader's Expertise*—Does the leader possess the necessary knowledge and expertise to make a good decision without follower input? *Likelihood of Commitment*—Is the group likely to commit itself to successful implementation of a decision alternative if it is chosen by the leader without their input? *Group Support for Objectives*—How well does the group support the organization's objectives that may be affected by the decision? *Group Expertise*—How much expertise do group members possess that can be useful in resolving the decision problem? *Team Competence*—How skilled are group members at working together to solve problems?

With this model, the leader must have the authority to make the decision and implement a solution, and there must be an identifiable group of followers who are available to participate in the decision process. The theory specifies four *criteria* for measuring the success of the decision process used. *Quality of the Decision*—Does the decision alternative chosen advance the achievement of group or organizational goals? This criterion is especially important when a decision is significant, and there are a large number of alternative solutions. *Acceptance of the Decision*—Do followers accept the alternative solution chosen and are they willing to commit themselves to implement the decision successfully? Participation usually increases follower commitment for implementation. *Costs of the Decision*—For a given decision problem, are the costs of a specific decision style greater than the benefits? Considerable time is required for group decision making, and this can be costly. *Development of Followers*—Is follower and/or team learning and development an important issue in this decision situation? Participation can build follower competence and improve team skills.

Research on the Normative Decision Theory generally supports its usefulness for leaders and is popular with managers. When leaders use the decision styles recommended by this theory, they usually make more successful decisions. This model is a contingency theory because its recommendations depend on the decision situation, even though it deals exclusively with the degree of participative leadership used by a leader. It is important to remember that this theory tells a leader which decision style to use in making a specific decision; it does not specify which decision alternative is optimal.

The Leader Member Exchange Theory

Another theory that addresses a specific aspect of the leadership process is the Leader Member Exchange (LMX) Theory, which evolved from an earlier theory called the Vertical Dyad Linkage (VDL) Model. Both of these models focus on the interaction between leaders and individual followers. Similar to the transactional approach described earlier, this interaction is viewed as a fair exchange whereby the leader provides certain benefits such as task guidance, advice, support and/or significant rewards and the followers reciprocate by giving the leader respect, cooperation, commitment to the task and good performance. However, LMX recognizes that leaders and individual followers will vary in the type of exchange that develops between them.

Over time, some exchanges between a leader and specific followers become very close, whereas other exchanges may be somewhat distant. This can create *in-groups* and *out-groups* of followers who vary significantly in their effort, commitment, and active cooperation. In-group members are said to have *high quality exchanges* with the leader who perceives these followers as being more experienced, competent, and willing to assume responsibility than other followers. The leader begins to rely on these individuals to help with especially challenging tasks. If the follower responds well, the leader rewards her with extra coaching, favorable job assignments, and developmental experiences. If the follower shows high commitment and effort followed by additional rewards, both parties develop mutual trust, influence, and support of one another. Research shows that in-group members usually receive higher performance evaluations from the leader, higher satisfaction, and faster promotions than out-group members. Great leaders like Ernest Shackleton and Abraham Lincoln developed high quality exchanges with followers, and these close relationships were invaluable in their success.

Time constraints and personal characteristics often result in the leader spending less time with some followers and entering in less intense and more distant exchanges than with in-group members. This can create out-groups whose members have *low quality exchanges* with the leader. In theory, low quality exchanges are considered fair since the leader expects no more than adequate job performance, good attendance, reasonable respect, and adherence to the job description in exchange for a fair wage and standard benefits. But the leader spends less time with out-group members, they have fewer developmental experiences, and the leader tends to emphasize her formal authority to obtain compliance to leader requests. Research shows that out-group members are less satisfied with their job and organization, receive lower performance evaluations from the leader, see their leader as less fair, and are more likely to file grievances or leave the organization.

Similarity of attitudes or socio-economic background and personal liking between the leader and follower help determine a follower's exchange. Research indicates that gender or race do not significantly affect the exchange. The quality of an exchange between leaders and their followers is usually established early in their relationship and is resistant to change, making it difficult for out-group members to achieve in-group status. When leaders are trained to develop high quality exchanges, performance of all followers increase but the largest increases are for out-group members. This may indicate that the capabilities and willingness of some out-group members were overlooked by the leader. These individuals may be ready and willing to contribute more and simply need to spend more time with the leader.

Research shows that high performance ratings for in-group members may occur regardless of their actual performance. This may indicate a halo effect where the leader has already decided the in-group follower is competent and deserving of a high rating. The reverse may occur for out-group members resulting on low performance ratings and resentment by these followers. This theory does not consider the effects of individual exchanges on the overall group's performance or the effects of one exchange on other exchanges in the group. Although high quality exchanges can result in positive attitudes by followers and possibly high performance and retention, leaders should leave open the possibility of high quality exchanges for all followers.

The Implicit Leadership Theory

Most people have an image in their heads of the characteristics of an ideal political leader, military leader, or business leader. These images are often called *prototypes* and they dictate who a person perceives as a leader or not a leader. This process is described by the Implicit Leadership Theory (ILT) which was first developed by Robert Lord and his colleagues. The great Apache war leader Geronimo embodied the characteristics of a fearless warrior who refused to surrender, yet was loyal and generous to his own people. The great football coach Vince Lombardi demonstrated the characteristics of toughness, hard work, and fierce competitiveness that epitomize the game of professional football. Followers of these leaders expected their leaders to have these characteristics since they were required for success. They demonstrate how ILTs can influence leader-follower relationships.

The ILT describes the perceptual processes used by followers and others to classify individuals as leaders or non-leaders, effective or ineffective leaders, or business or sports leaders. Lord and his colleagues argued that individuals' beliefs about the attributes and behaviors of leaders are clustered together in their memory in categories (also called schemas). The prototype is the individual's best example of the leadership category. When an observer or follower meets a person who holds a leadership position or a potential future leader, the person's attributes are compared against the observer's prototype. The better the match, the more likely the person is seen as a leader. This increases the person's social power and the observer likely assumes this individual has the ability to motivate and direct others. This can be an important factor in followers' decision to cooperate and actively carry out a leader's requests.

An individual's ILT likely develops over time, from early experiences with parents, coaches, siblings, friendship groups, and teachers as well as movies and books. These experiences cause us to encode specific attributes and behaviors as characteristic of leaders, effective leaders, or ineffective leaders. If we see a leader being kind to a follower, we may decide the leader is humane and encode this characteristic as an attribute of effective leaders. If we notice a leader effectively organizing a project and clarifying work assignments and expectations for followers, we may decide that good leaders are directive. As we mature and add experience, our learning process continues resulting in rich prototypes for different types of leaders. These prototypes are called "fuzzy sets" because they may overlap with one another so sports leaders may have some of the same characteristics as business leaders. Attributes such as dynamic, organized, and supportive may characterize many types of leaders in varying degrees.

Research shows that ILTs are affected by contextual factors such as cultural characteristics and identification with a group, as well as the leader's ethnicity. ILTs influence followers' expectations of leaders and affect the leader/follower relationship. If a follower expects a leader to be autocratic, a participative leader will likely be viewed as weak and have difficulty obtaining active cooperation from followers. This is true in countries that accept major power differences among individuals as normal and proper, such as Russia and Iran. In countries that do not accept power differences as normal and necessary, such as the Netherlands and Denmark, family and organizational leaders are expected to make decisions through extensive discussion and participation. Understanding followers' ILTs can be important in establishing a productive relationship between leaders and followers.

Substitutes for Leadership

Another leadership theory that is related to contingency theories is Substitutes for Leadership, which was developed in the late 1970s by Steve Kerr and John Jermier. These scholars noted that all leadership theories assumed some type of hierarchical leadership was important in all situations, although one leadership style might be effective in one situation and a different style in another situation. They proposed that there are characteristics of followers, their work task, or the organization that reduce the importance of hierarchical leadership. These characteristics essentially *neutralize* the effects of specific leader behaviors. Other characteristics were proposed to *substitute* for certain leader behaviors by having an important effect of their own on followers' performance and attitudes independent of the leader. Their model reflected the realization that numerous factors in organizations can provide guidance, motivation, and good feelings that followers need to complete their tasks effectively. Although Kerr and Jermier described the effects of neutralizers and substitutes on directive and supportive leadership, they noted that these characteristics also likely affect other leadership behavior patterns.

One example of a possible leadership neutralizer is *spatial distance* between a leader and follower that makes it difficult for the leader to effectively monitor the follower's performance and to provide useful guidance for the follower in carrying out her work tasks. Another example is a strong *need for independence* by the follower that can make the follower less willing to accept a leader's efforts to provide task guidance. An example of a leadership substitute occurs when followers have a high degree of *ability, experience, training and knowledge,* and a *professional orientation* that provides them with the capabilities they need to do their job well and the desire to work independently of their hierarchical leader. They may resist a leader's efforts to provide task guidance and be perfectly satisfied to work on their own. Another substitute occurs when followers belong to a *closely knit cohesive work group with high performance norms* they may receive all the task guidance, encouragement, and interpersonal support they need from other group members. In this situation, followers may prefer to interact with their group of peers and tacitly ignore task guidance and relationship oriented efforts by their hierarchical leader.

Some type of task guidance, encouragement and/or support is important for most organizational members, but the leader is not the only source of these factors. If the needed guidance, motivation, and support are available from non-leader sources such as leadership substitutes, then the leader may not need to provide them, and she can concentrate on other important activities. In recent years, management programs have become popular that emphasize non-leader sources of influence involving several types of leadership substitutes. Programs for *self-leadership, shared leadership,* and *self-managed work teams* incorporate substitutes such as increased followers' ability, experience, training and knowledge, self-administered performance feedback, and closely knit work groups. *Total Quality Management* involves continuous training to increase workers' ability and job knowledge and continuous feedback from customers and work tasks rather than from a formal leader. *Computerized workplaces* and *telecommuting* rely on networked computer systems and groupware that provide job guidance and information on demand without reliance on hierarchical managers.

Although research has provided mixed support for the existence of substitutes for leadership, the popularity of management programs like these that include substitutes attests to their importance. A recent development in the Substitutes for Leadership model includes adding leadership *enhancers,* which are situational and follower characteristics that increase a leader's influence on followers. Researchers have found substitutes, neutralizers and enhancers for other leader behaviors including charismatic/transformational leadership and leader reward and punishment behaviors. Research also shows that substitutes and neutralizers do *not* make all leadership unnecessary or irrelevant.

The great British Admiral Horatio Nelson relied on the ability, experience, training, and knowledge of his captains to achieve his success against Napoleon's navy. After providing direction for the overall strategy and tactics to be used during a particular battle, he left it to his captains to carry out the strategy as the situation developed. Although he was often spatially separated from their ships in the white heat of battle, the captains' experience, capabilities, and adaptability likely resulted in their tremendous victory over the French navy at the Battle of the Nile.

Ethical Theories

The last three leadership theories to be described were developed in recent years and have yet to be researched extensively. They are not contingency theories, but describe personal characteristics and behaviors that their developers believe all leaders should demonstrate. They emphasize issues of ethics and morality, integrity, personal character, trust, service to others, openness, humility, and self-knowledge/self-awareness. As such, nearly all the great leaders contained in this book can be described by one or more of these theories. The bad leaders demonstrate a conspicuous absence of the elements described in these models.

The Servant Leadership Theory

The Servant Leadership Theory was first developed by Robert Greenleaf in the 1970s and has slowly gained popularity. It specifies a *caring* and *ethical* approach toward others with a strong element of *supportive leadership behavior*. With this theory, the leader's primary responsibility is to serve the needs of followers and other organizational constituents with a special concern for the least privileged individuals. Assessing followers' needs requires *careful and active listening* and being viewed as *trustworthy*. Leaders are viewed as trustworthy when they are *open* and *honest* and *role model the values of empathy, fairness, altruism, humility,* and *trust*. Servant leaders are also said to inspire followers' trust by *demonstrating optimism, a firm belief in the importance of the group mission or goal, showing confidence, competence, openness to change,* and *granting autonomy* to followers in controlling their own actions.

The Servant Leadership Theory also emphasizes the importance of the *leader's self-knowledge* or *self-awareness* which emerges over time as the leader becomes aware of his strengths, core values, beliefs, and desires. Self-knowledge is discussed by other writers as resulting from *self-reflection* and *connection*. Self-reflection may occur with meditation, religious practices, or other techniques. Connection may be with the inner self, a higher deity or (in the case of servant leaders) with followers. Missions and goals reflect the leader's self-knowledge and connection with followers and servant leaders always place others above themselves.

Greenleaf predicted that servant leaders would have followers who are healthier, freer, wiser, more empowered and autonomous, and would likely become servant leaders themselves. Although research on servant leaders is at an early stage, results indicate their followers are satisfied, concerned with safety, trust their leader, and are committed to their organization. Little is known at this time about reliable effects of servant leadership on group or organizational performance. Mother Teresa, Ernest Shackleton, and Sitting Bull were great leaders who exemplified the Servant Leadership Theory. Each of these individuals gave themselves completely to the service of their followers and constituents.

Authentic Leadership

Authentic Leadership is a relatively new leadership theory that borrows heavily from positive psychology, which studies the capacities and virtues that help people thrive and make life more fulfilling. It stresses identifying and nurturing people's strengths and helping them live out these strengths. It focuses on enjoyment, engaging in activities that fit one's strengths and contributing to something worthwhile and larger than oneself. These factors are said to make life more meaningful and to promote well-being. Authentic leadership begins with certain psychological capacities of the leader including self-confidence, optimism, hope, happiness, resilience, emotional intelligence, and high moral character. With a supportive organizational climate these capacities result in self-reflection, self-awareness, and self-regulated behavior by leaders.

Self-awareness emerges over time as the leader recognizes his strengths, core values, beliefs, and desires. It is fostered by self-reflection described earlier with the Servant Leadership Theory. Self-reflection helps leaders assess their own emotions, motives, and goals within their organizational context and increases leaders' awareness of who they are, how they think and behave, and how others perceive them. It involves balanced processing, which is collection and interpretation of self-related information in an unbiased fashion—whether it is positive or negative. This assists with self-regulation where leaders align their values, motives, and capacities with their actual behavior. This is said to make leaders more transparent to followers and others which builds trust. Demonstrating integrity through open and honest communication, concern for followers' welfare, and respect for others also builds trust in the leader and encourages these behaviors in followers. A trusting atmosphere in organizations improves followers' attitudes, citizenship behavior, willingness to take risks, and performance.

Authentic leadership also emphasizes hope and optimism, which result from success experiences and social interactions with other hopeful individuals such as coaches, teachers, parents, or leaders. These leaders remain realistically hopeful and engender this in followers by sharing credible information, role modeling hope and commitment, clarifying paths to successful accomplishments, and matching followers' skills with tasks that make use of their strengths. These leader actions build followers' self-confidence and optimism, which result in persistent efforts and resilience to setbacks, they increase people's repertoire of solutions to problems, and make people more flexible and creative. Emotional intelligence by leaders helps them understand and identify with followers, which also assists in evoking self-confidence, optimism, and other positive emotions and beliefs in followers.

Authentic leaders realize their leadership role includes a responsibility to act morally and in the best interests of others. These leaders strive to do what is "right and fair" for followers and associates and they openly discuss their own weaknesses while emphasizing their own and followers' growth and development. Authentic leaders likely have a strong desire to serve others and to make others more capable and empowered, similar to the Servant Leadership Theory. They are aware that their ethical behavior is closely watched and affects what followers pay attention to, how they view their own roles, and eventually how they behave. Great leaders like Anita Roddick, Nelson Mandela, Leymah Gbowee, and Cesar Chavez all demonstrated authentic leadership. Bad leaders such as Al Dunlap and David Koresh were sorely lacking in the requisites of this model.

Most of the literature on Authentic Leadership focuses on theory building, with little empirical research to test the theory. Supporters of this theory point to research in other areas and in extreme settings that appears consistent with Authentic Leadership. Clearly, research is needed to verify the theory's assertions but interest in this model is growing among leadership scholars and practicing leaders.

Principle-Centered Leadership

Principle-Centered Leadership was developed by Stephen R. Covey based on his earlier book, *The Seven Habits of Highly Effective People.* Principle-Centered Leadership describes overall principles that all leaders can use to guide their decision making and interactions with followers and others. Covey maintains these principles apply in all situations and, when they are followed, they result in fair and kind leaders who develop trust and commitment among followers and efficient and effective organizations.

Principle-Centered Leadership emphasizes the *leader's character and competence* as essential for effective leadership. Covey describes character as composed of: (1) *integrity* which is knowing one's values and behaving consistently with these values, (2) *maturity* which is expressing one's true feelings and beliefs with courage and consideration in one's behavior and communications, and (3) *abundance mentality,* which involves believing that life is not a zero sum game and sharing recognition, responsibility, and profits. Competence is developed by prolonged effort and practice through useful experience.

Covey also emphasizes the importance of *personal and organizational values* in this theory. He defines *values* as our own personal convictions about what we believe are most important and desirable in our lives, our most basic priorities. Values are often classified as terminal or instrumental. Terminal values are desired end states we wish to achieve in life such as happiness, freedom, salvation or a comfortable life. Instrumental values are desirable characteristics of people that help them achieve terminal values, such as honesty, ambition, courage or politeness. Most of the values Covey describes are instrumental and he asserts that focusing on one's values will help leaders to be more self-aware and ethical in their behavior, to prioritize tasks, and to be seen by others as trustworthy and credible.

This theory emphasizes the principle of creating *trust* and *trustworthiness* which result from character and competence. The principle of follower *empowerment* results from the leader as helper, performance contracts with jointly set goals, follower participation in performance appraisals, and self-management. Covey asserts many other principles such as maintaining a *service orientation* by viewing life as a mission to serve others; *continuous learning* through reading, taking courses, listening, observing, and asking questions; *radiating positive energy* by being cheerful, optimistic, enthusiastic, and happy; *believing in others* by showing faith in their character and competence; *seeing life as an adventure* by taking risks and trying new methods and techniques; *showing humility* in all dealings with others; *listening* and *obeying one's conscience* in all actions; *refraining from speaking unkindly* to others to build relationships; and *keeping all promises* and *commitments* to build trust. He continually emphasizes that people must be treated as economic, psychological, social, and spiritual beings who want *meaning* in the work activities. Involving people in developing a mission statement that includes a vision and purpose for the organization can help provide this meaning.

Principle-Centered Leadership is popular with many managers who have participated in seminars conducted by the Covey Leadership Center. The model is appealing because it is based on Covey's best-selling book on personal development and it specifies guidelines that are easy to understand. It includes many elements that are similar to Servant Leadership and Authentic Leadership. The theory has not been carefully researched by other scholars so its overall validity is difficult to judge. However, great leaders such as Nelson Mandela and Ernest Shackleton appeared to embody many of the principles of this theory.

Conclusion

Each of the leaders described in the following chapters demonstrate different aspects of these theories. Some theories better describe a specific leader than others. Regarding leader traits, all the leaders (great and bad) were *determined* and *driven* to achieve their goals showing exceptional energy, initiative and perseverance. Most leaders were *self-confident* with *assertive* personalities. Most great leaders demonstrated *integrity* by being truthful, trustworthy, and loyal to their people and cause. Many leaders had strong *cognitive* and *social skills*. These leaders also demonstrated several of the leadership behavior patterns found in contingency leadership theories including directive, supportive, boundary spanning, participative and rewarding leader behaviors. Most leaders showed some elements of charismatic/transformational leadership. Many leaders relied on in-groups of followers while most fit the prevailing leader prototype for their time and type of organization. Some made use of leadership substitutes to influence followers. Nearly all the great leaders demonstrated ethical behavior and fair treatment of followers and other constituents. Ethics and fair treatment were conspicuously absent from the bad leaders.

Most of the leaders were flawed in some way. Steve Jobs' abrasive interpersonal style and willingness to take credit for others' work left much to be desired; Vince Lombardi's treatment of his son and his violent outbursts at players were extreme and very unpleasant; Napoleon's ruthlessness and deceptions were countless; Hayek's bluntness, explosive temper and tendency to take credit for others' work

TABLE 1.1 Matrix of Great Leadership and Leadership Theories

	Trait Theories	Fiedler's Contingency Theory	Leadership Grid	Path-Goal Theory	Normative Decision Theory	Situational Leadership Theory
GREAT LEADERSHIP						
Steve Jobs	X	X		X		X
Anita Roddick	X			X		
Ernest Shackleton		X	X	X		X
Mother Teresa	X	X	X	X		X
Abraham Lincoln	X			X	X	
Pat Summitt		X	X	X		X
Laymah Gbowee	X	X	X	X		X
Nelson Mandela				X	X	X
Geronimo	X	X		X		X
Winston Churchill	X	X		X		X
Vince Lombardi	X	X		X		X
Napoleon Bonaparte	X	X		X		X
Mary Kay Ash	X	X	X	X	X	X
Nicolas Hayek	X	X	X	X	X	X
César Chávez	X	X		X		X
Konosuke Matsushita	X	X	X	X		X
Bill Wilson	X			X	X	X
Mark Zuckerberg	X	X	X	X		X
Martin Luther King	X	X	X	X	X	X
George Washington	X	X		X	X	X
Luiz Inácio Lula da Silva	X	X	X	X	X	X
Mohandas Gandhi	X	X	X	X		X
Sitting Bull	X	X		X	X	X
Indra Nooyi	X	X		X	X	X
Horatio Nelson	X	X		X	X	X
BAD LEADERSHIP						
Adolf Hitler	X	X		X		X
Al Dunlap	X	X		X		X
Idi Amin	X			X		
David Koresh	X	X	X	X		X
Kenneth Lay	X			X		

Multiple Linkage Model	Leader Member Exchange	Charismatic/ Transformational Leadership	Servant Leadership	Implicit Leadership Theory	Substitutes for Leadership	Authentic Leadership	Principle Centered Leadership
X		X				X	
X		X				X	
	X	X	X			X	X
X		X	X		X	X	
X	X	X			X	X	
X				X	X		
X		X				X	
X		X	X			X	X
X		X		X			
X		X		X			
X		X		X	X	X	
X	X	X		X			
X		X			X	X	
X		X					
X		X				X	
X		X				X	
X		X	X				
		X		X		X	
X		X	X			X	
X		X		X			
X		X	X				
X		X	X				
X		X	X	X			
X		X					
X		X			X	X	X
X		X		X			
X	X			X			
X	X			X			
		X		X			
X	X	X					

were well known; Bill Wilson's depression, alcoholism, and infidelities were discouraging to all around him; and Gandhi's treatment of his family and extremist views about Jews sacrificing themselves to the Nazis were unpalatable to most observers. But these leaders exhibited major strengths that they relied on to lead their groups and organizations to amazing accomplishments. Each leader was unique due to their personal nature, background, and context. No single set of traits or behaviors characterize them all. Yet, they are viewed by most observers as examples of great leadership.

Hopefully, the leadership theory descriptions in this chapter along with the references to them at the end of each snapshot, will clarify how the great leaders achieved their amazing feats. If these theory descriptions increase the reader's understanding of the leadership process, then this chapter has served its purpose. The matrix (Table 1.1) relates the great and bad leaders described in this book with the leadership theories in this chapter.

References

Trait Theories

Bass, B. M. & Bass, R. (2008). *The Bass handbook of leadership: Theory, research, and managerial applications* (4th ed.). New York: Free Press.

Daft, R. L. (1999). *Leadership: Theory and practice*. New York: Dryden Press.

Kirkpatrick, S. A. & Locke, E. A. (1991). Leadership: Do traits matter? *Academy of Management Executive, 5*(2), 48–59.

Lord, R. G., DeVader, C. L., & Alliger, G. M. (1986). A meta-analysis of the relation between personality traits and leadership perceptions: An application of validity generalization procedures. *Journal of Applied Psychology, 71*, 402–410.

Lord, R. G. & Hall, R. J. (1992). Contemporary views of leadership and individual differences. *Leadership Quarterly, 3*(2), 137–157.

Northouse, P. G. (2004). *Leadership: Theory and practice* (3rd ed.). Thousand Oaks, CA: Sage.

Leadership Grid

Blake, R. R. & McCanse, A. A. (1991). *Leadership dilemmas—Grid solutions*. Houston, TX: Gulf Publishing.

Blake, R. R. & Mouton, J. S. (1964). *The managerial grid*. Houston, TX: Gulf Publishing.

Hersey, P., Blanchard, K. H., & Johnson, D. E. (1996). *Management of organizational behavior: Utilizing human resources* (7th ed.). Upper Saddle River, NJ: Prentice-Hall.

Contingency Theory of Leadership

Ayman, R., Chemers, M. M., & Fiedler, F. E. (1995). The contingency model of leadership effectiveness: Its levels of analysis. *The Leadership Quarterly, 6*(2), 147–167.

Bass, B. M. & Bass, R. (2008). *The Bass handbook of leadership* (4th ed.). New York: Free Press.

Fiedler, F. E. & Garcia, J. E. (1987). *New approaches to effective leadership: Cognitive resources and organizational performance.* New York: Wiley.

Fiedler, F. E., Chemers, M. H., & Mahar, L. (1994). *Improving leadership effectiveness: The leader match concept* (2nd ed.). New York: Wiley.

Schriesheim, C. A. & Kerr, S. (1977). Theories and measures of leadership: A critical appraisal of current and future directions. In J. G. Hunt & L. L. Larson (Eds.), *Leadership: The cutting edge* (pp. 9–45). Carbondale: Southern Illinois University Press.

Schriesheim, C. A., Tepper, B. J., & Terault, L. A. (1994). Least preferred co-worker score, situational control, and leadership effectiveness: A meta-analysis of contingency theory model performance predictions. *Journal of Applied Psychology, 79*(4), 561–573.

Situational Leadership Theory

Fernandez, C. F. & Vecchio, R .P. (1997). Situational leadership theory revisited: A test of an across-jobs perspective. *Leadership Quarterly, 8*(1), 67–84.

Goodson, J. R., McGee, G. W., & Cashman, J. F. (1989). Situational leadership theory. *Personnel Psychology, 43,* 579–597.

Hersey, P. (1984). *The situational leader.* Escondido, CA: Center for Leadership Studies.

Vecchio, R.P. (1987). Situational leadership theory: An examination of a prescriptive theory. *Journal of Applied Psychology, 72,* 444–451.

Path-Goal Theory

House, R. J. (1971). A path-goal theory of leader effectiveness. *Administrative Science Quarterly, 16,* 321–328.

House, R. J. (1996). Path-goal theory of leadership: Lessons, legacy, and a reformulated theory. *Leadership Quarterly, 7*(3), 323–352.

House, R. J. & Mitchell, R. R. (1974). Path-goal theory of leadership. *Journal of Contemporary Business, 3,* 81–97.

Multiple Linkage Model

Kim, H. & Yukl, G. (1995). Relationships of managerial effectiveness and advancement to self-reported and subordinate-reported leadership behaviors from the multiple linkage model. *Leadership Quarterly, 6*(3), 361–377.

Yukl, G. (1994). *Leadership in organizations* (3rd ed.). Englewood Cliffs, NJ: Prentice Hall.

Yukl, G. (2010). *Leadership in organizations* (7th ed.). Upper Saddle River, NJ: Pearson Education.

Charismatic and Transformational Leadership

Agle, B. R., Nagarajan, N. J., Sonnenfeld, J. A., & Srinivasan, D. (2006). Does CEO charisma matter? An empirical analysis of the relationships among organizational performance, environmental uncertainty, and top management team perceptions of CEO charisma. *Academy of Management Journal, 49*(1), 161–174.

House, R. J. (1977). A 1976 theory of charismatic leadership. In J. G. Hunt & L. L. Larson (Eds.), *Leadership: The cutting edge* (pp.189–207). Carbondale: Southern Illinois University Press.

Judge, T. A. & Piccolo, R. G. (2004). Transformational and transactional leadership: A meta-analytic test of their relative validity. *Journal of Applied Psychology, 89*, 755–768.

Shamir, B., House, R. J., & Arthur, M. B. (1993). The motivational effects of charismatic leadership: A self-concept based theory. *Organizational Science, 4*(4), 577–594.

Shamir, B., Sakay, E., Breinin, E., & Popper, M. (1998). Correlates of charismatic leader behaviors in military units: Subordinates' attitudes, unit characteristics, and superiors' appraisals of leader performance. *Academy of Management Journal, 41*(4), 387–409.

Yukl, G. (2010). *Leadership in organizations* (7th ed.). Upper Saddle River, NJ: Pearson Prentice Hall.

Normative Decision Theory of Participation

Howell, J. P. & Costley, D. L. (2006). *Understanding behaviors for effective leadership* (2nd ed.). Upper Saddle River, NJ: Prentice Hall.

Vroom, V. H. (2000). Leadership and the decision making process. *Organizational Dynamics, 28*(4), 82–94.

Vroom. V. H. (2003). Educating managers for decision making and leadership. *Management Decision, 42*(10), 968–978.

Yukl, G. (2010). *Leadership in organizations* (7th edition). Upper Saddle River, NJ: Prentice Hall.

Leader Member Exchange Theory

Fairhurst, G. T. (1993*).* The leader-member exchange patterns of women leaders in industry: A discourse analysis. *Communication Monographs, 60*(4), 321–351.

Hogg, M. A. (2004). Leader-member exchange (LMX) theory. In G. R. Goethals, G. J. Sorenson, & J. M. Burns, *Encyclopedia of leadership*. Thousand Oaks, CA: Sage.

Howell, J. & Costley, D. (2006). *Understanding behaviors for effective leadership* (2nd ed.). Upper Saddle River, NJ: Prentice Hall.

Scandura, T. A. (1999). Rethinking leader-member exchange: An organizational justice perspective. *Leadership Quarterly, 10*(1), 25–40.

Yukl, G. (2010). *Leadership in organizations* (7th ed.). Upper Saddle River, NJ: Prentice Hall.

Implicit Leadership Theory

Javidan, M., Dorfman, P. W., Howell, J. P., & Hanges, P. J. (2010). Leadership and cultural context: A theoretical and empirical examination based on project GLOBE. In N. Nohria & R. Khurana (Eds.), *Handbook of leadership theory and practice.* Boston, MA: Harvard University Press.

Offerman, L. R., Kennedy, J. K., Jr., & Wirtz, P. W. (1994). Implicit leadership theories: Content, structure, and generalizability. *Leadership Quarterly, 5*(1), 43–58.

Phillips, J .S. & Lord, R. G. (1986). Notes on the practical and theoretical consequences of implicit leadership theories for the future of leadership measurement. *Journal of Management, 12*(1), 321–341.

Substitutes for Leadership

Devries, R. E. (1995). Measuring substitutes for leadership using the concept of need for leadership: A cross-sectional research. Tilburg University, Work and Organizational Research Center, Netherlands.

Howell, J. P. (1997). Substitutes for leadership: Their meaning and measurement—An historical assessment, *Leadership Quarterly, 8*(2), 113–116.

Howell, J. P., Bowen, D. E., Dorfman, P. W., Kerr, S., & Podsakoff, P. M. (1990). Substitutes for leadership: Effective alternatives to ineffective leadership. *Organizational Dynamics, 19,* 21–38.

Kerr, S. & Jermier, J. (1978). Substitutes for leadership: Their meaning and measurement. *Organizational Behavior and Human Performance, 22,* 275–403.

Podsakoff, P. M., MacKenzie, S. B., & Fetter, R. (1993). Substitutes for leadership and the management of professionals. *Leadership Quarterly, 4*(1), 1–44.

Podsakoff, P. M., Niehoff, B. P., MacKenzie, S. B., & Williams, W. L. (1993). Do substitutes for leadership really substitute for leadership? An empirical examination of Kerr and Jermier's situational leadership model. *Organizational Behavior and Human Decision Processes, 54,* 1–44.

Yukl, G. (1994). *Leadership in organizations* (3rd ed.), Englewood Cliffs, NJ: Prentice-Hall.

Servant Leadership Theory

Avolio, B. J., Walumbwa, F. O., & Weber, T. J. (2009). Leadership: Current theories, research, and future directions. *Annual Review of Psychology, 60,* 421–449.

Greenleaf, R. K. (1991). *The servant as leader.* Indianapolis, IN: Robert Greenleaf Center.

Joseph, E. E. & Winston, B. E. (2005). A correlation of servant leadership, leader trust, and organizational trust. *Leadership and Organizational Development Journal, 26,* 6–22.

Yukl, G. (2010). *Leadership in Organizations* (7th ed.). Upper Saddle River, NJ: Prentice Hall.

Authentic Leadership

Avolio, B. J. & Gardner, W. L. (2005). Authentic leadership development: Getting to the root of positive forms of leadership. *Leadership Quarterly, 16*(3), 315–338.

Avolio, B. J., Gardner, W. L., Walumbwa, F. O., Luthans, F., & May, D. R. (2004). Unlocking the mask: A look at the process by which authentic leaders impact follower attitudes and behaviors. *Leadership Quarterly, 15*, 801–823.

Gardner, W. L., Avolio, B. J., Luthans, F., May, D. R., & Walumbwa, F. (2005). "Can you see the real me?" A self-based model of authentic leader and follower development. *Leadership Quarterly, 16*(3), 343–372.

Yammarino, F. J., Dionne, S. D., Schriesheim, C. A., & Dansereau, F. (2008). Authentic leadership and positive organizational behavior: A meso, multi-level perspective. *Leadership Quarterly, 19*, 693–707.

Principle-Centered Leadership

Covey, S. R. (1989). *The seven habits of highly effective people: Restoring the character ethic.* New York: The Free Press.

Covey, S. R. (1991). *Principle-centered leadership.* New York: Simon and Schuster. http://kleczek.wordpress.com/2008/06/14/principle-centered-leadership.

Part II

Snapshots of Great Leadership

Chapter 2

Steve Jobs
CEO and Cofounder of Apple Inc.

Steve Jobs was cofounder and CEO of Apple Inc. and founder and former CEO of Pixar Animation. He was a complex human being. Described as a brilliant megalomaniac, his vision for the personal computer and information technology combined with his intense focus on style and function made Apple "the temple of techno-cool." He was innovator, agitator, and egotist—but most importantly he was a charismatic speaker who captivated employees, potential employees, and crowds of technology buffs exactly like an evangelist or demagogue. He excited people to buy into his vision and inspired them to work absurd hours, days, and months to meet ridiculous deadlines to create what he termed "killer products" that will change the world. And the teams he created and inspired were usually successful.

He was born in San Francisco on February 24, 1955, and was adopted by Paul and Clara Jobs. He attended school in the San Francisco bay area and became interested in electronics. When he was 14 a friend introduced him to Steve Wozniak (known as Woz) who was 5 years older and was already building an early personal computer. Jobs was fascinated, and the two became friends. Both were solitary and self-absorbed individuals who could focus on a project they chose to work on and become lost in their work. Woz had the real engineering knowledge and Jobs had the drive and guts to do anything to achieve his goal. After graduating from high school, Jobs attended Reed College in Oregon for a short time, dropped out, and returned to California where he joined a computer club with Woz. Jobs took a job with Atari, manufacturer of computer games, to earn money. He was affected by the anti-Vietnam war era with its hip drug culture and he spent several months backpacking around India with a friend from college.

Back in the United States, he returned to Atari and was assigned to reduce the number of chips on a circuit board for a game called Breakout. He made a deal with the tech savvy Woz to reduce the number of chips, and they would split the commission evenly. Woz completed the project with incredible success, and Jobs paid him $350. Jobs did not reveal that Atari had actually paid him several thousand dollars for the job.

In 1976 Jobs and Woz formed a business partnership called Apple which would sell their first computer—Apple I. It was actually a circuit board that could be used to help hobbyists build their own computers. Jobs succeeded in selling the boards to an early computer parts store. Meanwhile, Woz was busy designing the Apple II—their first free-standing computer. Jobs worked hard at finding deals on parts, looking for investors, and promoting their computers. Together they attended the first personal computer festival and made key decisions about their next computer. In 1976 they met Mike Markkula who provided financing and in January 1977 they founded Apple Inc. There were four shareholders—Jobs, Woz, Markkula, and Rod Holt who specialized in power supplies. Jobs had wanted a business to build and now he had one.

When Apple became a corporation, Steve Jobs' management style came into focus. He was a perfectionist and very impatient. He could not wait for things to be completed and introduced to the public. Although Markkula insisted that an outside executive be hired as president, Jobs, Woz, and Markkula were the major owners and they had the power. Power is an issue that recurred throughout Steve's life. Over the next year, the friendship between Jobs and Woz deteriorated. Jobs was described by an early employee as primarily focused on the end user—he was most concerned with the appearance of the computer screen and the computer case. But the interpersonal style he used in conveying his desires often angered employees. At the West Coast Computer Faire, Jobs insisted the cases for Apple II be sanded and repainted the night before the show. They were a sensation and Apple received several hundred orders.

Jobs was insistent on having his ideas implemented at Apple. He fought with the president to include a one year warranty to promote customer loyalty and won after crying to have his way. He was a very tough negotiator with suppliers and bested many people with more experience. He repeatedly set unrealistic goals for product development, yet he had an almost unbelievable power of persuasion. People would "drink Steve's Kool-Aid"—a reference to LSD mixed with Kool-Aid and served at rock concerts in the 1960s. They believed in his perception of reality—that they could change the world—and accepted his ridiculous timetables. They called this Steve's "reality distortion field." He could infuriate and inspire small groups of hand selected engineers to do the impossible. One coworker described Jobs' power of vision as almost frightening. In the early years, Apple staff were not there for the money, they were changing the world.

In the late 1970s Apple had made the originators wealthy. Two years later Apple had its first public offering of stock, and they were made extremely rich. Jobs refused to offer stock options to loyal employees who had worked hard for Apple for years. He seemed determined to show his power. Woz initiated a private sale and gave away some of his own stock to deserving employees. Jobs insisted on a small computer case for Apple III, too small for the electronic configuration. It never worked well, and the engineers were blamed. Problems with the next Apple computer, titled Lisa and driven by Jobs, resulted in a revolt by the management. In 1984, Jobs was moved out of an operational role and given the titular role of Chairman of the Board. Jobs then found another project to build called the Macintosh. He had opposed this project as originally conceived, but now needed something to push and he was enthused about creating a small inexpensive computer for the masses. Through political maneuvering and tearful confrontation, he took over the project from its originator, Jef Raskin.

He micromanaged the project and insisted that the Macintosh be ready for market in 12 months. He interrupted ongoing work and was interested in every detail. His people said he would typically reject a new idea when first presented, but he would often return two weeks later with the same idea and claim he just thought of it. They could then incorporate "his" idea in their designs. They eventually used this tendency to influence his decisions. Steve made a dramatic presentation of the Mac at Apple's 1984 annual meeting, and the computer used a voice synthesis program to introduce Steve as "like a father to me." The early sales of the Mac were very good but they soon lagged due to problems with storage space. Steve had insisted on specifying the exact configurations without market research and he had missed key user needs. Continued sales declines and unhappiness with Steve's management led to his ouster as head of Macintosh. In May 1985 he tried to have John Sculley, then Apple CEO, ousted but failed. Jobs was then labeled "Chairman," and "Global Visionary," and was stripped of any management role at Apple. Woz had already left Apple; it was a different place now.

Steve then started a new company, NeXT Computer, with Ross Perot as a major investor. The new computer would provide advanced technology for the scientific and academic fields. He described the new machine as an "interpersonal computer" to facilitate communication and collaboration between people, and it sported improved email features. Jobs insisted on a small magnesium cube to house the machine which caused hardware problems, and it never sold well. The new company eventually transitioned to software development. In 1986, Jobs bought the Graphics Group from George Lucas for one third the asking price (due to Lucas' impending divorce). He named the graphics company Pixar. It was originally a sophisticated graphics hardware developer, but frustration in selling their graphics computer ended with signing a contract with Disney to produce several computer animated films. Its first product was *Toy Story* followed by several other box office hits that won Academy Awards. Jobs and Michael Eisner, Disney CEO, could not agree on renewing their partnership, but Eisner was ousted by the Disney board in 2005, partly due to Jobs' criticism. The new CEO patched things up with Jobs and Disney acquired Pixar from Jobs for 7% of Disney stock. Steve was now the largest shareholder of Disney.

In 1996 Apple bought NeXT for $429 million, and Steve was back at Apple as an advisor. Shortly thereafter, Apple was having trouble competing in the rapidly growing PC market and the board, with Steve's help, ousted the CEO. Steve was made interim CEO of Apple. He quickly terminated several projects and people and tried to implement other cost cutting measures. The board disagreed so he managed to force most members to resign, including Mike Markkula. He replaced them with some old friends. Employees developed a renewed fear of Steve, that he would fire them on the spot. He would lash out unexpectedly, even at his closest friends, and commanded loyalty. He craved respect yet he would often leave turmoil and bad feelings in his wake.

NeXT brought technology and skilled engineers back to Apple and they developed the iMac for the home consumer market which helped Apple's competitiveness. This was followed by iTunes music software, the iPod portable music player, and the iTunes music store which made use of the new technology at Apple and revolutionized music distribution. Apple then entered the cell phone business with the iPhone—a touch display cell phone, internet device, and iPod. Throughout, he continually reminded his employees that "real artists ship," meaning they must produce functional stylish products on time.

Jobs dropped the term "interim" from his title in 2000. He never desired or emphasized a salary for his work, some years he took $50 and other years he took nothing. He did believe in stock ownership and the power it bestows. He always sought to place Apple and his other companies at the cutting edge of information technology by anticipating and setting innovative and stylistic trends. He loved to quote Wayne Gretsky, "I skate to where the puck is going to be, not where it has been." He was temperamental, aggressive, and demanding and he radiated zeal for "killer" products while instilling fear in his employees.

He was an egotistical perfectionist who craved approval, as well as an insightful and masterful communicator. He had tremendous successes and huge failures, but his extreme self-confidence never waned. Perhaps most of all, Steve Jobs was an entrepreneur who saw that computers could be more than business and scientific tools, they could unleash human creativity and provide enjoyment for everyone. He had the ability to harness the most creative talent available and motivate employees to change the world. In early 2011, Jobs took an extended leave of absence from Apple to recover from an illness. In August of the same year, he resigned his position as CEO of Apple but remained as chairman of the board of directors. Steve Jobs died in October 2011.

Steve Jobs' leadership can be viewed from several theoretical perspectives. He was clearly a Charismatic/Transformational leader by providing a convincing *vision* of the importance of information technology in today's society, he reframed or *stimulated our thinking* about computers as more than scientific and business tools, and his *speeches inspired* audiences to create, write about, and buy his products. He might also be viewed as partly a *negative charismatic* by exhibiting narcissistic characteristics of extreme self-promotion and lack of consideration for coworkers. His leadership can be described by the Path-Goal Theory, Fiedler's Contingency Theory, Managerial Grid or the Situational Leadership Theory due to his precise *directive* leadership regarding product specifications and appearance and his *lack of support and consideration* for coworkers. His effective negotiating skills also reflect *boundary spanning* leadership from the Reformulated Path-Goal Theory and the Multiple Linkage Model. Jobs' leadership might be criticized from the Authentic Leadership perspective regarding his frequent lack of openness in dealing with others and some of his actions can be questioned from an ethical perspective. His determination, cognitive capacity and self-confidence clearly reflect Trait Theories of leadership.

Discussion Questions

1. What do you think of Steve Jobs' charismatic leadership style?
2. Would you be comfortable using Jobs' leadership style? Why or why not?
3. In light of his severe treatment of some colleagues and coworkers, why do you think he was so successful?
4. Are there unique characteristics of the computer/information technology and animated film industries that make Jobs' leadership style especially effective? If so, what are they?

References

Deutschman, A. (2000). *The second coming of Steve Jobs*. New York: Broadway Books.

Isaacson, W. (2011). *Steve Jobs*. New York: Simon & Schuster.

Steve Jobs. (n.d.). In *Wikipedia*. Retrieved January 16, 2009, from http://en.wikipedia.org/wiki/Steve_Jobs

Young, J. S. & Simon, W. L. (2005). *iCon Steve Jobs: The greatest second act in the history of business*. Hoboken, NJ: Wiley.

Chapter 3

Anita Roddick

*Founder and CEO
of The Body Shop*

Anita Roddick was often called the "Mother Teresa of Capitalism" or the "Queen of Green." She opened a small cosmetics store in Brighton, England in 1976, named it The Body Shop, and turned it into a multinational corporation selling natural cosmetics with over 1,900 stores in over 50 countries. But her reputation was primarily related to her extreme activism in advocating for environmental/ecological issues, human rights, and her opposition to product testing on animals. She used the organization she built as a powerful platform to pursue her agenda for social and environmental change. Described as "loquacious, wacky and opinionated," she never wavered in her moral outrage at the actions of some corporations and governments, her anti-establishment idealism, and her dedication to the causes she championed.

Trained as a teacher, Anita spent time early in her life traveling and working abroad in a library, a labor organization, and an Israeli Kibbutz. She traveled in the South Pacific before returning to England where she met her future husband, Gordon. The two of them ran a bed & breakfast and a restaurant for a time, but they grew tired of working seven days a week and having little time for their two children. Anita then hatched her idea for the cosmetics shop with natural products, Gordon helped her obtain her first loan for 4,000 pounds, and The Body Shop was born. Gordon took off for a horse back adventure in South America.

Gordon eventually returned and began helping with the business, but Anita *was* The Body Shop from the beginning. The business grew quickly, and in 1984 they had the first public offering of stock in The Body Shop. Anita was determined to use their success for the benefit of society. The first item in her mission statement read: "To dedicate our business to the pursuit of social and environmental change." She never wavered from her active pursuit of this mission. The business of The Body Shop, providing women worldwide with cosmetics, lotions, and soaps that are created from natural ingredients and are not tested on animals, became a vehicle for pursuing her true passion for change. She traveled extensively and created trading relationships with disadvantaged communities throughout the world to assist them in becoming self-reliant and sustainable.

In 1986, The Body Shop established an Environmental Projects Department and engaged with Greenpeace to support the Save the Whales campaign. Soon after this, they partnered with Friends of the Earth to combat acid rain and to preserve the ozone layer. Two years later, Anita led a Stop the Burning campaign to end massive burning of rainforests in Brazil. Her organization collected a million signatures from their customers, and Anita presented this petition with signatures to the Brazilian embassy. In 1990 The Body Shop Foundation was created to help fund human rights and environmental protection groups. One effective initiative was to help (with her husband) establish *The Big Issue* magazine which provided a platform and political presence for homeless people. Her organization helped finance the London headquarters for Amnesty International, initiated the use of biodegradable plastic bags, gathered over 4,000,000 signatures resulting in the British government's decision in 1998 to ban animal testing for cosmetic ingredients and products, campaigned to fight domestic violence, fought against carbon emissions in the mining industry, and the list goes on. She emphasized how these programs made employees proud of The Body Shop and had a huge effect on motivation and morale.

Roddick's vision of The Body Shop was a *stakeholder corporation* that was accountable not only to shareholders, but to all stakeholders including employees, customers, and communities. The stakeholder corporation would focus on three bottom lines—financial, social, and environmental. It was expected to deliver superior performance that benefited all of these groups. Her sales force held Body Shop at Home gatherings that provided word-of-mouth advertising. Anita believed that the absence of a marketing department at The Body Shop was a moral statement, but her public image was all that was needed for marketing her products. Her organization invested in a wind farm to use environmentally friendly electricity (ecotricity) in their headquarters and stores in the United Kingdom. It also supported a new management degree at University of Bath that combined training in business, environmental, social and ethical issues. In 2000 the Foundation established a human rights award to give recognition to grass-roots individuals and groups working on social, cultural, and economic problems around the world. The award provided financial support for the recipients. The first theme for the award addressed child labor and those who help children receive a basic education.

She was committed to leading an environmentally and socially responsible company that represented her values and she challenged other corporate leaders to be "true planetary citizens." Roddick modeled her socially active role by sacrificing profits—she would not do business in countries she believed were not attempting to address her social and environmental causes. She was considered an inspirational leader and generated passion among Body Shop employees. She invited ideas for the business and social programs from all employees through their Department of Damned Good Ideas (DODGI). She spent as much time with employees as possible and continually emphasized an image of female beauty that was realistic and not socially constructed by the media. She regularly sent video messages to employees regarding their organization's most recent advances in social causes and reminded them that their work efforts made an important contribution to larger environmental and social issues. Her organization financially supported employees who spent time working in community programs.

Her charismatic leadership style was focused on the future and the need for change from the status quo. Her office contained a sign that read "Welcome to the Department of the Future." Roddick referred to her style as "benevolent anarchism." She inspired creativity by inviting employees to examine what they were doing and how they were doing it, hoping to find better work methods. She encouraged employees to make their work enjoyable and to try novel and unique approaches to problems. Her passion for environmental and social causes, her personal belief and message that all women are beautiful, and her future oriented inspirational leadership style, all contributed to The Body Shop's amazing success.

In 2005 Anita announced she was giving away her 51 million pound fortune through her Foundation to support ethical entrepreneurs. In 2006 the Roddicks agreed to a buyout by the French company L'Oreal. Although she was criticized for this because of L'Oreal's record, she was later featured in a survey of the most admired powerful women. Anita Roddick died in 2007 from liver problems due to contracting Hepatitis C during blood transfusions in 1971.

Several leadership theories are demonstrated in Anita Roddick's leadership. Reformulated Path-Goal Theory and the Multiple Linkage Model are reflected in her *boundary spanning* behaviors as she was a constant advocate with employees, customers, and governments for environmental issues, human rights, and eliminating product testing on animals. She regularly corresponded with all employees through videos emphasizing the importance of their efforts for society and the latest environmental efforts of her organization. She embodied Authentic Leadership in her visible moral outrage at the actions of some corporations and her personal behavior consistent with her rhetoric (such as giving her fortune to a foundation to support ethical entrepreneurs). She displayed Charismatic/Transformational Leadership by constantly portraying a *vision* of women's beauty different from that defined by the popular media, by *inspiring* other organizations to be environmentally responsible, and by inspiring her employees to help create a better future for the world. Her determination, self-confidence and integrity reflect Trait Theories of Leadership.

Discussion Questions

1. Why do you think Anita Roddick focused her behavior so heavily on social and environmental issues?
2. Was her focus on social and environmental issues "good leadership" in her industry?
3. Which leadership theory do you believe best characterizes Roddick's leadership approach?
4. Would her leadership approach be effective in other contexts, such as automobile manufacturing, extractive industries (oil or mining), or tobacco?

References

Adler, N. J. (1997). Global leadership: Women leaders. *Management International Review, 37*(1), 171–196.

Anita Roddick. (n.d.). In *Wikipedia.* Retrieved November 25, 2011, from http://en.wikipedia.org/wiki/Anita_Roddick

Howell, J. P. & Costley, D. L. (2006). *Understanding behaviors for effective leadership* (2nd ed.). Upper Saddle River, NJ: Pearson Prentice Hall.

Kochran, N. (1997). Anita Roddick: Soap and social action. *World Business, 3*(1), 46–47.

Roddick, A. (1991). *Anita Roddick: Body and Soul.* New York: Crown.

The Body Shop (September 3, 2002). Retrieved November 20, 2008, from http://everything2.com/index.pl?node_id=1131866&displaytype=printable&lastnode_id=0

Chapter 4

Ernest Shackleton
Antarctic Explorer

The Antarctic expedition of 1914–1917 led by Ernest Shackleton became one of the most amazing feats of adventure and leadership in the 20th century. Shackleton was an Irishman born in 1874 who sailed as a naval lieutenant on Robert Scott's first expedition to the South Pole in 1902. Shackleton became ill early in the Scott expedition and was forced to return to England. Shackleton later led the Nimrod expedition to the Antarctic in 1908 but was forced to turn back for lack of food. Undeterred, he organized a third expedition in 1914 with the goal of crossing the Antarctic continent from one coast to the other via the South Pole. Although this expedition also failed, Shackleton's determined leadership and dedication to the welfare of his crew became the focus of an incredible story of survival and rescue under the harshest conditions imaginable.

Shackleton was inundated with volunteers for his third expedition and chose the Norwegian ship *Endurance,* which was built for Arctic cruises. They left England bound for the Antarctic in August 1914. After stops in Buenos Aires and a whaling station on the sub-Antarctic island of South Georgia, they left South Georgia on December 5, 1914, for the Weddell Sea on the northern edge of the Antarctic continent. The *Endurance* struggled through a thousand miles of icy seas over the next six weeks and was 100 miles from the Antarctic continent when the ice closed in and froze her solid. The ship drifted southwest with the ice and all efforts to free her failed. Temperatures fell to minus 20 degrees Celsius yet the crew had faith in "the boss"—their nickname for Shackleton. They played soccer and hockey games on the ice and hunted for seals and penguins for meat until the long dark winter set in. The sun returned in July along with blizzards, more low temperatures, and ice flows that "rafted" atop one another posing severe danger to the ship. In October the *Endurance* had become so badly damaged they were forced to abandon ship. Shackleton then wrote in his journal that his task was to reach land safely with all members of his expedition.

Their ship had drifted nearly 1,200 miles during the 281 days they were lodged in the ice. They were about 350 miles from the nearest land and possible shelter. They had no chance of contacting the outside world or of rescue in their present position. They had limited supplies and the ice was starting to break up—making their position even more perilous. During their first night camping on the ice, they had to move camp three times due to cracks appearing beneath them. When their ship broke up in the ice, Shackleton made a characteristic speech to encourage the men. He spoke simply and briefly, but told them not to be alarmed, but through hard work, cooperation, and loyalty they would reach land. The speech immediately caused the men to adopt a more cheerful view of their situation, even though they had only thin linen tents that did not keep out the cold and had to sleep on the ice in sleeping bags that were not waterproof. They simply believed that if any man could lead them to safety, it was Shackleton.

On December 20, 1915, Shackleton and his 27 men began a march westward on the ice, pulling three 22-foot lifeboats in relays as they went. He knew that if the ice began to disappear under them, the boats would be essential to their survival. Many times they took to their boats and hauled them up onto large ice floes to pitch their tents for the night. On April 12 they discovered that instead of actually traveling westward, the drifting ice had carried them 30 miles eastward during nearly 4 months of their march. This produced frustration, irritability, and outbursts of anger among the men. But Shackleton had a keen sense of how one man or a small group could influence the morale of the entire crew. He tactfully redistributed certain men among the tents on different pretexts, reminded them they needed to work together, and insisted on an optimistic attitude that was contagious. At one point they were camped on a long ice flow and, while sleeping, the ice turned so the sea swell began to crack the ice through the middle of their camp. They heard this and ran outside to see a tent being split in half, one half on each side of the crack. Shackleton immediately looked into the crack and saw a man in his sleeping bag that had fallen in. He quickly leaned down into the crack and pulled the man out before anyone realized the situation. Seconds later, the two pieces of ice were jammed together again with a huge thud. Actions such as this became symbolic and solidified the men's faith in their leader. On April 14, after several days of rowing through treacherous icy seas, they sighted Elephant Island and the next day they reached the island—497 days since they had last set foot on land. Shackleton's dedication to his men and understanding of the importance of maintaining their morale kept them together through months of pulling their laden lifeboats across broken ice flows and in and out of the water.

The crew was safer than they had been since leaving the ship, but Shackleton realized they would not be rescued from Elephant Island. No ships used that passage and they had no radios to call for help. Winter had set in again and they did not have enough supplies to last the winter. Shackleton had a patriarchal view of his crew and believed everything that happened to them was his responsibility. The men had trusted him and he felt morally accountable for their welfare. He decided he needed to travel to the nearest habitation to get help. This was the whaling station on South Georgia Island, which was 800 miles away and across the stormiest expanse of ocean in the world. Waves as high as 50 feet, known as "Cape Horn rollers," frequented these seas and their navigation would rely on a sextant and chronometer. But these tools required sighting of the sun that may not be visible for weeks at that time of year. It was clearly a very risky trip but essential if he was to save his men. When he told the men of his plan to go for help, all 28 immediately volunteered to accompany him. He was almost overtaken with emotion from their faith in him, and finally managed to say only, "Thank you, men."

He chose five experienced seamen and the lifeboat, *James Caird,* for the trip. The men worked on the boat to make it as seaworthy as possible, using canvas and odds and ends to create a partial covering. The canvas required thawing over a seal blubber fire before it could be sewn in place. The wooden boat seams were caulked using lamp wicks, oil paints from the ships artist, and seals' blood. Launching the boat was difficult because of water and supplies for the estimated 30 day trip and the rough seas. The boat rolled over on the first attempt throwing two of the men overboard. Those remaining on the island used the other two boats to make a hut because the wind had shredded their tents. They heated the hut and cooked with a smoking seal blubber stove.

The six men left Elephant Island on April 24, 1916, the day before the ice closed in on the island. The sea constantly washed into the boat, making the reindeer hide sleeping bags and everything else wet. They were soaked with seawater an average of every 3 to 4 minutes. Reindeer hair from their sleeping bags clogged the manual pump they used to empty the seaweater. Ice formed on the boat that was 15 inches thick, making it sluggish in the enormous waves, strong winds, and "cross seas" that battered them about. They chipped away at the ice but eventually had to throw items overboard including all but two sleeping bags to lighten the load. Shackleton insisted on hot meals every 4 hours using a tiny stove that two men had to hold in place while boiling water for the "hoosh" they drank from mugs. After 7 days they determined they had traveled 380 miles toward their destination and concluded they would make South Georgia Island in good time—if their navigation was correct. On the 11th day they were nearly swamped by the most enormous wave any of them had ever seen. All six bailed water for dear life and after 10 minutes they realized they would not sink. On the 14th day they sighted South Georgia Island, half as long as they expected the journey to take. They were out of drinking water because their last container became contaminated with sea water. They finally landed two days later after fighting their way through treacherous surf and reefs and were able to obtain fresh ice to melt for drinking water. They had navigated the 800 miles using only four sightings of the sun—an amazing feat. If they had missed South Georgia Island, they would have been swept into the south Atlantic to perish and the men on Elephant Island would have had no chance of survival.

When they finally landed on South Georgia Island it was nearly dark. They stripped the boat of all supplies and hauled it up as far as possible on the rocky beach. Finding a cave in the rocks fringed with 15-foot icicles, they rested, ate, and slept. The boat was nearly destroyed that night, and they all had to hold it onto the land for the rest of the night. Shackleton got a laugh from the men by thanking them for joining his little party. The next day the boat received further damage, and they decided they had enough of sailing.

They needed to travel overland 22 miles to reach the whaling station and obtain a ship to rescue their crewmates on Elephant Island. This required crossing the main mountain range on the island, which was totally unmapped, covered with snow and ice, and had never been traversed. Some of the men were too weak for the trip so Shackleton set out with two others to cross the mountains. They crossed glaciers, icy slopes, and snow fields with fog closing in behind them. As night fell, they knew they had to descend to a lower altitude or freeze, since they had no sleeping bags. Because they were so high and the slopes so steep, Shackleton proposed they take a chance and slide down a very steep snowy slope in the dark, hoping they did not go off a cliff or hit rocks. He took the lead, and they survived without injury. They then warmed a hot meal of hoosh and the other two exhausted men fell asleep. Shackleton realized they would freeze and never wake up, so after 5 minutes he awakened them and told them they had slept for an hour and it was time to go. The two then noticed that Shackleton was not wearing the warmest boots designed for their trip, but a lighter weight boot that was less warm. They realized this was typical of their leader, as there had been a shortage of boots on their trek and his rule was any deprivation should be experienced by him before any of the men.

At first light, Shackleton climbed a ridge and thought he heard a steam whistle from the whaling station. It was repeated at 7:00 am and they rejoiced. They roped themselves down and cut steps in the ice to get off the ridge, then had to lower themselves down through a drenching waterfall in the ice cliffs to reach solid ground. When they approached the whaling camp with unkempt beards and hair, tattered clothing, and unwashed for a year, the first two people who saw them were young boys who ran in terror. But the manager recognized them, took them in and helped them recover.

After recovering, they first took a boat to rescue the three men on the other side of South Georgia Island. Shackleton sent them home to England as soon as possible. He then arranged for a ship to rescue the rest of the crew on Elephant Island. But the ice pack forced them back to the Falkland Islands, where Shackleton got another ship from the Chilean government. Once again the ice was too much and they had to turn back. British and Chilean citizens then donated enough money to Shackleton to commission another ship, which broke down in route. Shackleton then petitioned the Chilean government for a fourth ship, which was finally successful in reaching the men on Elephant Island. When the first lifeboat was lowered to rescue the men on the island, Shackleton was one of the first in the boat. As it neared shore he yelled, "Are you all well?" The men answered immediately, "All well!" All had survived 105 days on the island in spite of hardships, which included amputation of one young crewman's toes. Shackleton was surrounded by his men who pummeled his back and arms in gratitude. Within half an hour they were all on the ship headed north and eventually back to England.

Frank Worsley, skipper of the *Endurance* and close confidant of Shackleton, attributed their survival to Shackleton's constant care for the men and his general watchfulness concerning their welfare. He would attend personally to the smallest details and had unending patience and persistence regarding their well-being. He was viewed by the men as exceedingly brave but never foolhardy. He always approached dangerous tasks with caution and careful planning. In 1921 Shackleton returned to Antarctica on a scientific expedition but died suddenly from a suspected heart attack while at anchor on South Georgia Island. He was 47 at the time of his death.

Fiedler's Contingency Theory, Path-Goal Theory, the Leadership Grid or Situational Leadership Theory can be used to discuss Shackleton's extreme concern and *consideration* for the safety, welfare, and survival of his crew. He was also highly *directive* in the dangerous and highly uncertain situation they faced when their ship broke up in the ice. He exhibited Charismatic/Transformational

Leadership by *inspiring* his men with short speeches and personal *risk taking*. This caused them to cheerfully carry out his directives and maintain their supreme confidence in his leadership. His absolute belief in assuming *moral responsibility* for their situation, in assuring their safety and escaping danger reflects elements of Principle Centered, Authentic Leadership and Servant Leadership. One might also consider him from a Leader Member Exchange perspective in that he had an *in-group* of confidants he frequently consulted on important decisions, but he always included all the men in any benefits possible—*out-group* members did not suffer under his leadership.

Discussion Questions

1. How did Shackleton's situation and environment on the Antarctic expedition affect his leadership approach?
2. Why was Shackleton's supportive and considerate leadership approach especially important to the crew?
3. Do you believe Shackleton's leadership style would be effective in organizational environments such as government, business, labor or sports? Why or why not?
4. Which leadership theory do you believe most accurately characterizes Shackleton's leadership approach?

References

Cool Antarctica. (n.d.). Shackleton, Sir Ernest (1874–1922) Trans-Antarctica Expedition 1914–17. Retrieved December 7, 2008, from http://www.coolantarctica.com/Antarctica%20fact%20file/History/Ernest%20Shackleton_Trans-Antarctic_expedition.htm

Ernest Shackleton. (n.d.). In *Wikipedia*. Retrieved April 20, 2011, from http://en.wikipedia.org/wiki/Ernest_Shackleton

Worsley, F. A. (1931). *Endurance*. New York: W. W. Norton & Company.

Chapter 5

Mother Teresa
Servant to the Poor

Mother Teresa was a Roman Catholic nun who obtained Indian citizenship while devoting her life to serving the poorest of the poor. From Calcutta, in the state of West Bengal, she created and led a worldwide organization titled the Missionaries of Charity that operated over 600 missions in 123 countries at the time of her death in 1997. Mother Teresa and her organization provided caring service and dignity to the destitute, sick, orphaned, and dying without any concern for their religious beliefs. During her life, she received countless awards including the Nobel Peace Prize and India's highest civilian honor. Gallup polls consistently found Mother Teresa to be the most admired person in the United States.

Mother Teresa was born Agnes Gonxhe Bojaxhiu in 1910 in the city of Skopje, now the capital of the Republic of Macedonia. Her father was a contractor and was known to be very charitable to the poor but he died before she was 10. Her mother supported three children with an embroidery business of her own and raised her children as devout Catholics. Agnes became involved in the church and was fascinated by reading stories of missionaries helping the poor in India. When she was 12 she knew she wanted to be a nun and at 18 she left her family for Ireland to join the Sisters of Loreto who prepared her for a teaching ministry in Bengal, India. She arrived in India in 1929 and took her vows as a nun in 1931, choosing her new name Teresa from the patron saint of missionaries. She taught in the Loreto Convent school in Calcutta for 17 years, the last 11 of which she served as school principal.

At the convent school, Teresa was described as hard working, selfless, dedicated, and very practical. During World War II, Calcutta became filled with refugees. A famine and the war resulted in food supplies being cut off from the city, causing rampant poverty and starvation. When East Pakistan (now Bangladesh) became independent, this resulted in over 1 million more refugees fleeing to Bengal and Calcutta. Conditions for the poor became even worse. In 1946, Mother Teresa had an epiphany while traveling on a train. She realized she must leave the Loreto Convent and devote her life to serving the poorest of the poor. She petitioned her superiors and was granted permission two years later to work as a nun outside the convent. She chose a white sari with blue borders as her dress, obtained some medical training, and left the convent in December 1948 to begin work in the slum of Calcutta.

She began her service by starting a school for small children in an open area under the shade of a tree. She had no chairs, tables, or blackboard, but drew on the bare ground with a stick to teach the alphabet. The first week she visited two priests who donated a small amount of money she used to rent two small rooms for her school and a dispensary with medical supplies for the poor. The school quickly grew and teachers began to volunteer when they could spare the time. Others made small donations including furniture, books, and a little money. She gave baths to the children and awarded bars of soap for good attendance. She began what she called her "begging expeditions" to local churches, influential officials, and local pharmacies for whatever medical supplies or other resources they could spare. She quickly developed a policy of refusing government grants that placed restrictions on how the money was spent. When she saw a need, she tried to meet it at that time and spent little effort planning or scheduling for the future.

After one week she opened a dispensary with medicines to serve the multitude of people suffering from leprosy, tuberculosis, cholera, tetanus, meningitis, and plague. She had already begun visiting the sick and began screening visitors to the dispensary for TB. One month after leaving the convent, she opened a second school and dispensary in another area of the city. Her missionary service became well known in the area and her begging expeditions became famous and more productive.

At first she lived in a single room, which was donated to her, with nothing but a box for a chair and table. Soon some furniture was donated, and a cook from her convent joined her as a companion. More volunteers appeared and in 1950 her mission was designated a congregation by the Vatican. Within two years, 30 women joined the Missionaries of Charity to serve with Mother Teresa. She sent them out in pairs to hospitals and the streets to pick up the dying, seriously ill and drunk. They tried to have the sick and dying admitted to the hospital but were often refused and had to treat people in the streets. Mother Teresa once sat in the doorway of a hospital until they agreed to admit a dying woman. Sisters of Charity carried only a water bottle and refused any refreshment, traveled like the poor, and were recognized and respected even in the roughest areas of the city.

Mother Teresa's spiritual advisor advertised her ministry in a newspaper and more donations began arriving. A property with three modest buildings was donated to the archbishop of Calcutta who loaned Mother Teresa the money to purchase the property. It became the center for the Missionaries of Charity and was known as Motherhouse. Missions multiplied in number and spread all over India. In 1965 she was invited for a visit by the Bishop for Venezuela and was struck by the poverty of landless people of African descent. She then opened a Mission of Charity in Cocorote, Venezuela to serve these people. This became a pattern for her in opening overseas missions. A local bishop would typically invite her for a visit, she would assess the situation, and frequently sponsor another overseas mission to serve the local need. Her second mission was in the Vatican, to serve the poor living in that segment of Rome. Her facility was provided by the Pope who visited her mission at times and served food to the poor. Other missions were opened in Rome, Australia, London, Jordan, Bangladesh, Northern Ireland, New York, and the Soviet Union (after she sent a personal note to Mikhail Gorbachev).

In 1953, she opened a home for the dying in southern Calcutta, to allow suffering beggars, rickshaw pullers, and the unwanted to die with dignity and love. There they received medical attention and last rites according to their own faith. In the 1950s nearly all those admitted eventually died, in the 1960s and 1970s about half died, and in recent years only one fifth of those admitted have died. Soon the citizens of Calcutta no longer ignored the sick and dying, but called for an ambulance or brought them to a hospital or the Missionaries of Charity.

As her Missionaries of Charity became well known, Mother Teresa was welcomed by government officials and influential individuals in different countries. She gave talks, sent messages, and visited these people often, resulting in donations and permission to open more missions. She also visited war zones and disaster sights to help bring aid to the injured and homeless. At the end of each day, when the other sisters were in bed, she dealt with administrative issues and correspondence. Eventually Mother Teresa spent about half of her time visiting and opening other missions. She decided difficult issues for the sisters as they sought and followed her directions. She led their prayer services and taught them how to handle the problems they would face.

Mother Teresa received the Nobel Prize for Peace in 1979 and asked that the traditional banquet be cancelled and the money given to serve the poor. Her request was honored and inspired more giving throughout Europe, resulting in 40,000 pounds in donations. People worldwide flocked to see her and asked for an autograph. She inspired those around her with her complete dedication to serving the poor. She was granted free airline tickets around the world, and people scrambled to help her make connections, holding flights when necessary. Like Mohandas Ghandi, she understood the effective use of symbolism as an inspirational tool—wearing only a loincloth and sari of coarse cloth woven by lepers. She understood that identifying with and ministering to the innocent suffering people of the world could inspire action by others to help.

In 1963 the Brothers of Charity was formed when Mother Teresa realized some work was best done by men, such as tasks requiring physical strength and role modeling for young boys in orphanages. Although they wore no distinctive dress, the Brothers of Charity served the same poor populations as the Sisters. Coworkers of Charity were volunteers who worked part time and for short periods to allow them to serve and decide if they were suited for this life of service. The Missions of Charity eventually included child welfare and education services, food programs, night shelters, natural family planning centers, medical dispensaries, leprosy clinics and rehabilitation centers, as well as schools, sewing and handicraft classes, prison visiting, family counseling, and religious teaching. They also provided homes for abandoned, crippled, and mentally handicapped children, unwed mothers, alcoholics, sick and dying destitutes, and AIDS sufferers. Donations streamed in from around the world and a committee of coworkers allocated resources to missions that requested help. These resources included millions of pounds of food items, clothes and financial assistance. Sister Superiors were appointed for each region of the world and a constitution was created to govern the behavior and activities of all Missionaries of Charity.

This small humble woman with no university education, a limited vocabulary, and misshapen bare feet in rough sandals maintained a cheerful disposition and aroused the emotions of all who met her. She was perceptive, incredibly hard working, always practical, and exhibited the grace and deliberateness of one who has not a single doubt about her calling. She believed in taking one step at a time, that no act was too small, and often said big things can be done by other people. Her Missionaries undoubtedly have saved millions of lives throughout the world.

Mother Teresa exhibited several important leadership behaviors that are addressed by leadership theories. She is likely best described by the Servant Leadership Model due to her complete *dedication* to serving the poorest of the poor and *empowering* and *nurturing* the Sisters of Charity to carry out their work. Her actions were always consistent with their mission and she constantly put their *mission ahead of any personal goals.* Her *optimism, resilience, high moral character,* and *"walking the walk"* reflect the Authentic Leadership model. Her *integrity* and *determination* are described in Trait Theories of Leadership. Her inspiration of followers, donors, and recipients of her service through *role modeling, risk taking, inspirational speeches, spirituality,* and use of *symbolism* are addressed in Charismatic/Transformational Leadership Theories. Her *boundary spanning* behaviors through "begging expeditions" to obtain resources, to gain designation from the Vatican as a congregation, and to spread her service to worldwide locations is addressed in the Multiple Linkage Model and Reformulated Path-Goal Theories. Her *supportive* leadership with the Sisters and charity recipients are described in several contingency leadership models including Path-Goal Theory, Situational Leadership Theory, Fiedler's Contingency Theory and the Leadership Grid. *Substitutes for Leadership* might also describe Mother Teresa's strategy for sending her teams of missionaries to serve the poor.

Discussion Questions

1. Why was Mother Teresa so effective in serving the poor and building an organization to serve the poor?
2. In what ways was Mother Teresa a Servant Leader? In what ways was she a Charismatic/Transformational Leader? Do you think it would be difficult for a leader to be both Servant and Charismatic/Transformational with followers? Why or why not?
3. Did Mother Teresa and the Missionaries of Charity make use of substitutes for leadership? If so, in what ways? Were there any possible leadership neutralizers that might have inhibited her influence on some Sisters of Charity? If so, what were they?
4. What do you think of Mother Teresa's policy of refusing government grants to support her work with the poor?

References

Chawla, N. (1992). *Mother Teresa—The authorized autobiography.* Boston, MA: Element Books.

Mother Teresa. (n.d.). In *Wikipedia.* Retrieved November 23, 2009, from http://en.wikipedia.org/wiki/Mother_Teresa

Chapter 6

Abraham Lincoln
16th President
of the United States

Abraham Lincoln is often described as the greatest president in United States history. He was first elected to the presidency in 1860 when the United States was on the brink of being torn apart. Economic strife between northern and southern states, changing attitudes toward slavery, and rapid western expansion all combined to create an explosive social and political division in the country. This situation eventually led to a civil war that destroyed over 600,000 lives as well as countless families, livelihoods, and the collective fabric that holds a nation together. The Civil War began one month after Lincoln took office and occupied his entire time as president. His insightful and skilled leadership held the northern states together and eventually ended the war, while showing empathy and compassion for all the soldiers and families involved.

Lincoln was born in 1809 in a frontier log cabin in Kentucky. His father farmed, and Lincoln described his early life as poor but apparently rich in affection, especially from his mother who died when he was 9. His father remarried and his stepmother encouraged Abraham in his efforts to educate himself. He developed a lasting fondness for her. His youngest brother died in infancy and his last sibling, a sister, died when he was 19. These early tragedies undoubtedly affected the young Abraham, creating a somewhat melancholy demeanor and philosophical perspective on life. Abraham had very little opportunity for formal schooling but he showed persistence early in life as he read and reread anything he could find. His love of literature and fondness for reading aloud for an audience continued throughout his life. He held many jobs in his early years including storekeeper, postmaster and surveyor while he studied law. He was popular and respected due to his honesty and sincerity, his physical strength, and his ability and willingness to tell humorous stories that delighted his audiences.

He ran unsuccessfully for the Illinois state legislature in 1832 but was elected in 1834. That same year he became partner in a law firm, the first of three law partnerships that allowed Lincoln to develop a high level of legal competence and a reliable income. He married Mary Todd, daughter of a successful banker, in 1842. He served for eight years in the state legislature where he voted and spoke out against slavery. In 1846 he was elected to the United States Congress where he opposed the war with Mexico. The issue of slavery emerged in a proposed amendment to legislation banning slavery in any territory acquired from Mexico. Lincoln supported the amendment, and it became a battle with southern states that feared eventual abolition of slavery. He drafted legislation banning slavery in the District of Columbia but did not receive the needed support and it was never introduced to Congress.

In 1849 he did not seek reelection and returned to his law practice. He ran unsuccessfully for the United States Senate two times and helped organize and lead the new Republican Party in Illinois. In the second Senate race, he participated in the famous Lincoln-Douglas debates over slavery in the new territories. Public speaking and debating were major forms of entertainment at that time, and Lincoln was gaining fame and confidence as a master orator. In 1859 he positioned himself for a presidential nomination through long speaking tours where he exposed himself to thousands of voters. He deftly engineered the nominating convention toward Chicago, in his home state of Illinois. At the convention in May 1860 he managed to secure the presidential nomination over several major rivals, all of whom had longer and more distinguished careers. He did this by letting the more famous candidates fight it out with each other and positioning himself as the second choice for everyone. His election team also packed the hall with his supporters. Using friendly and complimentary requests, Lincoln convinced his former rivals to speak on behalf of his campaign for election. They did a magnificent job while Lincoln worked on keeping the party factions together through writing letters, resolving disputes, carefully avoiding commitments for patronage, and gathering and sharing information for the election. He was elected in November 1860 as 16th president of the United States. He had finally reached his lifelong goal of being respected and esteemed by his fellow men. He now needed to prove himself worthy of that esteem.

Lincoln immediately set about establishing his cabinet of close advisors. Lincoln knew the country was in jeopardy and that incredibly difficult problems lay ahead. He wanted individuals who were highly intelligent and experienced, were well-respected, and represented different factions in their new Republican Party. He chose as his top cabinet members the three individuals who had also sought the Republican Party nomination for president—his former competitors. His self-confidence allowed him to select men with more education and longer records of public service than his own. He knew he would need their information, perspective, and insight to help solve the problems they faced. He selected the remainder of his cabinet with the same criteria in mind. He constantly consulted with these advisors, individually and as a group, throughout his presidency. He became especially close with Secretary of State William Seward and relied on his advice and suggestions many times.

Lincoln had shown his ability and willingness to mediate among powerful factions within his party to maintain its cohesion throughout the election. Now he needed to fulfill the same function to span boundaries among northern states and keep them together as southern states began to secede from the Union. Seven southern states seceded between Lincoln's election in November 1860 and March 1861. Lincoln had consistently maintained he did not seek to eliminate slavery in states where it existed, but only in the new territories. He believed that slavery would die if not extended to these territories where southern growers planned new plantations. On his first day in office, the first item on his desk reported that the federal Fort Sumter in South Carolina was being threatened by Confederate troops and a resupply ship had been fired upon and forced to turn back. The military recommended surrendering the fort and Lincoln polled each member of his cabinet separately for their opinion. He then gathered more information, shared it with his cabinet, and polled them again. They decided to try to resupply the fort again with the support of their best warship. Unfortunately a communication error resulted in the ship being misdirected and the fort was attacked and eventually surrendered. The South had fired the first shots, the country was now divided and engaged in a civil war. Lincoln had shown his willingness to listen carefully to his advisors and to use them to help make major decisions, a pattern he would demonstrate repeatedly during his administration. He was a skilled communicator and now realized the critical importance of accurate communication in the war effort.

He frequently acted as mediator between military generals and among members of his cabinet, who differed in their opinions of the correct actions during the Civil War. He supported individuals even when he disagreed with them and defended officers who were attacked by the press or other officials. He often took personal responsibility for mistakes that were caused by others, to show his support. And he visited the Union troops often and after every defeat to show his kindness and concern, sometimes taking his young son Tad on these visits. At 6 feet 4 inches tall plus his tall stove pipe hat, he actually looked comical atop a horse with his long legs dangling down when he made these visits. The overall effect was to endear him to the troops and develop great loyalty from the military and his advisors.

A key factor in the North's war effort was preventing Britain from recognizing the Confederate States as a separate country. Lincoln diplomatically softened Seward's approach in negotiating with Britain to successfully prevent their recognition of the South. Early defeats of the Northern forces caused resentment among military officers and cabinet members, which Lincoln continued to mediate. He became frustrated with General McClelland, his main military commander, for lack of action against the South's forces. McClelland continually insisted on the need for more personnel and supplies with predictions of future victories, while living a lavish lifestyle in camp and overestimating the enemy's forces. In January 1862 Lincoln issued a General War Order directing McClelland to move on the South. His directive was soon followed by the death of his beloved son, Willie, who succumbed to Typhoid Fever. Lincoln and his wife suffered incredibly in their grief. His melancholy persisted when the Union Army suffered several defeats. Lincoln replaced General McClelland with General Burnside who was then out-maneuvered and badly defeated at Fredericksburg. Lincoln consulted Seward on how to raise more troops. He eventually accepted Seward's idea of having the northern governors offer the additional troops from their states, thereby removing Lincoln from any public criticism for wanting more troops. It became clear that slaves were being used by the South to build defensive positions for the Confederate forces, freeing up Southern whites for active combat. In January 1863 Lincoln issued the Emancipation Proclamation freeing all slaves in the Confederate States and allowing them to join the Union armed forces. He countered significant Northern feelings of discrimination by publically pointing out that blacks were needed for the war effort. The Emancipation Proclamation resulted in huge numbers of former slaves entering Northern lines and joining forces in military companies of their own. These companies soon distinguished themselves in battle and became highly respected by other soldiers and officers.

These were difficult times for all those involved with the war effort including Lincoln's administration. Cabinet members and many generals were proud men under stress, and often resented if their advice was not taken by Lincoln. In addition to his reputation as a great speaker and humorous story teller, Lincoln was a master at "smoothing their feathers." He was always charitable and showed kindness, respect, and provided generous compliments for offended individuals. He showed tremendous emotional control and understanding of those around him by never retaliating against those who attacked his ideas and never holding a grudge (even though Secretary of War William Stanton had humiliated Lincoln early in his political career). Although outwardly he appeared melancholy, Lincoln dealt effectively with stress by frequently reading great and popular literature and poetry (often aloud to friends), by visiting Seward and his two secretaries, and trips to the theater. As the war dragged on, his appearance became more careworn, pensive, and haggard, but his face would always lighten and often smile in the presence of friends and acquaintances who he usually entertained with his never ending store of humorous stories and anecdotes.

Lincoln continued to try new generals until he appointed General Meade three days before Union forces confronted Lee's army that had invaded the North. It was July 1863, and Meade held the high ground near the town of Gettysburg. In a horrible three-day battle that claimed over 60,000 lives, the Union Army defeated Lee's army and forced a retreat. Lincoln's hopes for hastening the end of the war were dashed when Meade failed to follow up and capture Lee's army. But the victory was quickly followed by the capture of Vicksburg and a large Confederate force by General Grant. At last the tide was turning in favor of the North. In November 1863 Lincoln delivered the famous Gettysburg Address at the site of the battle. Some believe this brief address is the greatest speech in United States history.

His overall goal from the beginning was to preserve the union and he eventually resolved to end slavery throughout the country. With excellent writing skills, he wrote public letters addressing policy issues to be read by officials at gatherings. These complemented press releases and speeches which he and cabinet members gave on tours of the Union states. Lincoln often inserted material in the speeches delivered by his advisors. He continued to support Secretary of the Treasury Salmon Chase, when he criticized Lincoln and the administration's handling of the war during his own pursuit of the presidency in 1864. Chase had done an outstanding job financing the war and Lincoln was grateful, while realizing that keeping him close and involved in the war effort would likely minimize the damage he could inflict on Lincoln. He regularly obtained input from influential individuals including congressmen and senators, governors, military officers, cabinet members and those outside the government such as anti-slavery advocate Frederick Douglass (who spoke very highly of Lincoln).

Lincoln placed General Grant in charge of the Union Army in March 1864. Grant avoided the public eye, lived very frugally, and took the initiative against the South. He soon fought a seven-week battle of attrition against Lee's army in Virginia, inflicting major damage on the Confederate forces. General McClelland opposed Lincoln as the democratic candidate for president, but Union victories at Atlanta, Mobile, and Virginia made peace imminent and confirmed Lincoln's reelection. Lincoln and Grant worked together to develop a program to give land and assistance to freed slaves. Lincoln pushed the Thirteenth Amendment of the Constitution through Congress abolishing slavery throughout the United States, using patronage to sway Democratic senators to vote for the amendment. The Thirteenth Amendment was ratified after Lincoln's death. He negotiated from strength with Southern peace commissioners, insisting on three points—all the states were part of a single country, with no slavery, and any suspension of hostilities must include the Confederacy's full surrender and a complete end to the war.

Lincoln was reelected in November 1864 and in March 1865 he gave a conciliatory inaugural address directed toward the Southern states—"with malice toward none, with charity for all." Grant and Sherman pursued Lee's army and occupied Richmond, Virginia, the Confederate capital. Lincoln followed Grant's progress and visited Richmond where blacks called him their savior. He left Richmond in a joyful mood. Secretary of State Seward, who had become Lincoln's close friend and ally and had worried about Lincoln's safety as the war was ending, was seriously injured in a carriage accident. Lincoln returned to Washington to see Seward, and Robert E. Lee surrendered the following day. Always self-confident, Lincoln became more cheerful and neatly groomed in the following days. He read literature and writings by his favorite humorists aloud to visitors and planned a visit with Mary to his favorite playhouse, Ford's Theater. On April 14, 1865, five days after Lee's surrender, they visited the theater and Lincoln was fatally shot by a well-known actor who easily gained admittance to the theater. Seward was also attacked but survived his injuries. Lincoln died the next morning. He had stated his ambition was to be esteemed by his fellow men and to prove himself worthy of their esteem. History shows Lincoln clearly achieved his ambition, since his reputation as an honest, caring and intelligent leader who was a great speaker and abolitionist, has spread throughout the world.

Lincoln's leadership has often been described as Charismatic/Transformational due to his *vision* for preserving the United States union, his outstanding *rhetorical skills*, and his ability to create loyal and devoted followers to support his candidacy and programs as president. His *boundary spanning* activities are clearly evident in his political maneuvering during his candidacy and time in office, as well as his effective mediation among politicians and military generals. His *caring* and *consideration* for all people were evident in his *supportiveness* for troops, widows and concern for the Southern states as he opposed all punitive actions against Southern states once the war ended. He exhibited *directive leadership* by issuing General War Orders requiring specific action by the Northern forces. These actions demonstrate important leader behavior patterns described in Reformulated Path-Goal Theory, the Multiple Linkage Model, Situational Leadership Theory and Fiedler's Contingency Theory. Lincoln demonstrated Leader-Member Exchange Theory by developing an *in-group* of trusted advisors composed of several members of his cabinet who became fiercely loyal to him. His reliance on this cabinet also demonstrated *Substitutes for Leadership*. He also demonstrated a *participative* approach in making complex decisions with trusted cabinet members during the Civil War. This approach is addressed in the Normative Decision Theory. Lincoln was clearly an Authentic Leader and his *cognitive complexity, determination, self-confidence, sociability,* and *integrity* all reflect Trait Theories of leadership.

Discussion Questions

1. Try to think of specific situations in Lincoln's life that he demonstrated Charismatic/Transformational Leadership? Describe these situations.
2. In what ways did Lincoln show his consideration and concern for people?
3. Why was Lincoln's boundary spanning behavior so important for his administration and the country?
4. Why was a trusted in-group of individual advisors, as described in Leader Member Exchange Theory, so important for Lincoln during his presidency?

References

Abraham Lincoln. (n.d.). In *Wikipedia.* Retrieved December 11, 2010, from http://en.wikipedia.org/wiki/Abraham_Lincoln

Goodwin, D. K. (2005). *Team of rivals: The political genius of Abraham Lincoln.* New York: Simon and Schuster.

The White House. (n.d.). *Abraham Lincoln.* Retrieved December 10, 2010, from http://www.whitehouse.gov/about/presidents/abrahamlincoln

Chapter 7

Pat Summitt
Women's Basketball Coach

Pat Summitt was the head basketball coach for the University of Tennessee Lady Volunteers (Vols). She coached at Tennessee since 1974 and recently became one of only two collegiate coaches with over 1,000 victories. Her teams have won more games than any other NCAA basketball coach in history. Summitt was a consummate competitor who won eight NCAA national championships (second only to John Wooden from UCLA who had 10 titles) and 27 Southeastern Conference championships. Her program has produced 19 Olympic athletes and 43 professional players. She was admitted to the Basketball Hall of Fame the first year she was eligible and she was the first women's basketball coach to break the $1,000,000 salary ceiling. Perhaps most important for her players, every Lady Vol who completed her basketball eligibility at Tennessee has graduated with a degree.

Patricia Head Summitt was born in 1952, the fourth of five children, in Clarksville, Tennessee. She spent most of her early years working with her family from sunrise to sunset on their dairy and tobacco farm. Her father was a severe disciplinarian who built a small plot of farmland into a thousand acre farm before branching into several other businesses. Pat described her early days as filled with school, church, and field work. But her father did build a basketball court in the hayloft of their barn and strung lights so Pat and her brothers could play at night. The entire family was tall in stature, and Pat grew up playing against her athletic brothers. When she was in high school, her father moved the family to another county so Pat could play for a school basketball team. By then she could dribble circles around the boys.

She excelled on the court and attended the University of Tennessee at Martin where she was selected as an All-American. In 1974, her senior year, she severely injured her knee and was sidelined. That same year she became a graduate assistant basketball coach at the University of Tennessee, Knoxville. Soon after this the head coach left, and she was named head coach of the Lady Vols. She was not much older than her players. They were all from Tennessee and had played only six-person women's basketball in high school—three on defense, three on offense—which required very little running. They were now playing five person full court basketball—a new game for these players. The athletic funds for the team were minimal so Pat drove them to their games and washed their uniforms. She told the undergraduates who showed up for the first tryout how demanding it would be to be a Lady Vol and many never returned. She was accustomed to hard work, she role modeled this for her players, and she expected their maximum effort at all times.

In her first year coaching the Lady Vols finished with 16 wins and 8 losses, this was followed the next year with a similar record. During this time Pat finished her master's degree and served as co-captain of the 1976 Olympic basketball team, earning the United States a silver medal. Billie Moore coached the Olympic team that year and she drove Pat like a tough taskmaster with harsh words and challenges. Pat attributes her aggressive verbal and physical style of coaching to Moore. It is also likely her upbringing with a domineering father influenced her style. After her first two years of coaching, Summitt's teams never won less than 20 games per season.

Summitt believes that life is competition and those who believe they will win, usually do. She states that winners are not born, they are made, and told her players they must always go for what they want and have no fear of failure. They must learn from mistakes and correct them for the next opportunity. She was animated, intense, and demanding during practice and games—shouting directions and waving her arms. She met with each player at least four times per year to direct them in how to perform their roles. She then held them accountable for meeting her expectations such that they learned self-discipline and began to "own their role" on the team. She also met with the team captains early in the year to set goals for the team in writing. She believed the goals must require great effort to achieve, but not be so high that the players lose morale and self-discipline. She set goals for the team each day and held them accountable, with rewards for achieving the goals and punishment for non-achievement. One example was decreasing the number of turnovers during practice scrimmage, which was often against male players. If this goal was met, they ended the practice with an easy shooting drill. If the goal was not met, they ran sprints. She had few rules for her teams, but enforced them consistently with negative consequences for violations. One key player who was destined for a successful professional career was dropped from the team when she repeatedly violated team rules. Summitt insisted that her players always give their best effort and maintained that this makes others respect them. She constantly challenged her players by scheduling a large percentage of their games against nationally ranked opponents. She noted that the pressure of these games prepared her team for NCAA tournament competition.

She learned from her parents that you win in life with people, so she consulted with her players and listened. Early in the year, she asked the players what style of play they wanted to use during the season. They nearly always said they wanted to run, press, play hard, fast, and smart. Later in the year, when they were gasping for breath after running sprints, she reminded them of their decision. She also used her captains' input in setting team goals and establishing rules. John Wooden stated that Pat knows people as well as she knows basketball. She got to know each player and tried to understand their goals and motivation. Early in her career, she realized that her constructive criticism and aggressive style was destroying some of her players' confidence and ability to play to their potential. At her husband's suggestion, she instituted a program called Rebound and Two Points. Whenever a Lady Vol received a compliment from Summitt, they responded with "Two Points!" When they received a criticism, they stated "Rebound!" This made them keep track and realize that they received compliments along with the criticism. By being honest, she built mutual trust and respect. She showed that she cared for her players, who called her "Pat," and she always gave them the major credit for their successes.

Summitt knew that to be successful, she must constantly change and update her strategy and tactics. Tennessee has a long standing rivalry with the University of Connecticut, a basketball powerhouse. When the Lady Vols lost to Connecticut in the final game of the NCAA tournament in 1995, Summitt studied the triple-post offense UConn used to defeat her team. She then took her staff to Chicago and met with coaches for the Chicago Bulls who used that offense at the professional level. They learned the Bull's strategy and implemented portions of this offense in their team's play the next year, resulting in three consecutive NCAA national championships.

Pat Summitt knew that all leaders have weaknesses and believed they should surround themselves with people who are better than the leader in those areas. They should then rely on those people for decisions and guidance when needed. She believed in role modeling good citizenship and was extremely active in representing her program and university to the local, state, and national community. She was an active fund raiser for University of Tennessee and served in numerous capacities for the Smithsonian Institute, United Way, Verizon Wireless Hopeline (which benefits domestic violence advocacy organizations), Big Brothers Big Sisters, Easter Seal Society, American Heart Association, Race for the Cure of Juvenile Diabetes, Basketball Hall of Fame, United States Olympic Committee, and other organizations. She was a popular motivational speaker for numerous organizations such as the CIA, Federal Reserve, and Victoria's Secret, and she served as consultant to the Women's National Basketball Association. Summitt's achievements and service brought her widespread recognition and numerous national leadership awards. Her players describe the life lessons they receive from her as just as important as their coursework and degree from University of Tennessee. Pat Summitt was diagnosed with early onset dementia in 2011 and stepped down as head coach in early 2012.

Pat Summitt was a highly *directive leader* when she assigned roles and clarified expectations for individual players. She also used *participative leadership* by consulting with her captains on goal setting, rule specification and style of play. She was *supportive* of her players by getting to know them and showing she cared for them as individuals. She used *reward* and *punishment behaviors* by implementing a system so they remembered how she complimented them for meeting goals, gave them credit for their successes and punished them for rule violations. These leader behaviors are discussed in the Multiple Linkage Model, Situational Leadership Theory, Path-Goal Theory and the Leadership Grid. Her fund raising and volunteer activities for worthy causes demonstrate effective *boundary spanning* for her university and sports program. This leader behavior is described in the Reformulated Path-Goal Theory and the Multiple Linkage Model. Her aggressive verbal and physical style fits with common expectations for a leader in highly competitive sports, demonstrating the Implicit Leadership Theory for this type of leader. She made use of *Substitutes for Leadership* in hiring staff members who could fill in for her weaknesses and provide leadership in their areas when needed. Her *determination, self-confidence,* and *integrity* reflect the Trait Theories of leadership.

Discussion Questions

1. Do you believe Pat Summitt's highly aggressive verbal and physical style is necessary in leading a national contender in university level sports competition? Why or why not?

2. Do you believe there are athletes who would be unable to play for Summitt? If so, why?
3. How important are Summitt's boundary spanning activities for the success of her program at University of Tennessee?
4. In what ways does Summitt make use of substitutes for leadership in the teams she coaches?
5. What are the leadership characteristics and behaviors that make up an implicit leadership theory for a top level university sports coach? Are these characteristics and behaviors any different for a professional sports coach?

References

Frick, Lisa. Summitt, Patricia Head. *Notable Sports Figures*. 2004. Retrieved August 6, 2011, from Encyclopedia.com: http://www.encyclopedia.com/doc/1G2-3407900547.html

Pat Summitt and the Tennessee Lady Vols. (n.d.). Retrieved on November 6, 2009, from http://thethunderchild.com/LadyVols/Photos/BioPhotos/Biography.html

Pat Summitt. (n.d.). In *Wikipedia*. Retrieved August 7, 2010, from http://en.wikipedia.org/wiki/Pat_Summitt

Chapter 8

Leymah Gbowee
Liberian Leader of Women in Peacebuilding Network

Leymah Gbowee is a Liberian social worker who initiated and led a mass movement of Christian and Moslem women to end many years of civil war and carnage between fighting factions in Liberia. They succeeded in ousting the despot Charles Taylor from the presidency and exiling him from the country. They then supported a transitional government, which held democratic elections resulting in the first popularly elected female head of state in Africa.

Leymah was born in Liberia and grew up in the capital, Monrovia. Her parents were Liberian and poor, and she experienced civil war from the time she graduated from high school. Charles Taylor had been a major African warlord who launched a rebellion against the president of Liberia in 1989. He had a checkered past, having been educated and arrested in the United States twice and was fired for embezzlement when serving as an official for the Liberian government. Beginning in 1989, the population was subjected to a continual campaign of rape, mutilation, and murder of non-combatants by child soldiers with automatic weapons from both sides of the conflict. The "boy soldiers" (9–15 years old) were given guns and drugs and told to take what they wanted—resulting in horrible atrocities committed in front of families. Taylor eventually emerged the victor and was elected president in 1997. People voted for him because they feared him and a continuation of the war. His administration was marked by diamond smuggling, gun running, supporting terrorism, conscription of children as soldiers for the war in Sierra Leone, as well as abduction, torture, and murder.

Shortly after Taylor became president, another rebellion began in northern Liberia for his overthrow. The war continued with boy soldiers decimating the population and hacking off limbs of civilians to prevent them from fighting. Innocents fled to Monrovia for protection as the rebels took over most of the countryside. The refugees were placed in camps of displaced persons where they faced lack of drinking water, sanitation facilities, and food. Many other Liberians faced these issues as well, including Leymah and her family. She had become a social worker in 1994; and her young children had felt hunger all their lives. She saw the horrible conditions in the camps and how the children suffered. She had counseled former child soldiers and the damage done to Liberia's children was becoming too much for her. In 2003 over 200,000 people had died in the wars, and she had a dream that someone told her to organize the women in her church to pray for peace.

She asked to speak to her Christian church congregation and described the terrible life of the Liberian people, that they were tired of war and what it was doing to their children, and it was time to rise up and speak together about the need to end the fighting. A Muslim woman, who was an official in the Liberian National Police, was in the church and became inspired by Leymah's speech. She offered to carry the message to the other Muslim women in her mosque. They listened and agreed that bullets did not discriminate, so they joined with the Christian women and formed the Women in Peacebuilding Network (WIPNET) with Leymah as their leader.

Taylor's government was embarrassed by the refugee camps, and he told the inhabitants to return to where they were born. They refused because there was still fighting in the countryside and he threatened them. He hypocritically professed to practice Christianity and the rebels were largely Muslim. So the women pressured their ministers, bishops, and imams to pressure government officials and rebels to conduct peace talks. Leymah had the women meet to demonstrate for peace at an open air fish market in Monrovia, where Taylor's convoy drove past every day. They all dressed in white (to symbolize peace) with placards and banners saying that the women wanted peace now. On the first day, 2,500 women overcame their fear and demonstrated as Taylor's convoy slowed but did not stop. She led them in singing, and their words rang out that they were tired of running, suffering, and dying and that they wanted peace for their children. They demonstrated every day for a week and Taylor announced that no one would be allowed to embarrass his administration. The women became more cohesive and declared a sex strike—denying sex to their men until they did something to help stop the war. Husbands began to join the women in praying for the end of the war.

Rebels were getting close to Monrovia and apparently attacked the refugee camps. Taylor sent soldiers supposedly to protect the inhabitants, but both sides committed atrocities on the people living there and the camp populations fled. The international community began to call for peace talks, but both Taylor and the rebels refused. WIPNET decided to submit a position statement to the government demanding they meet with the rebels to discuss peace. It stated that they must stop the carnage, rape, hunger, and disease and save the children's future. They insisted on an unconditional cease fire and a fruitful dialogue to end the war. Taylor realized the women were supported by the Liberian population and the international community and he agreed to meet with them. Leymah read their statement and presented it with careful respect to a government representative who gave it to Taylor. Leymah knew Taylor could smile one minute and have them killed the next. But she vowed they would continue sitting in the sun and rain at the fish market until Taylor responded. The women left the meeting with Leymah leading them into the street. As they marched, more women joined them at every intersection, all dressed in white. The march grew and grew and Taylor knew he could no longer ignore them. He agreed to attend peace talks in Ghana.

Leymah and her followers then needed to convince the rebels to attend, so they conducted a fundraising campaign to send WIPNET representatives to Freetown, in Sierra Leone, where the rebels were meeting. Money came in from all over Liberia, and in Sierra Leone they organized women from that country. Together they lined up outside the hotels and along travel routes—all dressed in white to symbolize their solidarity and all calling for peace. Some of the women knew several rebels and told them their mothers and sisters had traveled a long distance to talk with them. The women told the rebels that if they did not attend peace talks that many innocent people would die in Monrovia and that they would be responsible for the deaths. The women of WIPNET were there to demand that all human rights abuses must stop and the rebels eventually promised to attend the peace talks.

The women knew they needed to keep up the pressure so they raised money to send a group to Ghana to mobilize the refugee women there. Peace talks began with pressure from many other countries to stop the fighting that was destabilizing much of Africa. The women in white demonstrated across the street from the conference center where negotiations took place—singing and holding placards. Leymah described the demonstrators as the "conscience" of the negotiators and called on them to do the right thing for Liberian women and children. Several

African leaders spoke at the conference calling for an end to the fighting. On the first day, the BBC reported that Taylor (who was attending the conference) had been indicted for war crimes in Sierra Leone. Fearing arrest, he fled back to Liberia and left his delegation to negotiate. Rebel leaders gave orders to attack Monrovia and full scale war began around the city while the negotiations proceeded. Taylor's boy soldiers rampaged through the city and threatened to destroy Liberia if Taylor was arrested. His forces repelled several incursions by the rebels and the war continued.

In Ghana, Leymah talked with the mediator (the former president of Nigeria) who saw the women as an important ally. They went to different hotels and spoke with the warring parties, asking them what they could be comfortable with in a settlement. They realized the real issues were power, positions in government, and control of resources that would allow them to profit from any settlement. A high level rebel officer told the women they planned to kill all the people in Monrovia, bring in more women and replenish the population. After six weeks, the talks were stalled with little or no progress. Both sides wanted more power and control in Liberia.

Leymah and the other women despaired for their families in Monrovia where they heard of mass graves and soldiers leaving the front to return and rape civilian women. She sent for more women for a showdown. She instructed them to engage in a "sit in" at the entrances and exits to the main conference room, to lock arms, and to allow no one to leave until a peace accord was signed, even if it took days. Security guards told Leymah that the women were obstructing justice, and she exploded, telling the guards she would make it easy to arrest the women. In Africa, it is considered a curse to see the naked body of your mother, especially if she disrobes deliberately. Leymah began removing her clothes and stated they would all do so unless a peace accord was signed. At this point the mediator arrived to calm the situation. Leymah pointed out that many of the negotiators were having a dream vacation, after sleeping in the bush for most of their lives. She told the mediator about the rebels plans to kill the population in Monrovia and replenish the population. She stated the women wanted the negotiators to feel the hunger and thirst that Liberian people were feeling.

At this point, one rebel warlord tried to jump over the women and they pushed him back into the conference room. He prepared to kick them, and the mediator dared him to try it. The mediator told the warlord the women were treating him like a boy because he was not acting like a real man. He was told to return to the conference table and no one could leave until the women were satisfied. Then the security officer, who had threatened to arrest Leymah, came to her and told her they needed to send some women to block a window where some negotiators were trying to escape. They did so. Leymah and the mediator talked and she decided to give the negotiators two weeks to reach an agreement or they would return with more women and block the doors again. She insisted that the talks must move forward, all delegates must attend every session, and they must not insult the women demonstrators. From this point on, the talks became very serious and sober. The international community continued to apply pressure and threatened financial reprisals if no peace agreement was reached. A peace agreement was finally signed two weeks later. As part of the agreement Taylor was exiled to Nigeria, United Nations and other peace keepers entered Monrovia to supervise the disarmament, and a transitional government was set up to supervise democratic elections of a new permanent government.

The women of WIPNET returned to Liberia as heroes. The transitional government contained many rebel leaders, and the women immediately let them know that they would carefully monitor implementation of the peace agreement. They continued demonstrations for the implementation, wore their white clothing, and displayed placards. Disarmament did not go well until the women asked for calm and began talking with the fighters to assure them of their safety and that the women would help them receive their benefits under the agreement. Many of the fighters told the women they appreciated them and surrendered their weapons. The women worked at accepting former young combatants, knowing they must forgive to move forward. Leymah counseled them and realized they too had been victimized by the military leaders. Leymah and WIPNET worked to support the democratic elections—registering voters and supporting peace candidates. In 2005 Liberia elected Ellen Johnson Sirleaf as president—the first popularly elected woman head of state in Africa. In her inauguration speech, she acknowledged the women of WIPNET who brought peace to Liberia.

Leymah later earned a master's degree in conflict transformation from Eastern Mennonite University in Virginia and received a Blue Ribbon Peace Award from Harvard University, the John F. Kennedy Profile in Courage Award, as well as other awards for her leadership role in bringing peace to Liberia. She currently directs the Women Peace and Security Network Africa located in Ghana. This organization works to build relationships and peace in West Africa by supporting women's efforts to prevent and resolve conflicts. Leymah was awarded the Nobel Peace Prize in 2011.

Leymah Gbowee is clearly an effective *boundary spanning* leader, as she represented the women of Liberia in confrontations with Charles Taylor's government and the negotiators in Ghana. This leader behavior is discussed in the early Multiple Linkage Model and Reformulated Path-Goal Theory. She also exhibits Charismatic/Transformational Leadership in her *inspiring speeches, risk taking, emotional appeals,* and focus on a *vision* and *mission* to achieve peace in Liberia. Her compassion for women and children during the struggle for peace and her activities since then demonstrate a *considerate* and *supportive behavior* pattern addressed in the Situational Leadership Theory, Path-Goal Theory, Fiedler's Contingency Theory and the Leadership Grid. Her *resilience, emotional intelligence, high moral character,* and carefully *self-regulated behavior* also point to Gbowee as a truly Authentic Leader in a very difficult situation. Her *determination* and *integrity* clearly reflect Trait Theories of leadership.

Discussion Questions

1. Why do you think Leymah Gbowee chose to appeal primarily to women in the peace movement in Liberia?
2. Why was her leadership strategy with WIPNET successful in finally ending the fighting?
3. Which of Gbowee's leader behaviors do you believe were most important? Why?
4. Would Gbowee be successful as a business leader? Labor leader? Military leader? Why or why not?

References

Charles Taylor. (n.d.). In *Wikipedia.* Retrieved December 5, 2010, from http://en.wikipedia.org/wiki/Charles_Taylor_(Liberia)

Disney, A. E. (Producer), & Reticker, G. (Director). (2008). *Pray the devil back to hell* [Motion picture]. United States: Fork Films.

Leymah Gbowee. (n.d.). In *Wikipedia.* Retrieved December 5, 2010, from http://en.wikipedia.org/wiki/Leymah_Gbowee

Macaulay, S. (2008). Women create peace in Liberia. *Amazing women rock.* Retrieved May 16, 2010, from http://www.amazingwomenrock.com/role-models/women-create-peace-in-liberia.html

Reeves, S. (February 3, 2011). Liberian activist tipped to win 2011 Nobel Peace Prize. *Nordic Africa News.* Retrieved from http://www.nanews.net/MAIN.asp?ID=4304

Second Liberian Civil War. (n.d.). In *Wikipedia.* Retrieved November 3, 2010, from http://en.wikipedia.org/wiki/Second_Liberian_Civil_War

Women of Liberia Mass Action for Peace. (n.d.). In *Wikipedia.* Retrieved November 3, 2010, from http://en.wikipedia.org/wiki/Women_of_Liberia_Mass_Action_for_Peace

Chapter 9

Nelson Mandela
*Human Rights Leader and
President of South Africa*

Nelson Rolihlahla Mandela was the primary leader of the decades-long anti-apartheid movement in South Africa which opposed the systematic segregation and subjugation of Black Africans by an all-White minority. He led a largely peaceful, but sometimes violent, movement to establish equal rights for all South Africans and was imprisoned for 27 years for his activities. He sponsored negotiation and reconciliation with the dominating and often ruthless White minority and led the transformation toward a democracy for all races in South Africa. He eventually became the president of that country in the first truly representative democratic election with all South Africans' participation.

Nelson Mandela was born July 18, 1918, in the village of Mvezo in the Union of South Africa. His father was descendent of a king in that district and, although not in line to become king, he served as the king's advisor. The nation was only eight years old at the time and Black Africans were controlled and restricted by the White former British colonials and Afrikaner population. Afrikaners were former northern European settlers (mostly Dutch and German) who spoke their own language and made peace with the British after several years of war. Nelson's father died when he was 9 and he was adopted by the acting king who became a role model for Nelson's leadership. He watched as this tribal leader listened patiently to members as they criticized and argued and he then tried to render a consensus decision that showed respect to all parties. Mandela later described this as a true democracy that allowed voicing of diverse views and kept the tribesmen together. This type of participative leadership style reflects the African cultural value of *ubuntu,* a belief in the brotherhood of all people, compassion, mutual respect and openness to others, and the idea that nothing important can be accomplished without the support of others.

Mandela attended Methodist missionary schools run by the British and was given the name Nelson by a teacher, following the colonial practice of naming African boys after famous British citizens. He then enrolled in Fort Hare University, the only Black university in the country, which was heavily attended by bright students from aristocratic tribal families. He began to flourish and eventually led a boycott to protest poor food. This resulted in his being expelled after refusing to give up his objections, which were supported by the students. His adoptive father arranged marriages for Nelson and the future king, and they both fled to Johannesburg to avoid the unwanted marriages. There he worked in a law office, completed his BA degree and began studying law. He also met members of the African National Congress (ANC), which was established in 1912 by tribal chiefs and religious leaders to promote the rights and freedom of African people. Like most Black Africans, he had always viewed Whites as interlopers who unfairly suppressed the Black majority. He joined the ANC in 1944 and began his political career protesting extreme segregation of Black Africans by the ruling White government through their program of apartheid (literally meaning "separation"). He was married the same year to Evelyn Ntoko Mase who was from the same area as Mandela. She was a very religious woman who later stated she thought Mandela was a student and did not approve of politics.

When he was 25, he helped form the ANC Youth League to encourage more mass action by the organization for the rights of Africans. The White government viewed the ANC members as communists, violently cracked down on strikes by Black miners, and began limiting the ability of Indian residents to acquire property. The ANC supported the Indians, who practiced the peaceful resistance of Gandhi, and they joined forces in demonstrations. The same type of alliance occurred later between the ANC and the communist party when the latter was outlawed in South Africa. Gandhi's peaceful tactics were followed by Mandela during much of his early political activities, to be changed later when he decided they had been ineffective. Nelson rejected communism but did advocate nationalization of large industries prior to running for president.

In 1948 a new Afrikaner government was elected with severe segregation policies to combat what they saw as "Black peril" and communism among Black Africans. Every person was to be classified by race, different races were required to live in separate parts of the cities, mixed marriages were forbidden, non-Whites were removed from voting rolls, and "pass laws" severely limited the movement of non-Whites when they left designated areas. Mandela helped organize a Defiance Campaign to protest the new restrictions, resulting in his arrest with many other ANC protestors. He was charged under the anti-communist laws and found guilty but given a suspended sentence. Arrests became a badge of honor in the ANC but Mandela was banned from attending their meetings. In 1952 he became a legally qualified attorney, established a practice with an old friend and ANC colleague, and began representing the ANC and other Black clients for little or no fees.

He developed a flamboyant speaking style in court—assertive and theatrical. He treated racist magistrates with contempt and defied apartheid restrictions. He became prominent in court rooms and in politics, but was banned from holding public office and public speechmaking. He relied on his court appearances and image to stay visible. In 1953 he was restricted to Johannesburg and required to resign from all organizations and he began to believe that violence was needed to change apartheid. The same year a former professor of Mandela's proposed a conference for African people of all races to develop a "freedom charter," which eventually denounced racist policies and laws, asserted that the state government must be based on the will of all the people, and argued for public ownership of large monopolistic business organizations ("nationalization"). Apartheid continued to spread to schools and universities, cutting off opportunities for young Blacks. In 1956 Mandela and other supporters of the freedom charter were arrested and charged with treason. This widely watched trial lasted until 1961 and gave Mandela the opportunity to present carefully prepared and inspiring descriptions of his own and the ANC's experience of subjugation and their goals of equal rights for all Africans. All were acquitted but he knew the government would not stop their apartheid policies.

In 1961 he co-sponsored an armed wing of the ANC which carried out sabotage against government offices and facilities, but avoided attacks on people. He stated it was a last resort when nonviolent tactics made no progress. He had divorced his first wife who disapproved of his political activities and married Winnie Madikizela—a strong-willed social worker who became an activist and political revolutionary herself. Both dressed extremely well (he had acquired this habit from his adoptive father), and the handsome couple developed a glamorous public persona. Demonstrations, arrests, and killing of protestors increased and Mandela decided to go into hiding, knowing the government sponsored security officers who constantly followed him would eventually move in. He helped organize a national stay-at-home strike of trains and buses which hurt the government, coordinated sabotage bombings, and was eventually arrested (probably from a CIA tip to the South African government). Nelson was charged with inciting an illegal strike and leaving the country without a passport. When he entered the court, he noticed the magistrate in charge appeared spellbound by his appearance and he realized his own power. He represented himself in the court room to increase the symbolism of his work, delivering inspiring speeches to justify his actions and those of his colleagues. He was found guilty and given five years in prison, the heaviest penalty ever given in the country for a political offense. He became the militant martyred leader who had defied the apartheid system, was hunted, and remained devoted to his people. To Black Africans, he was the primary symbol of the injustices to native Africans by the White South African government.

Nine months later, the government seized ANC papers proposing a violence campaign and overthrow of the government. Mandela and others were charged and tried. He again used the court room as his theatre, retracing his background and the ANC objectives of equal rights, multiracialism, and the end of White domination. His speech was reported throughout the world. He and eight others were found guilty of sabotage but not of conspiring to overthrow the government and were sentenced to life in prison. He had become a powerful spokesman and symbol of the anti-apartheid movement and his sacrifice for this movement was unquestionable.

Mandela and the others were imprisoned on Robben Island. For the next 27 years he was largely cut off from the world but was surrounded and supported by his ANC colleagues. He now had the time to examine himself as others saw him—an aggressive and militant revolutionary—and he learned to control his temper and strong will, to use persuasion and emphasis to convince others, and to slowly build his influence over other prisoners and the White guards. He was treated with respect, probably due to his connections and royal family, and was able to continue his legal studies through correspondence with the University of London. His legal background, court experience, past leadership in the ANC, and assertive personality made him a natural leader of other prisoners. He was visited by dignitaries, explained ANC policies to visiting officials, wrote to prison officials about the poor treatment of prisoners, and inspired others to take courses and continue their education. Robben Island became known informally as Mandela University. This atmosphere of self-improvement and education gave them confidence and a type of authority over the White guards who were as young as 17 and not well educated. Mandela listened to others' life stories and learned to appreciate and understand their perspectives, including the guards. He impressed them with his assertiveness, respect, and legal knowledge and he learned to maintain his dignity in all situations. He respected the guards as fellow humans, but carefully refused to be subservient and he assured that he and others worked in the rock quarry at their own pace.

Nelson heard about the increasing violence by other anti-apartheid groups outside the prison. He recognized the need for reconciliation in South Africa to achieve a true democracy. He developed the capability to see the best in people, emphasized respect for all people, and advocated forgiveness. He became less arrogant and autocratic, and more democratic in his dealings with others. He stayed in excellent physical condition and always maintained self-control while being sensitive to others' insecurities and resentments.

Winnie struggled with government harassment of her and their children and was becoming increasingly rebellious and violent in her associations and actions. But she kept Mandela informed of the anti-apartheid movement, which now included White liberals, church officials, and many students in South Africa. A Free Mandela campaign was building around the world which involved other countries limiting investments and loans to South Africa. This and the increasing violence were seriously damaging the economy and Whites were leaving the country. Nelson was moved to a nicer location with more visits from journalists and eminent individuals. In a closely held government report, he was described as the number one Black leader in South Africa whose influence as a charismatic inspirational leader had increased while in prison. He was celebrated in songs, international concerts, street names, and was adored by African children. The government decided he was helping the ANC and anti-apartheid movement more as a symbolic martyr in prison than if he were free. A team of government officials began several years of negotiations with Mandela concerning the creation of a more democratic South Africa.

In 1989 a new White president took office in South Africa. F. W. de Klerk represented the Afrikaners and knew that Mandela must be released to save the country from civil war and economic collapse. In February 1990 he stunned his party by unbanning the ANC and other political organizations, releasing all political prisoners not guilty of violent crimes, and suspending all executions. Mandela and others were freed as the world watched. He had won but he humbly gave credit to the ANC for all the work they did during his imprisonment. He entered prison when he was 46 and emerged when he was 71. He returned an eminent moral leader who had stood by his fundamental principles of liberty and equal rights for all and he gave hope to all oppressed people around the world.

Mandela began traveling the world speaking and asking for financial support for the ANC. His relaxed charm and serious moral arguments commanded respect and disarmed listeners. He was successful at fund raising, was elected president of the ANC, and resolved to reorganize that organization to attain political power. He was more moderate and pragmatic than prior to his imprisonment and younger ANC members worried about his effectiveness. Mandela and the ANC members met with the government and offered to cease their violent campaign. He also withdrew his call for nationalizing large industries and supported a development program to generate foreign investment. Independent groups within the South African police and security forces continued terrorizing and killing anti-apartheid workers. His wife Winnie was implicated in violent activities involving torture and murder that hurt the movement, and Mandela eventually divorced Winnie in 1995.

In December 1991, a conference with all political parties in South Africa was held in Johannesburg where de Klerk spoke of the need for power sharing in government. The eventual result, after months of negotiation, was a new constitution and a planned popular election with all major parties represented, including the ANC. When another Black ANC leader was fatally shot by a White man, a White Afrikaner woman saw the assassin's license plate and reported the number to the police who caught the killer (a European immigrant) within 15 minutes. Mandela's speech described her actions and asked for calm, which avoided widespread rioting and made it clear that most South Africans wanted peace and equality. Mandela and de Klerk were jointly awarded the Nobel Peace Prize and Mandela was elected president of South Africa at the age of 75. The constitution provided that de Klerk would be one deputy president and Mandela picked Thabo Mbeki, his long-time ANC colleague, as his other deputy president. Mandela was inaugurated in May 1994, four years after leaving prison, determined to show that Africans could govern effectively.

During his presidency, he quickly won the respect and support of his staff, many of them from the previous administration. He was noted for his humility and preferred one-on-one meetings and personal contacts with other leaders, thereby skipping bureaucratic protocol. He thus made use of his convincing and supportive interpersonal style honed during his many years in prison. His speeches were written by a multiracial staff and often stiff, but he always followed the scripted material with his own stories often making fun of himself ("I'm just a sinner who keeps on trying"). This caused his audience to continue to identify with him as a man of the people. He was inclusive with his multiracial cabinet, listening carefully to their discussions before stating his position or decision, which generally reflected much of the cabinet members' discussion (similar to his adoptive father's participative style with tribesmen). His friendly smiling style was often contagious, and his multiracial cabinet members worked surprisingly well with a focus on problems and issues rather than partisanship and ideology. His vision and mission as president was to transform the nation from a White oligarchy to a multiracial democracy. In 1995, he actively supported the Springboks, a largely White South African rugby team, who hosted and won the World Cup final game in Johannesburg. Mandela presented the cup to the Springboks captain after the game, wearing a Springboks jersey with the captain's name on the back. This symbolic act became a critical turning point for the reconciliation of the White and Black populations in the new multiracial democracy of South Africa.

Although Nelson liked to socialize with business executives and movie stars, he lived a relatively simple life. He gave one third of his salary to the Nelson Mandela Children's Fund, which he founded in 1995 to improve the conditions of children in the world. He visited high profile Afrikaners, Afrikaner churches, and met with widows of deceased Black and White leaders. He adamantly supported a free press, even though he sometimes disagreed with the reporting. He directed the creation of a Truth and Reconciliation Commission in 1996 to investigate past crimes involving apartheid policies and ANC activities. If perpetrators revealed the truth, they were granted amnesty if they could prove their actions were politically motivated. This Commission was chaired by Archbishop Desmond Tutu and caused tremendous pain for families of tortured and murdered victims, but it revealed violent acts by both parties and helped resolve long term resentment.

In 1996 de Klerk's party withdrew from the government, making Mbeki the sole deputy president. De Klerk's party lost coherence when he later resigned from public office due to personal issues. Mandela stepped down as president of the ANC and in his last speech he warned the members against the corruption and greed of "predatory elites" in Africa who looted their country's national wealth and he called for moral renewal as part of an African renaissance. In 1998 he married Graca Machel, widow of the former President of Mozambique, who helped him relax from the strains of office. He traveled extensively with Graca and saw his moral mission as spreading peace and tolerance around the world.

Graca described him as being very aware of his basic values and many of his colleagues pointed to his strong sense of human dignity. Others view Mandela as a symbol of moral authority and a peace maker in a continent rife with racial and tribal conflict. He set the direction for South African diplomacy insisting that human rights must be the core of international relations. He became a charismatic symbol for all of Africa seeking to escape the colonial past to achieve a fair and democratic society. He negotiated and forged economic alliances with Asia and other countries and often criticized the United States for its actions in the United Nations and elsewhere. He confronted powerful myths of Black inferiority, White invincibility, and incompatibility between races and gave confidence to people in the world who had been conditioned into submission. He also personified African dignity and self-respect by avoiding the arrogance, pretension and paranoia that characterized many leaders in developing countries. He used the term "we" in speeches, much more than "I." His mistakes were often in trusting and seeing the best in people who later disappointed him, but he was able to bring the best out of some former enemies during reconciliation. He also adapted his leadership style as the situation dictated, shifting from an early aggressive militaristic approach to a negotiating and conciliatory style after his release from prison. This latter style included participation of all parties while recognizing their fears and respecting their dignity and sensitivities. He served his five-year term as president and chose not to seek another term, being succeeded by Thabo Mbeki.

In retirement, he became an important advocate of social causes—especially those focused on poverty and children's living conditions. He acted as mediator for numerous conflicts and disputes outside South Africa. He received awards and acclaim throughout the world. Above all else, Mandela's integrity, values and dedication speak more about him as a leader than any other aspect of his life.

Mandela is often described as a Charismatic/Transformational leader because of his *inspirational sacrifice, moral rhetoric,* and *symbolic* role in Black Africans' struggle to overcome apartheid. He emphasized a clear *vision* and *mission* for the anti-apartheid movement with which he was identified. He modified this vision when released from prison to allow for reconciliation and a true democracy for all South Africans. He therefore also reflects contingency/situational leadership theories such as Situational Leadership Theory, Path-Goal Theory, or the Multiple Linkage Model, which advocate modifying a leader's style to fit the situation. These leadership theories also address Mandela's *directive leadership* in initiating early militant campaigns of sabotage and demonstrations and eventually negotiation and reconciliation. His *supportive behaviors* are clear in the respect shown for all persons, encouraging fellow prisoners to pursue their education in prison, support for colleagues in court and after imprisonment, and interpersonal relations as president. His inclusive *participative leadership* as president is described in the Normative Decision Theory. Mandela's negotiating behavior, reflecting *boundary spanning leadership,* was critical to overcoming anti-apartheid policies after his imprisonment and in gaining foreign support for the ANC movement as well as South African investment when he was president. The Multiple Linkage Model and Reformulated Path-Goal Theory address this leader behavior. The Authentic Leadership model also addresses much of Mandela's *self-confidence, hope, optimism,* and *resilience* during his long campaign for Africans' rights. His *self-reflection* and awareness, as well as *self-regulation* and careful *listening* behaviors are included in the Servant Leadership model. His *character, competence, trustworthiness,* and *empowerment* reflect Principle Centered Leadership.

Discussion Questions

1. Which leadership theory do you believe most accurately describes Mandela's behavior prior to his imprisonment? What about after his imprisonment?
2. What do you believe are the most important things Mandela did to overcome the apartheid policies of the White government of South Africa?
3. As president, some criticized Mandela for tolerating government inefficiencies in favor of reconciliation. Was this good leadership? Why or why not?
4. How important was Mandela's supportive and friendly interpersonal style to his long term success as a leader?

References

Mandela, N. (1994). *Long walk to freedom: The autobiography of Nelson Mandela.* New York: Little, Brown.

Nelson Mandela. (n.d.). In *Wikipedia.* Retrieved May 4, 2010, from http://en.wikipedia.org/wiki/Nelson_Mandela

Sampson, A. (1999). *Mandela: The authorized autobiography.* New York: Alfred A. Knopf.

Chapter 10

Geronimo
*Apache Native American
War Leader*

Geronimo (whose birth name was Goyathlay, meaning "one who yawns") was born in about 1829 in the mountains of what is now eastern Arizona and southwestern New Mexico. He was fourth in a family of eight children and was part of the Bedonkohe group of the Apache Indians. He grew up in the traditional Apache culture, learning to pray to their high God Usen and hearing stories of brave deeds of warriors and glories of the warpath. The Apaches were nomadic and lived primarily on wild game, berries, acorns, roots, and other foods available in their surroundings. They also traded with other tribes and villages. They typically traveled throughout the mountains of eastern Arizona, New Mexico, and the Mexican states of Chihuahua and Sonora. Until 1852, these were all part of Mexico. His father died when he was young and he assumed responsibility for his mother.

Geronimo was admitted to the council of warriors when he was 17 as he had met the requirements of killing dangerous animals alone and participating in raids on those outside the tribe. He immediately married his first wife, Alope, who was from the Chiricahua band of Apaches, and they had three children during the next five years. In spring of 1851 their group traveled to Mexico and camped near a small Mexican town to trade with the locals. While most of the men were in town, Mexican soldiers raided the camp and killed nearly all who were there, including Geronimo's wife, three children, and mother. Left with nothing, the survivors immediately returned to their homeland in the Arizona-New Mexico mountains. Geronimo described himself as unable to speak or act, he simply followed his tribesmen home. He burned all the possessions he had shared with his wife, children, and mother. He had lost more than anyone else. He had nothing.

Geronimo's small Bedonkohe band joined forces with the Mimbreno Apaches whose chief, Mangus Colorado, called a council; all members wanted war. Geronimo was sent to other Apache groups (including the Chiricahuas who were led by Cochise), and they agreed to join his group in seeking vengeance on the Mexicans. Apache raids on Mexicans dated from the 17th century. In the early 1800s, Mexico began paying a $100 bounty for each scalp of an Apache warrior, $50 for an Apache woman, and $25 for an Apache child. The Apaches willingly traveled to the town where Geronimo's group had been attacked and his family murdered and they lured the soldiers out to meet them. Geronimo was allowed to direct the battle because he had lost so much to these Mexicans. In the fight that followed, the Apaches wiped out the Mexican soldiers, and he earned the name Geronimo, which is Spanish for Jerome, the patron saint of the Mexican soldier. He was so fierce that he attacked the soldiers with his knife after he ran out of arrows and was without his spear. The soldiers called on their saint so often during this and later battles with these Apaches that he was labeled Geronimo. He later reported that he was given the title Apache War Chief after this battle—a sign of great respect.

Although many other Apaches were satisfied with their vengeance, Geronimo could not get enough. Repeatedly over the next 25 years, he convinced various groups of warriors to accompany him on brutal raids to Mexico. At times the Mexican soldiers attacked Apache villages with equal brutality. Many of Geronimo's raids were successful and he would return with booty of cattle, horses, mules, and other supplies to be distributed to his tribe. This earned him great respect among his people. Britton Davis was a United States Army lieutenant who lived with Geronimo's tribe on the reservation, came to know Geronimo, and later pursued him through much of Mexico. He wrote that Apaches viewed raids as an exciting adventure, a way to attain glory and respect with their people. Geronimo's raids in Mexico were that and more—he sought revenge on the Mexicans throughout his free life after the death of his family.

Geronimo reported that his first meeting with White men was in the 1850s when a group of surveyors came through their country. He described them as friendly. They traded with the Apaches and were well liked. In the early 1860s a column of Union soldiers came through to protect supply lines from Confederate forces. The United States had obtained possession of Arizona and New Mexico territory in the Gadsden Purchase of 1852, and the soldiers claimed the areas traditionally occupied by Apaches for the United States government. Some historians report that soldiers were instructed to kill Apache men but not women and children. This set the Apaches against the White soldiers and settlers.

Geronimo's mistrust of Whites was permanently fixed by two incidents. One involved an invitation by United States soldiers to meet peaceably with Chiricahua Apache Chief Cochise and other subchiefs regarding a missing White boy. When the Indians entered the soldiers' tent, the soldiers tried to place them in chains. Cochise and others cut their way out of the tent and escaped but others were taken prisoner and executed. Geronimo and his group had always been close to the Chiricahuas, and he was later married to Cochise's niece. The other important incident occurred when White miners lured Geronimo's chief, Mangus Colorado, with a peace offering but imprisoned and eventually murdered him. These incidents cemented Geronimo's hatred and distrust for White people.

The Mescalero Apaches, who occupied land east of Geronimo's band, resisted the White invasion first. They were defeated and forced onto a reservation where they were unable to support themselves and were inadequately supplied and fed. Geronimo now expanded his list of enemies to include Whites, and conducted hit-and-run attacks on soldiers, miners, and settlers throughout southern Arizona and southeastern New Mexico. He also continued his raids into Mexico. He was viewed by Apaches as epitomizing their male warrior culture. Time and again he was courageous in battle, he was cunning in planning his raids, and he never relinquished his desire for his people to live their free nomadic life.

In 1876 the United States government tried to move the Apaches to reservations, which were barren desert and completely unlike their mountain homeland. When the Chiricahuas were forcibly removed to the San Carlos Reservation in Eastern Arizona, Geronimo fled to Mexico with a group of followers. He was arrested soon after and taken to San Carlos. The Indian Bureau assigned many agents who were political appointees and unqualified for their positions. This was true for Geronimo's band and many supplies intended for the Indians were siphoned off to Whites and sold for private profit. When an Apache prophet was slain by Whites in 1881, Geronimo's band left the reservation and went to the Sierra Madre Mountains of Mexico to continue their traditional way of life. They also continued their raids against Mexicans and Whites.

In 1882 General George Crook was called to Arizona to conduct a campaign against the Apaches who were still outside the reservation and waging war. Through continuous pursuit and harassment, Geronimo was persuaded to surrender and return to the reservation. He did so with 350 Mexican cattle, which were taken from him at the reservation to be used by the Indian Bureau. He resented this for many years. Life on the San Carlos Reservation, where Geronimo and his tribe were located, was not pleasant. Although they were allowed to select a location in the mountains of their homeland, their hunting grounds were restricted and they were subjected to inadequate supplies and further graft by the Indian agents. The reservation Apaches resented being prohibited from making and drinking Tiswin, a Native American alcoholic drink made from corn. The men protested at not being permitted to discipline their wives through physically beating them or cutting off their nose when they were unfaithful. They protested that they had kept their bargain with the military by living on the reservation and keeping the peace. Nothing had been said in their agreement about how they lived and conducted their private affairs. They were not allowed to raise stock, which appealed to their skills, but were told they must farm. The country they inhabited was not well suited for farming and it was not a major part of their traditions. Although General Crook and some of his officers recognized these difficulties, they enforced the government requirements and battled with the Indian Bureau to try to assure the Indians received their promised food and supplies. The Apaches were often losers in these bureaucratic battles. They were idle much of the time, which was totally foreign to their nomadic subsistence oriented culture. These factors bred mistrust and defiance by the Indians.

In spring 1885 Geronimo and about 150 other Apaches again left the reservation. Many of the Apache chiefs who had first resisted the Whites had died by then, and although he was not a hereditary chief, Geronimo was a respected leader due to his courage, unwavering determination, and skill as a war chief. He was viewed by his people as having special powers such as walking without leaving any tracks and having visions of the future. It was believed that guns could not kill him, and he reported late in life that he received eight gunshot wounds during his war years. He had also been related to several of the great chiefs by marriages subsequent to his first family's death. Geronimo's group conducted several raids on White settlers before again entering the mountains of Mexico. General Crook was replaced by General Miles in pursuing the Apaches along with 5,000 soldiers who had permission to follow the Indians into Mexico. Several groups split from Geronimo in the months that followed over disagreements and the fact that they were constantly harassed by both Mexican and United States troops. The Indians knew that smaller bands would be harder to surprise by the soldiers. But they were worn down by constant pursuit and attacks that continued to decrease their numbers. Apache women, children, and young boys were frequent casualties of the soldiers' attacks.

In fall 1886 Geronimo let it be known he would meet with General Miles to discuss surrender. Lieutenant Charles B. Gatewood first met with the Indian leader and arranged the meeting with the general. Miles told Geronimo that many Apaches had already been moved to Florida, these included many relatives of Geronimo and his band. The Apaches were very concerned about their families and wanted to be with them. Miles said Geronimo's group would be sent to the east where they would be reunited with their families. After two years, they would be returned to the reservation, which included many of the mountains of their native homeland. Geronimo and his band surrendered and several days later were placed on a train for Florida.

The United States government did not keep its word. Geronimo and his followers were placed in hard labor and were not reunited with their families for nearly a year. Later they were all sent to Alabama for seven years where they suffered badly from disease. They were ill suited for the humid climate and living conditions in the south and many died. Eventually the Comanches and Kiowas, who had been traditional enemies of the Apaches, invited Geronimo's band to share their reservation in Fort Sill Oklahoma. They arrived in Fort Sill, and Geronimo lived there the remainder of his life. He appeared in a presidential parade and at state fairs and dictated his life story to S. M. Barrett in 1905. After much wrangling with the United States government, his story was published in 1907. Despite repeated requests, he was never allowed to return to his homeland. He died of pneumonia in 1909 after drinking heavily and lying overnight in a cold wet road.

Geronimo's leadership can be considered using several leadership theories. He was apparently highly *directive* with followers, especially during the raids they conducted. Path-Goal Theory emphasizes directive leader behavior in high stress situations. Fiedler's Contingency Theory, Multiple Linkage Model, and Situational Leadership Theory also describe similar leader behaviors. Reformulated Path-Goal Theory is also seen in his *boundary spanning behavior* through negotiations with other Apache groups to join in his raids and in his repeated negotiations with United States soldiers over their surrender. Charismatic/Transformational Leadership is clearly evident in his *inspiration* of warriors to accompany him on his continued raids, especially against the hated Mexican soldiers. As a *charismatic* leader, he was viewed as having special powers which were greater than other Apaches. Implicit Leadership Theory can also be applied to Geronimo's leadership, since he embodied the traditional Apache beliefs and values of an ideal warrior-leader. He was fearless in battle, unrelenting in the face of diversity, cunning in his planning, and generous with his tribal group with booty obtained on his raids. His *determination* and apparent *cognitive capacity* reflect Trait Theories of leadership.

Discussion Questions

1. Some writers believe a specific experience early in a leader's life is critical in shaping the leader's behavior throughout his/her life. Is this the case for Geronimo? Explain.
2. Some Indian leaders acquiesced to the U.S. government demands and struggled to make a life on their reservation. Do you think Geronimo's defiant stance toward the military and Indian Bureau was good for the Apaches?
3. Given the situation facing the Apaches in the mid 1800s, what type of leadership behaviors do you believe would have been most effective?
4. Try to describe an Implicit Leadership Theory for the ideal Apache leader in the mid to late 1800s.

References

Barrett, S. M. (1907). *Geronimo's story of his life*. New York: Duffield and Company.
Davis, B. (1929). *The truth about Geronimo*. Lincoln: University of Nebraska Press.
Geronimo. (n.d.). In *Wikipedia*. Retrieved May 26, 2009, from http://en.wikipedia.org/wiki/Geronimo

Chapter 11

Winston Churchill

British Prime Minister, Wartime Leader, and Statesman

Winston Churchill served as Prime Minister of the United Kingdom during World War II and is known as an outstanding wartime leader. He actively opposed Hitler from the beginning of the German aggression and imposed his imagination and will on the British public to defeat Nazi Germany and the Axis powers. He was also an officer in the British Army, a war correspondent, writer, historian, statesman, orator, and filled many other top level government positions. He received the Nobel Prize for Literature in 1953 and was the first person to be granted honorary citizenship in the United States.

Churchill was born on November 30, 1874, on a huge family estate in Oxfordshire, England. He was a descendent of the famous first Duke of Marlborough and spent part of his youth in Ireland while his father was Viceroy to Ireland, prior to Irish independence. His father was a flamboyant and outspoken member of British Parliament who served as Chancellor of the Exchequer (in charge of economic and financial matters) for Britain when Winston was 12. His father also possessed an incredible memory, loved luxury, and had a mercurial personality, traits inherited by his son Winston. Winston attended three private schools where he showed an early interest in fencing, shooting, and a military career. He was not a good student but loved history and studied English for several years because he could not master Latin or Greek. In school he was competitive and mischievous, stubbornly independent, indifferent to authority, and developed skill as a public speaker. He attended the Royal Military College where he further improved his skills at public speaking and argument, although he had a slight speech impediment that he worked hard to overcome. He was commissioned a Coronet (second lieutenant) in cavalry in 1895, the same year his father died at age 46.

Winston seemed to believe he would also die young and became known for his impatience. As a military officer and government official, he insisted on immediate action. He obtained an assignment as a war correspondent to observe and write about the Spaniards' fight against Cuban guerillas. He was under fire there for the first time. Soon after, he was posted to India where he was known for his polo playing and engaged in action against rebellious Indians who were fighting British rule. He received praise and notoriety for rescuing a wounded officer and for his war related articles published in Britain. When the action subsided, he wrote his first novel about political intrigue and sold the serial rights to a British magazine. Winston's mother (originally from the United States) was wealthy and socially connected in Britain. She helped him obtain postings to war zones for his war correspondence and to build his popularity and sent him extra money to support his developing addiction to luxury. He obtained a position in the Sudan where a British force was sent to retaliate for the murder of a British officer by an extremist ruler. He participated in a cavalry charge there that broke the enemy's force and exposed Winston to terrible carnage. While in the Sudan, he entertained other officers with his stories and amazing memory, he read extensively on history and politics and became known for his cleverness with words. He returned to Britain and published another book on the Sudan campaign, resigned his commission, and ran for a position in Parliament for the first time. He was defeated but gained confidence because of the positive responses to his speeches.

In 1899 a war broke out in British-controlled South Africa between Dutch/German settlers (known as Boers) and the British who wanted to participate in the Boer diamond mines. Winston obtained a commission as a war correspondent, traveled to South Africa, and accompanied a scouting expedition on a train that was attacked. He helped the wounded escape on the train and was captured. The Boers learned his identity and treated him well, calling him "Lord's Son." After numerous attempts, he escaped and traveled nearly 300 miles (mostly by train) to a friendly neighboring state where he was welcomed by the British Consul. He resumed reporting on the war and criticizing the British military leadership—something he did often throughout his life. He returned to Britain in 1900 to a standing ovation and planned to pursue a political career.

He gave 150 speeches in two months and was elected to Parliament, followed by a lucrative lecture tour in Britain and the United States. His speaking style was self-confident, sincere, and vehement showing his total belief in his message; he had an excellent sense of humor. His grasp of history, excellent memory, intelligence, and skill with words entertained his listeners, including Parliament members who appreciated good rhetoric. He was a favorite at dinner parties and loved the social scene in London. He changed political parties in 1906 and was appointed to his first government cabinet post as Undersecretary to the British Colonies. Over the ensuing years, he was reelected to Parliament several times and served in cabinet positions. He championed bills in Parliament dealing with issues that helped working people such as limiting miners' work days, an unemployment act, and an old age pensions act. As President of the Board of Trade he worked harder than any predecessor. In 1908 he married beautiful Clementine Hozier from a distinguished family. She became his frugal partner for life who helped them survive financially despite Winston's lavish life style. In 1910 he was appointed Home Secretary, one of the four highest offices in the government, responsible for internal affairs in England and Wales, immigration, citizenship, policing, and national security. He faced several severe strikes. His tactic was to bring disputing parties together (since they all loved to hear him speak), feed them plenty of drink, and usually their mood improved leading to more friendly talks and an agreement.

In 1911 Germany began belligerent actions with other countries and Winston began preparing Britain for war. The combination of intelligence and memory gave him a vision of the future course of international events that few others possessed. He directed a push to pass a bill allowing the government to intercept any correspondence, eventually resulting in every major spy being captured during World War I. He wrote a description for Parliament of likely developments with a timetable in case of war, predicting the complete defeat of the French army. The document was criticized and ignored but predicted the course of events three years later almost exactly. When the Prime Minister realized war was unavoidable, he transferred Winston to become head of the Admiralty—in charge of naval forces. Churchill directed the construction of warships with 15-inch guns, larger than the standard size. Naval officials objected that they might be unworkable, but he persisted, and the British Navy outgunned all German warships throughout the war. He also directed the change from coal to oil in powering warships and the creation of a fast division of battleships used in both world wars. He directed the creation of a Royal Naval Air Force, built the largest navy in British history, and declared a full mobilization to war footing (without the permission of the king or cabinet) just prior to the declaration of war.

Winston was also placed in charge of Aerial Home Defense and he immediately sent their planes to Europe to take the offense with the objective of winning the war. This resulted in several successful raids on the enemy. He directed the first development of tanks, which were new weapons that would alter future warfare. He spent time at the front encouraging and inspiring soldiers in their fight. He then designed a plan to invade Turkey and help Russia to defeat Germany from the east. The plan failed when the admiral in charge withdrew his ships after three were lost to mines. This resulted in terrible losses for Allied ground troops and a huge defeat on the Gallipoli Peninsula. Churchill was blamed for the defeat and removed from the admiralty. He then asked for a military commission to command front line troops to reestablish his career. He was appointed Lieutenant Colonel in charge of a Scottish battalion in December 1915.

As a military officer, he took good care of his troops, insisted on their health and cleanliness, made sure alcohol was available, dined with his officers in high style (mostly at his personal expense), and learned all their names and details of their lives. He insisted they sing whenever in motion, organized community sings, commanded several artillery barrages, and insisted on his own method of sandbagging trenches—which his men dutifully carried out and then changed to a more effective design after he left. His troops saw little action but they all liked him and cheered him when they were disbanded and sent to other units. Winston spent days making sure his officers obtained favorable assignments before he left for Britain and a new appointment. A new government had been formed and named Churchill, Minister of Munitions and later Minister of War and Air. For the remainder of World War I, he arrived at his office early, worked several hours, flew to France to deal with war matters, and often then flew in a small plane over the front lines, dropping in on commanders to offer advice—all in one day.

He despised the suppression and mass murder in Russia led by the Communists Lenin and Trotsky. In Parliament he opposed the Communist Revolution and supported the anti-communist White Russians while much of Britain was noncommittal. In 1920 he became Colonial Secretary—in charge of Britain's colonies—because the government could see their empire in danger of coming apart. He quickly hired T. E. Lawrence (the mysterious Lawrence of Arabia) to help him settle postwar disputes in the Middle East. Though the British government was stunned with the presence of Lawrence, he was able to resolve the problems in an amicable manner and then refused any other governmental appointment. As Colonial Secretary, Winston directed the push for an eventual treaty granting self-rule to Ireland. In 1924 he became Chancellor of the Exchequer. He was not a strong financial type and implemented a return to the gold standard for British currency, which added significant costs to British exports and led to major strikes and economic decline. He was blamed, later stating it was his biggest mistake, and resigned his position.

At age 55 he had fought and/or reported on five wars, held nine cabinet positions and made 8,000 speeches. Between 1929 and 1939 he wrote and engaged in lecture tours—producing a biography of his famous ancestor, the first Duke of Marlborough, a *History of the English Speaking Peoples*, numerous newspaper articles, and a collection of essays. Winston fought to maintain the British Empire with England as a benevolent governor of the colonies. His continued opposition to Mohandas Gandhi's peaceful disobedience revolt for Indian independence alienated him from the British government and he held no appointed office for much of the 1930s.

As early as 1932, he actively opposed allowing Germany to rearm to achieve parity with France. Hitler had ignored the peace agreement from World War I that limited the German army and formed an alliance with Mussolini in Italy. Churchill advocated rebuilding the Royal Air Force and creation of a Ministry of Defense, but only a few believed his warnings about Hitler. In 1936, Germany occupied the Rhineland and began its conquest of Europe, but Britain was divided on how to respond. He continued his vocal criticism of Hitler who apparently feared Churchill's power. When Germany's conquests continued and Britain finally declared war, Winston was reappointed to head the Admiralty. He advocated occupation of Norway and its key iron ore port, which was important to support a war machine. He was opposed, and Germany conquered Norway. In 1940, Prime Minister Neville Chamberlain lost the support of his Conservative Party colleagues. As a result, the king asked Churchill to serve as Prime Minister and form an all party government. He was now head of the British government and refused to sign an armistice with Hitler's Germany. His tough carefully crafted rhetoric galvanized the British people against Hitler and they prepared for a long war.

As Prime Minister, Winston directed the creation of a Ministry of Defense and filled the position himself. His incredible energy showed in his constant travel to keep track of the war effort. He placed an industrialist friend in charge of aircraft manufacturing, and production soared, which became a key to winning the war. Ignoring the risks, he would sneak up to the roofs of buildings in London to watch the air raids and battles over London. His speeches continued to inspire and stimulate the British people to defeat Hitler's armies. In summer 1940, he initiated the rescue of 338,000 British, French, and Belgian troops when they were cornered by the Germans on the beaches of Dunkirk. Awakened at 6:30 a.m. and alerted to the situation, he immediately began directing a phone campaign that mobilized up to 1,000 naval and private boats and ships to complete the rescue. In addition to the soldiers lost, Britain had left behind huge amounts of equipment and materials, France had fallen, and the United States remained officially neutral. Britain was alone.

During this crisis, Churchill reached the height of his charismatic effects on the British public. With his rhetoric, he inspired them to identify with the noble cause of freeing the world from the threat of totalitarian rule. He dramatized their lives by seeing themselves as carrying out a moral mission. They were somehow better, more noble, and moral than they were before the war. He emphasized simplicity in his speeches and explanations, often using only one or two syllable words to assure that his listeners understood. His famous tribute to the Royal Air Force pilots in their defense of Britain is a good example: "Never in the field of human conflict was so much owed by so many to so few." His mastery of the English language and the art of persuasion were unequaled at the time.

Churchill courted other nations' leaders to obtain their assistance in the war effort. He loved talking, eating, and drinking and used his personal experience and memory of history to tell fascinating stories. People were curious about him, and his mood always improved when people surrounded him to hear him speak. He was a master salesman for Britain and established a close relationship with U.S. President Franklin D. Roosevelt to obtain needed food, oil, and munitions for Britain. Later, when the United States entered the war, he facilitated the Allied invasion of Europe from England. Roosevelt liked Winston, but the two were competitive talkers. Roosevelt nagged Churchill to grant independence to India and abandon the British Empire system. When Japan attacked the United States at Pearl Harbor, Winston immediately issued a statement to the American public that Britain was declaring war on Japan.

Near the end of World War II Churchill met with the Russian leader, Joseph Stalin, several times. Both were strong willed and competitive, both had insight into the path of political developments, both were patriotic and mutually distrustful, and both loved to eat, drink, and smoke in huge amounts. British supplies had flowed to Russia when Hitler invaded their territory. Both knew that Stalin wanted to dominate the world while Churchill wanted to maintain the balance of power and preserve the British Empire. Churchill was effective at negotiating treaty agreements for European and Asian boundaries after the war, although he later spoke decisively against Russian dominance in Eastern Europe.

Winston loved to visit the battle front in boats, planes or on the ground and often was held back by his colleagues. When the war ended in May 1945, he received the greatest ovation ever given in the British Parliament. Two months later he was voted out of office. The public apparently was ready for change from a war leader to one who was devoted to helping the underprivileged. Winston was always compassionate but viewed complete egalitarianism as a socialist dream.

He led the government opposition in Parliament for several years and in 1946, while in the United States, he gave his famous Iron Curtain Speech at Westminster College in Fulton, Missouri. He used the term "Iron Curtain" to describe the division between powerful Western countries and the countries controlled by the Soviet Union. He pointed out that Soviet communists were active throughout the world and desired to spread their power sphere worldwide. He stated that the United States and other Western countries must oppose the communist movement but that Soviet leadership respected military power most of all. His speech marked the beginning of the cold war arms race between the United States and the Soviet Union.

Churchill was reelected as Prime Minister in 1951 and served until his resignation for health reasons in 1955. During this time a decolonization movement progressed in Europe, starting after World War II and continuing into the later 20th century. Most of Britain's colonies gained independence during this period, including India. Although Churchill used violence at first to try to quell rebellions in the colonies, the British Empire was not sustainable and disappeared. He experienced a series of strokes, resigned from Parliament in 1964, and died in 1965 at his home. Known primarily for his outstanding wartime leadership, he was also loved as a statesman, historian, writer, and orator.

Two types of leadership theories are highly descriptive of Churchill's leadership. He undoubtedly demonstrated Charismatic/Transformational Leadership in his impact on the British people during wartime. His *inspirational speeches* describing a moral mission and reflecting his mastery of the English language, his *vision* of future events, his *risk taking*, extreme *self-confidence*, and *foresight* are all charismatic qualities. The fact that he was a heroic leader during wartime and rejected during peace demonstrates the principle behind Contingency/Situational theories of leadership, which predict that different leadership approaches are needed in different situations. Theories such as Fiedler's Contingency Theory, Situational Leadership, and Path-Goal Theory all reflect this principle of effective leadership. The British public's reaction to his leadership after wartime reflects Implicit Leadership Theory's notion of followers' image of an effective peacetime leader. Churchill was also highly *directive* during wartime as the crisis situation required quick decisive action. This is described in the Multiple Linkage Model, Path-Goal Theory, and Situational Leadership Theory. His *boundary spanning behavior* was critical to settling strikes in England and in obtaining cooperation and support from other nations during war time. This leader behavior is also described in the early Multiple Linkage Model and Reformulated Path-Goal Theories of leadership.

Discussion Questions

1. Why was Churchill such an effective war time leader?
2. Why do you think the British public did not believe Churchill could adjust his leadership style to peacetime?
3. Which leader behavior do you think was most important in leading war time Britain: charismatic, directive or boundary spanning?
4. Why did Churchill find it so difficult to relinquish control of Britain's colonies?

References

Coleville, J. R. (1996). The personality of Sir Winston Churchill. In R. C. Kemper III (Ed.), *Winston Churchill: Resolution, defiance, magnanimity, good will* (pp.108–125). Columbia: University of Missouri Press.

Taylor, R. L. (1952). *Winston Churchill: An informal study of greatness.* Garden City, NY: Doubleday.

Winston Churchill. (n.d.). In *Wikipedia*. Retrieved May 24, 2010, from http://en.wikipedia.org/wiki/Winston_Churchill

Chapter 12

Vince Lombardi
Professional Football Coach

Vince Lombardi coached American professional football for 10 years and compiled an astounding record of 106 wins, 36 losses, and 6 ties. For nine seasons he coached the Green Bay Packers who had a long record of poor performance before Vince took over. In nine years with Lombardi, the Packers won five National Football League championships and the first two Super Bowls ever played. He was admitted to the Professional Football Hall of Fame, labeled Coach of the Century by ESPN, and the Super Bowl trophy was named in his honor. Lombardi was sought after by countless organizations as a motivational and leadership speaker and he set the standard for success in leading professional sports teams.

Vince Lombardi was born in New York City on June 13, 1913, the first of five children. He was raised a devout Catholic and attended daily mass and Catholic schools. He worked in his family's food wholesale business, muscling big sides of beef with his brother. His mother was a perfectionist and used the back of her hand to discipline her children. His Catholicism, strict upbringing, and parochial education combined to make Vince an extremely hard working, control-oriented individual. He was a good student and was apparently favored by his parents, being given the job of disciplinarian with his younger siblings in his teen years. His bossy style extended beyond his family to include his cousins and friends. He had the body of an adult at age 15, loved competitive sports, and was elected president of his section of 35 students four years in a row. His early plans to become a priest were abandoned after two years of study and he changed schools to obtain a scholarship to play football, his favorite sport, during his last year of high school.

His performance on the field earned him a scholarship to Fordham University where he became a guard in the offensive front line. That line became famous in New York City collegiate football. Lombardi loved the physical contact of football, and throughout life he referred to the game as primarily a "hitting" sport. Vince was heavily influenced by a Jesuit professor named Father Cox who taught that too much freedom could ruin men, and they achieved nobility only by suppressing their own desires and joining with others in the pursuit of a worthwhile group goal. Lombardi was an above average business major, graduated from Fordham in 1937 and began work at a finance company. His playing skills did not qualify him to play professional football, but he played for a semi-professional team for two years.

After an unsuccessful try at law school, he accepted a teaching/coaching position in 1939 at St. Cecelia Catholic High School and began his career as an assistant coach. He taught physics, chemistry, and Latin and coached basketball and football. He soon realized he loved coaching football and became obsessed with the game and winning. He spent late nights revising plays and strategy. After losses in the team's first two games, the head football coach invited Vince to give a pep talk to the team before their next game. He mesmerized the team and head coach with the force of his talk. With rapidly blinking eyes that bulged as he spoke and clinched fists, he told them they had not impressed him in practice and asked what they would do in this game to win. They were stunned and the rest of the season they were undefeated. During eight years at St. Cecelia, he learned that he must teach his football tactics so they were completely understandable to even the slowest player, and, when his players were in better physical condition than the opponents, his team usually won. He eventually became head football coach and taught his teams to play fair, but not to be good losers. He carried these lessons with him his entire career. Lombardi married Marie Planitz in 1940 and their first child, Vincent, was born in 1942. Lombardi developed a reputation for coaching and obtained a position as an assistant football coach at Fordham University in 1947, the same year their daughter Susan was born.

Vince spent two years at Fordham coaching freshman and assisting the varsity with the exact techniques of the T-formation offense. He moved players by inches this way and that, timed plays by split seconds, and drilled the exact size and number of steps each player was to take on a play. He emphasized repetition until every move was ingrained in the minds of his players. In 1949 Vince accepted a position at the United States Military Academy to coach the varsity offensive line. The military environment seemed to fit Vince's authoritarian personality. When Lombardi yelled at players for not carrying out their role according to his instructions, they were accustomed to this in the military academy. The head coach was Colonel Red Blaik who was considered the best college football coach of the 1940s. Lombardi learned from Blaik to use a limited number of simple plays that could be repeatedly drilled and well learned by players, to seek perfection in play execution, and to study films of their own team and opponents. They both had an overwhelming will to win and were terrible losers. Lombardi had little time for his family and did not hesitate to hit his son when disciplining him. This created an estrangement that lasted into his son's adulthood. Marie understood that football came first for her husband but she was still uncertain where she stood and she developed a drinking problem.

In 1954 Lombardi was hired by the New York Giants professional football team as an assistant coach. The head coach let Lombardi have control of the offense and Tom Landry, another future Hall of Fame coach, controlled the defense. The two assistant coaches competed with each other, became known as the Giants' "brain trust," and both had a relentless desire to win. Lombardi quickly learned that professional players were quicker, stronger, and much more talented than college players. He spent time with the players and learned from a great running back, Frank Gifford, that "running to daylight" was superior among professionals than simply running through a hole in the line as dictated by a playbook. He was also impressed by the mentality of many professional players and adjusted his coaching strategy based on their input. His new mantra was giving offensive players "freedom within structure" by having options within plays based on their reading of the defense. When the offense did poorly, he became depressed. When they did well, he was elated. Landry and the players began calling him "Mr. High-Low" because of these extreme mood swings. This label stuck with Vince through his career. Three years after joining the Giants they won the National Football League championship.

After five years with the Giants, Vince longed to be a head coach. He first thought of returning to college coaching, but in 1958 he accepted a head coaching job with the Green Bay Packers who had won only one game the previous year. He immediately began teaching his assistant coaches about football as he knew it. He directed them in the basics of blocking and tackling, he then covered the plays that they would run. Assistants each created their own notebooks and files, all based on Lombardi's teaching. They referred to these files as their brains, but they were really Lombardi's brain. This formed the basis they used to teach the players. Vince identified young running back Paul Hornung as the center of his offense. Hornung had spent two years with the Packers being shifted around to different positions but was unhappy and ready to leave football. Lombardi convinced him to stay as a running back and Hornung became an incredible Hall of Famer. He traded players who he saw as divisive and added to his defensive roster. He took charge of the entire Packer organization and the press described him as a chart carrying teacher of a "thinking man's" football.

With players, he emphasized their playbooks were their Bibles, twice daily practices that were one and a half hours long and carefully planned, and Lombardi time, which meant be there 10 minutes early or be yelled at. He promised to drive them to become the best players they could be and that included being in prime physical condition. He told them that fatigue made cowards of everyone and he had no tolerance for half-hearted effort. With maximum effort and dedication, he would make them champions so they must dress like champions. Practices involved brutal physical conditioning with some players losing as much as 30 pounds and repeating drills until they ran plays exactly as directed every time. Players were punished with extra laps for dropping a pass or not following a play in practice. He referred to football as "controlled violence" that involved inflicting and experiencing pain and he pressed his players to confront pain. He preached and coached repetition, confidence, and passion, and when they suited up for their first game they were unusually confident—they could feel themselves being transformed. He spoke to them of pride in being a Packer and he pulsed with emotion. He told them to win and they did—with emotion—and the fans were ecstatic that their Packers were winners. That year they had a winning season and in three years they were National Football League champions. That was the beginning of the Packer dynasty that lasted his entire time as their coach.

Lombardi's players described his speeches as emotional and enthusiastic, selling the players on themselves by making them feel special as a Packer and inspiring confidence. When he spoke, everyone listened. He described opponents as coming to Green Bay to whip the Packers and embarrass them in front of their families, thereby inspiring their power motive to beat the opponent severely. They viewed him as a teacher and commander. He showed them what he wanted done, how to do it, explained why and then repeated it and had them practice it over and over. He pushed, yelled and punished them during practice so they could take it during games. The plans for each game were all designed by Vince and he told each player exactly what to do. Options were provided in his plans so players could adapt to the other teams' play. He controlled everything on the team and, with his volatile temper, no-one challenged his authority. There was one way to do things on the team, and it was his way. He sometimes lost consciousness and required oxygen when extremely angry and players were always fearful of being cut from the team, traded or benched.

Lombardi would sometimes compliment players in private after yelling at them in front of the team. His compliments were brief but highly valued by the players. At times he helped players he cut by getting them a position on another team. And he laughed often when players played practical jokes on him. He would sometimes put in a joke play with six pass receivers and the fullback throwing the ball—to loosen the team up in a game. By focusing on fearlessness and disciplined willpower, he taught players the habit of winning. Over time, they became dedicated to Lombardi and his methods. Paul Hornung believed that Lombardi's leadership was worth at least seven points in every game. His Hall of Fame Packer quarterback, Bart Starr, described Vince's consistent unwillingness to accept anything less than excellence as his greatest gift to those around him. Lombardi's famous saying has often been repeated, "Winning isn't everything, it's the only thing." But he did not believe in cheating to win.

After nine winning seasons with the Packers, Lombardi retired in 1967 as active coach and remained as general manager. He was unhappy in this position and accepted the coaching job for the Washington Redskins and led them to their first winning season in 14 years. A short time later, he was diagnosed with intestinal cancer and died on September 3, 1970.

Lombardi was a highly *directive* leader with an *authoritarian* style that seemed to fit in the sport he coached. Other head coaches with more easy going styles often failed in this position, unless they had assistants who could fill the commander role. Directive leadership is described in several leadership models such as Fiedler's Contingency Theory, Multiple Linkage Model, Path-Goal Theory, and Situational Leadership. Vince was clearly Charismatic/Transformational as he transformed the Packers and Redskins into teams that believed they were winners and did win, despite their previous losing records. His *inspiring speeches* clearly raised players' self-image and beliefs in themselves to a higher level. His leadership can also be viewed from the perspective of Authentic Leadership as he continuously espoused his values of hard work, sacrifice, team loyalty and dedication (which he called "love") throughout his career. He lived these values and infused his players with them. His leadership style could also be described with Implicit Leadership Theory as exemplifying the leader commander role that is typical of violent sports and military combat situations. He sought to create a team of closely knit cohesive football players with high performance norms, which is described in *Substitutes for Leadership* Theory. Lombardi's *determination, drive, dominance, cognitive capacity,* and *integrity* regarding the game of football reflect Trait Theories of leadership.

Discussion Questions

1. Was Vince Lombardi's commanding directive leadership style essential for his success as a professional football coach? Why or why not?
2. Would Lombardi's leadership style be effective in other organizational situations? If so, describe these situations.
3. Why did his players become so loyal to Lombardi?
4. Would Lombardi's leadership style be successful today for a professional sports team? How about a college sports team? Why or why not?

References

Maraniss, D. (1999). *When pride still mattered: A life of Vince Lombardi*. New York: Simon and Schuster.

Vince Lombardi. (n.d.). In *Wikipedia*. Retrieved May 26, 2009, from http://en.wikipedia.org/wiki/Vince_Lombardi

Wiebusch, J. (1971). *Lombardi*. Chicago, IL: Follett Publishing.

Chapter 13

Napoleon Bonaparte
French Military and Political Leader

Napoleon Bonaparte was a military leader and eventually emperor of France whose conquests determined much of the European geopolitical landscape during the late 18th and early 19th centuries. He may be the best example to demonstrate that major events are determined by the personal drive and leadership of men and women rather than by environmental forces such as economics and geography. Napoleon was a highly talented opportunist who took advantage of the French Revolution to propel himself into a position of great power. He used force and political maneuvering to expand his power throughout Europe. He also made significant contributions to judicial law and public administration. He is credited with cultural advances, many of which resulted from art works that were looted by his armies and brought to France. His military campaigns demonstrated true genius at strategy and tactics and are studied in military academies throughout the world.

Napoleon was born in 1769 on the island of Corsica, just one year after France obtained the island from the city state of Genoa. At age 9 he benefitted from family connections and obtained an appointment to the royal military school in France. This was followed by four years at the military college and one year at the officers' academy in Paris. At 16 years of age he became a professional military officer in the French king's army, specializing in artillery. He was gifted in mathematics and learned to take a calculative approach in effectively planning military campaigns and in placing and using cannons during battle. He also became a master at map reading and was able to visualize and exploit terrain to develop battle strategies better than any other officer. His father died the same year he was commissioned, and he took charge of the family with seven siblings.

The next few years he returned to Corsica several times, occasionally engaging in political wrangling, until his family was forced to flee by the insurgent leader, Pasquali Paoli, who obtained dictatorial power in Corsica. But Napoleon observed that Paoli imposed order and passed legislation that benefitted Corsicans—thus giving a reason for his revolutionary success. Napoleon kept this model in mind during his career, though his penchant for military campaigns and conquest overshadowed his role in governance.

In the 1780s, change was thriving in Europe. Legal reforms were instituted, outdated tariffs eliminated, feudal labor and slave trade was abolished, and commerce was promoted peaceably in Denmark, the Netherlands, and Germany. But France's King Louis XVI was slow to respond and was dedicated to its image as "the Great Nation." The King provided financial support for the Americans in their revolution and prepared for a war with Britain while severely taxing his own people. Food prices increased steadily causing major financial hardships and in 1789 an assembly of representatives from the three classes in French society (commoners, clergy, and noblemen) was called by the Minister of Finance. From this point, the revolution gained momentum. The assembly of representatives became the National Assembly to form a French constitution, the nobility refused to pay more taxes, and the Bastille (the royal prison in Paris that symbolized the King's tyranny) was attacked by a mob and its seven prisoners freed. Larger mobs formed, other prisons were stormed to obtain guns, and Paris became the scene of general insurrection with many French soldiers joining the revolutionaries. Eventually, King Louis XVI was stripped of his powers and the National Assembly declared France to be a republic and the end of the monarchy.

Napoleon watched these developments until it was clear the monarchy was doomed and then he took the side of those supporting the Republic. France declared war on Austria and Sardinia in 1792, which delighted Napoleon since war meant promotion and a larger command. He was promoted to captain and sent to Toulon where royalists, who supported the King and were joined by British troops, had taken possession of that important French port. His ingenuity and aggressive nature gave him control of the assault, which he directed to retake the port. This action propelled Napoleon to brigadier general, skipping the ranks of major and colonel, and started his rise to power.

Napoleon's desire for power is reflected throughout his life. He saw his cannons as a source of power that inspired fear in opponents. He was not patriotic, in fact he considered himself Corsican. He viewed the French as frivolous and volatile, with short attention spans, and believed they were easily diverted from major issues by temporary excitement. He exploited these traits later in his career when he gained control of the media and used clever propaganda campaigns to bolster his heroic image with the French people.

He led several successful military campaigns against the Austrians and Prussians capturing enormous amounts of land and looting treasuries, which were removed to France. His personality was belligerent in nature and he viewed war and battles as his way of gaining and exerting power. He saw people with detachment and believed they needed competent leadership to accomplish anything worthwhile. He inspired his troops to believe in his military campaigns and tactics. His approach was always to attack and never assume a defensive position. He emphasized rapid movement of troops and artillery, the element of surprise by attacking before the opponents were deployed, the use of ruse to confuse the enemy, and rapid improvisation with high risk maneuvers. He visited his troops before a battle to show his confidence in them and his infantry wore hats that were nearly two feet tall to make the soldiers appear larger and intimidate the enemy.

As Paris was shaken by riots and bloody coups, those in power realized Napoleon was their most dynamic and influential general. Fearing his aspirations for power, they plotted to keep him away from Paris. They thus approved his plans to invade Egypt and the Orient to take India from British control. He landed in Egypt in early July 1798 with a major naval fleet, troops, and 200 scientists and artists to document their expedition. He won a major battle near Cairo, but three days later his entire naval fleet was destroyed by the British Admiral Nelson at Alexandria. His army was then without naval support and he proceeded to invade Syria but was repulsed at Acre. Retreating to Egypt, he lost many of his remaining troops in sand storms. In Egypt, he presented several carefully prepared speeches to his generals outlining how he was needed in Paris and they eventually agreed he must leave. He returned to Paris where he carefully spun a story of the cultural successes of his "scientific" expedition, which included discovery of the Rosetta Stone and incredible art works that documented ancient Egyptian civilization. The following year he participated in a coup and was given control of the army, but he managed to get himself appointed First Consul of the Republic, which was actually a dictatorship with Napoleon at the top. All of the restraints on political power had been swept aside during the Revolution—church, courts, aristocracy, universities—leaving all the power to Napoleon. He led the French military to other victories against coalition forces from Russia,

Austria, Sweden, Prussia, and other parts of Europe. He was made First Consul for life in 1802 and appointed himself Emperor in 1804.

His soldiers identified with Napoleon and trusted their future to him. He demonstrated amazing energy as he wore out his officers in long meetings to plan his battles. He was totally self-confident in his decisions and actions and he delivered carefully planned speeches to inspire his troops to victory. He exploited the terrain effectively by choosing his battlefields carefully and implemented an effective signaling system to communicate among officers during battles. He directed his armies from a high hill or rooftop to view the battles as they developed and during the action he wore a dark green uniform with gray overcoat with no decorations to attract enemy fire. His daring and aggressive style of warfare became his trademark and Wellington (who finally defeated Napoleon at Waterloo) described him as the greatest general in Europe.

In addition to his aggressive style, inspirational speeches and repeated victories, Napoleon motivated his troops with the promise of great rewards, which they frequently obtained. He promised them riches from looting as well as honor and glory in victory. He offered promotion based on merit in battle where an infantryman could become a high level officer. When he appointed himself Emperor he rewarded successful generals by making them princes and dukes with enormous estates. He also made it easy for soldiers to send home their looted riches so families in France shared in the rewards of his victories. He eventually made the military a privileged class in French society. The entire country benefitted from the riches he sent home from looting the treasuries of Europe.

Napoleon was a highly authoritarian commander as he directed his generals to carry out his plans. He had an excellent chief of staff who translated his strategies into clear orders. His generals rushed to obey his directions and were obsequious in their praise. He appointed all his senior officers without consulting other officers. Wellington believed his commanding type of direction decreased disputes among his generals, something Wellington and other military leaders struggled to resolve. When Napoleon became Emperor, he answered to no-one. He was not a considerate leader as he repeatedly deserted his army when his plans were not successful. This happened in Egypt and again when he invaded Russia and was defeated in a long winter campaign. He later deserted his troops again when he was defeated at Leipzig and he returned to Paris, allowing 100,000 French troops to be captured. He constantly drove horses to death, whipping them as well as the horses his aids rode. He urged his cavalry to do the same, which depleted the French horse population and caused his cavalry to become less effective over time.

Scholars indicate that Napoleon learned during the terror of the Revolution that people did not bother to keep their word, honor was not respected, and treachery and murder were commonplace. Napoleon and his troops did not spare the populations they invaded—rape, murder, and pillage were commonplace. One general looted the Swiss treasury and murdered 500 citizens who objected— men, women, and children. In Syria, Napoleon had over 4,000 prisoners slaughtered because he feared they might rise up against him. He had at least one innocent individual murdered because he suspected him of plotting another coup. His armies lost 50,000 men a year during his campaigns, and he stated he would gladly sacrifice a million lives to attain the power he sought.

Napoleon was active in revising administrative and legal systems of the conquered territories. He implemented a new legal code in all countries he conquered, abolished the remains of the feudal system in Europe, and theoretically made all persons equal before the law. But he also reversed progress on women's rights that had been attained during the revolution, reinstituted slavery in French possessions, and solidified powers of the central government. Wellington said that Napoleon was much too impatient to govern over a long term. This impatience also prevented him from fighting a defensive campaign against coalition forces that defeated him at Leipzig and again at Waterloo. If he had done so, he may have been able to negotiate a settlement with these forces and remain in power.

After his defeat at Leipzig and the coalition forces invaded France, Napoleon was exiled in 1814 to the small island of Elba in the Mediterranean near Italy. He had a small force of 1,000 soldiers and a staff. He was not provided with the financial support France promised and became bored. In France, the monarchy had been restored but the King did not treat the people well, a major recession occurred, and the remaining soldiers had lost their status and were unemployed. Napoleon sensed an opportunity, secretly left Elba and marched to Paris. French soldiers joined him in route after he lied to them that members of the government and several European powers wanted his return. As they approached Paris, the King and his family fled to Belgium. Napoleon gathered the army together and moved north where he was met at Waterloo by Wellington and the coalition forces. The fighting raged for three days with Napoleon's army finally retreating. He left the army two days later and eventually surrendered to the British. He was exiled to St. Helena, a small island in the Atlantic, when he was 45 and lived there six years before he died of stomach cancer.

Napoleon has been described as an incredibly talented military leader without a trace of humility and no patience for governing. His pattern of dedication to force and war, a totally powerful state government, centrally controlled propaganda to justify a single head of state, and marshalling an entire society behind a single dictator was followed by numerous leaders in the 20th century. In the end, the people subjected to this type of leadership generally suffered.

Napoleon's military leadership can be viewed as highly *charismatic*—whether or not it is Transformational is debatable. He reflected the Multiple Linkage Model and Reformulated Path-Goal theories with his soldiers by *rewarding* them for their conquests. Leader Member Exchange Theory could be used to analyze his relationship with his troops. His *directiveness* was extremely authoritarian. Elements of directive leadership are addressed in contingency leadership models such as Situational Leadership Theory, Path-Goal Theory, Fiedler's Contingency Theory and the Multiple Linkage Model. However, these models generally avoid authoritarian elements in their prescriptions for directiveness. Implicit Leadership Theory might be invoked to analyze how his leadership style matched the expectations of military leaders at the time of Napoleon. His *determination* and *dominance, cognitive capacity,* and *self-confidence* demonstrate Trait Theories of leadership.

Discussion Questions

1. What aspects of Napoleon's leadership would you describe as charismatic/ transformational? Would you consider him a "dark" charismatic? Why or why not?
2. What other leader behaviors or traits do you see in Napoleon's leadership that can be linked to specific theories of leadership?
3. In what ways did Napoleon likely fit an implicit leadership theory for military leaders in his time?
4. Would you describe Napoleon as an authentic leader? Why or why not?

References

Johnson, P. (2002). *Napoleon*. New York: Penguin Books.
Napoleon I of France. (n.d.). In *Wikipedia*. Retrieved October 14, 2009, from http:// en.wikipedia.org/wiki/Napoleon_I_of_France

Chapter 14

Mary Kay Ash
Founder and CEO of Mary Kay Cosmetics

Mary Kay Ash was born in 1918 in Hot Wells, Texas, to a family of modest income. As a young girl, she helped care for her father, who had tuberculosis, while her mother worked. She was a good student, but the family could not afford to send her to college. She married at 17, eventually had three children, and began working in direct sales for Stanley Home Products in Houston, Texas. She possessed tremendous energy and learned quickly, while conducting demonstration "parties" for homemakers where she sold Stanley's cleaning and personal care items. She eventually became a unit manager and held this position from 1938 until changing companies in 1952.

After her divorce from her first husband, she began working for the World Gift Company, another direct sales firm in Dallas. She became national training director for this firm and developed her own ideas about managing a sales organization. She held this position until 1963 when she was passed over for promotion in favor of a man she had trained and who had less experience and job knowledge than her own. Tired of being under rewarded, she quit (actually retired) and decided to write a book to help women in business deal with the discrimination they faced on a daily basis.

Her planned book turned into a business plan for an "ideal company" that would help women succeed and flourish while maintaining a healthy family life. The plan emphasized the need for work-life balance by advocating three priorities for all employees—God, family, and career—in that order. She believed all managers must model these priorities, even though she eventually began rising at 5:00 a.m. to extend her workday. Mary Kay purchased formulas for specialized skin care products developed by the family of a previous customer. She knew they were excellent products and a good base from which to start her business. Her second husband helped her plan her new business, but died of a heart attack before it opened. Her son then stepped in and helped her open Mary Kay Cosmetics in a Dallas storefront in 1963 with her total savings of $5,000 and nine sales women who she termed "beauty consultants."

From the beginning, Mary Kay emphasized a caring and supportive style in managing her employees and sales force. She believed that caring for people was completely consistent with a profit making organization as long as its operations added value to her beauty consultants, customers, suppliers and the business. She was a vocal advocate of the moral principle known as the Golden Rule: Do unto others as you would have them do unto you. Although she speculated that women might be more responsive to a caring supportive leadership style, she believed that this approach would yield positive results in nearly any organization. Her company had a flat organization structure with most of its people operating as independent entrepreneurs in direct sales through "parties" or "shows" they presented in private homes. These beauty consultants bought their products from Mary Kay (everyone paid the same prices) and sold them for twice their cost. The worked as hard as they wanted and earned as much as they could. There was very little management hierarchy so promotions were not emphasized—only sales. Mary Kay provided extensive and continuous training and coaching as well as ideas for sales presentations. Beauty consultants recruited new sales persons and earned a percentage commission on the sales of those they recruited. This encouraged recruitment and built Mary Kay's business.

Mary Kay Cosmetics grew quickly as women seized the opportunity to be in business for themselves. Regional directors were appointed to help with training and coaching in their areas. Mary Kay invited groups of directors to her headquarters once a month for sales training and always had them to her home where she cooked and served them homemade cookies. She always emphasized treating people fairly and helping them achieve their goals. She believed strongly that praise and recognition as well as substantive rewards were powerful motivators. She looked for things people were doing right and praised them, emphasizing that this showed appreciation and helped build the person's self-esteem. She noted that this was critically important for new sales people just starting out.

She gave pink Cadillacs to sales persons for reaching specific sales goals, referring to these awards as "trophies on wheels." She also awarded diamond bracelets and first class trips to foreign cities. She believed these awards should be things the salespeople would not buy for themselves and they should demonstrate to others their success. Over the years she awarded literally thousands of Cadillacs.

She clearly emphasized financial rewards as a motivator because of the profit margin built into the products they sold. But she believed that public recognition was a more powerful motivator than substantive rewards. At her regular sales conferences, her salespeople wore designer suits and color coded outfits to signify the level of sales they achieved. She published a company magazine titled *Applause* where top sellers were described and publicized. At times she speculated about whether this type of recognition was most powerful with women. Within two years of opening Mary Kay Cosmetics, her beauty consultants had sold over $1 million in product, and by 1992 it was one of the Fortune 500 largest companies in the United States.

Mary Kay was very free with advice and directions about how to conduct sales shows, but she respected her consultants as independent entrepreneurs and did not force them to use her techniques. She did require that they always be well groomed and dress appropriately. Pants suits were not encouraged. She emphasized that all Mary Kay personnel must be proud of their products, the company, and themselves and show this in their appearance and demeanor. She believed this was an important part of role modeling for customers and sales people. She was always enthusiastic and emphasized a positive attitude, believing that a positive interpersonal style was contagious and sales people would mimic this style if it was shown by directors. She made extensive use of her directors in solving problems, often asking questions during meetings until they developed a solution. She believed that new ideas originated primarily from the sales people, and taught her directors that people will support programs and changes that they participate in creating.

Mary Kay's vision for her business was to fulfill two needs—to allow women to achieve success and still have time for their families, and to provide beauty products that would make women feel good about themselves. She emphasized this vision at every opportunity and made frequent speeches about her business model as her fame spread. The sales women owned their own businesses, they were not in partnership with their spouse. However, at her conferences she provided seminars for husbands to teach them how to help their wives in their Mary Kay business. There were no sales territories in Mary Kay, sales people and directors could sell and recruit new beauty consultants anywhere. Regional directors helped train all sales people in their district, whether they received a percentage of their sales or not. They did this because they knew other directors were training their recruits in other areas. The organizational culture she created is often described as "can do" and frequently involved sales people asking "What would Mary Kay do in this situation?"

Mary Kay authored three books and received dozens of national and regional awards, including distinguished recognition from major business schools and Fortune magazine for her business leadership. Her company is often discussed in a case at the Harvard Business School. She had over 800,000 sales people in 37 countries with total revenue of over $2 billion when she died in 2001. In 2008 her company had over 1.7 million sales people worldwide. She frequently helped raise money for charities and established the Mary Kay Ash Charitable Foundation to combat domestic violence and to support research on cancers that frequently affect women.

She suffered a stroke in 1996 and this affected her overall health. When she died in 2001, she left $15 million to her Foundation. She had become a symbol for many women in how to achieve success on their own, especially those who felt discriminated against in strongly male corporate cultures. Her inspirational speeches, determination, hard work, enthusiasm and passion for helping women succeed became her legacy for many women around the world.

The leadership of Mary Kay Ash fits well with the Authentic Leadership model, as she emphasized *self-confidence, enthusiasm, optimism, hope* and *determination*. Her message of God, family, and career in that order carried a *moral* tone and her positive behavior to support her sales people were prominent in her leadership style. Her caring and *supportive style* reflects Situational Leadership Theory, Multiple Linkage Model, Path-Goal Theory, the Leadership Grid and Fiedler's Contingency Theory. Her *inspirational speeches, role modeling, vision* for her company, and *symbolic role* clearly represent Charismatic/Transformational Leadership theories. Providing constant *recognition* and *rewards* for high sales performers are also described in the Multiple Linkage Model and Reformulated Path-Goal Theory. Her use of *participative* decision making is addressed in the Normative Decision Making Model. Mary Kay's continual emphasis on increasing her associates' training and knowledge to improve their independent sales presentations reflects *Substitutes for Leadership*. Her *determination, sociability, integrity,* and *self-confidence* all reflect Trait Theories of leadership.

Discussion Questions

1. What are the main reasons Mary Kay Ash was able to create and lead such a successful business organization?
2. Describe how her leadership style reflects the Authentic Leadership Model.

3. Why did she emphasize such a caring and supportive style with Mary Kay salespeople?
4. What elements of Charismatic/Transformational leadership did she demonstrate in her leadership?
5. Did Mary Kay utilize substitutes for leadership in her organization? If so, which ones and how did they work?

References

Ash, M. K. (1984). *Mary Kay on people management*. New York: Warner Books.

Mary Kay Ash. (n.d.). In *Wikipedia*. Retrieved February 3, 2010, from http://en.wikipedia.org/wiki/Mary_Kay_Ash

Stefoff, R. (1992). *Mary Kay—A beautiful business*. Ada, OK: Garrett Educational Corporation.

West, S. E. (2011, May). Mary Kay Ash. Retrieved from http://www.theleadershipresource.com/WomenLeaders04.php

Chapter 15

Nicolas Hayek
Swiss Watch Executive

Nicolas Hayek was the major founder, CEO and Chairman of the Board of Directors of the Swatch Group, the largest manufacturer of finished watches in the world. He and his staff engineered one of the most amazing industrial turnarounds in the world and saved the Swiss watch industry from oblivion. He also played a major role in the creation of the Smart Car, a small green European automobile built by Mercedes Benz for city driving. Hayek's strategic leadership is at odds with contemporary thinking about how companies must compete in the global market place, but his strategic vision and outstanding communication skills resulted in Switzerland retaking the leading role in the global watch industry.

Hayek was born on February 19, 1928, in Beirut, Lebanon to a prosperous family. He attended a Lebanese Christian university and graduated with a diploma in math, chemistry, and physics. He was a nonconformist in his youth and fell in love with a young Swiss woman who was working as an au pair in Beirut. His parents did not approve of their marriage, so Hayek immigrated to Switzerland when she returned home shortly after his graduation. They were married two years later. In Switzerland he faced suspicion and hostility as an outsider so he chose to downplay his background and focused on becoming a Swiss citizen. His fierce independence made him comfortable with risk taking with little fear of failure. Throughout his career he was never discouraged by opposition or setbacks, using them as energizers to work harder to achieve his goals.

Shortly after moving to Switzerland, his father-in-law, who owned and ran an iron foundry, had a major stroke. The family asked Nicolas to take over management of the foundry, even though he had no management experience. He accepted and began working in the shop where he had much direct contact with staff and foundry workers. As his Swiss German language skills improved, he slowly overcame the early lack of acceptance. He eventually attended an international foundry fair in Germany where he concentrated on networking with customers and others in the industry, landing a large contract with the Swiss Railway system. This allowed their family foundry to carry out a much needed expansion and improvement of their facility. His father-in-law soon recovered and returned to the foundry, resulting in a significantly reduced role for Hayek who had enjoyed his new management experience and the independence he had as head of the company.

Throughout Hayek's career, he excelled at networking and representing himself and his organizations to other business people, governments and unions. While working at the foundry, he met an American engineering consultant named Lester B. Knight who respected Hayek's capabilities. When his role at the foundry became too confining, Knight suggested that Hayek start a branch office of his consulting firm in Switzerland. Hayek obtained a loan and rented office space and in 1957 began as a consultant in Zurich. His wife and two children joined him later when he could afford a living space for the family. At this time, Germany was still rebuilding from the destruction it experienced in World War II. Hayek had made many contacts in the foundry industry in Germany and began getting contracts in Germany. His reputation grew and so did his business. He added staff members to support the growth and six years later he parted with Knight to open his own consulting firm, taking many of the staff members from the branch office with him. His networks and consulting practice continued to grow with Swiss and international contracts and offices in other countries. His associates described him as highly intelligent with an excellent memory, a master at analyzing production, cost and financial data, extremely energetic and diligent in his work, with an intuition for market trends and developments. He also preferred to be in control of his operation by making all major decisions himself and using an autocratic type of directive leadership. He was highly self-confident in his judgment and enjoyed public recognition for his accomplishments.

In 1981, Hayek was asked by major Swiss bankers to undertake an analysis of the two major Swiss watch manufacturers who were nearing bankruptcy. The Swiss watch industry dated from the early 1800s when jewelry and watchmakers fled religious persecution in France to live in Switzerland. After an early concentration on expensive luxury watches, less expensive models were developed that were affordable to a larger market. At this point the watch industry became a major industrial sector in Switzerland. During the economic depression of the 1930s, the Swiss government began protecting the watch industry through legislation and investment which provided monopoly power to a few companies. They were protected from international competition and the management became complacent, concentrating on accuracy and precision in watches that sold themselves. They failed to adopt new technology as it became available and in the late 1960s they did not recognize that new electronic and quartz watch movements produced adequate accuracy for most consumers. In the 1970s Asian manufacturers mass produced and marketed these inexpensive electronic watches worldwide and the Swiss market share declined rapidly. The Swiss concentrated on luxury watches, but this market niche was decreasing in size, many Swiss watch manufacturers went out of business, and the others were in trouble. Major Swiss banks were the dominant shareholders of the two biggest Swiss manufacturers and they were considering selling their best brands to Japan. At this point, they asked Hayek to evaluate the companies and advise them of the best course of action.

With his colleagues, Hayek identified problems in products, policies, and distribution as well as outdated leadership that required changing. He advised merging the two watch companies to avoid duplication and recommended establishment of three divisions—finished watches, parts and components, and diversified industrial products. He also recommended replacing the entire leadership group with a five-member committee containing a senior member of his consulting group—Ernst Thomke. He opposed selling the best brands to foreign watchmakers and emphasized keeping watch-making knowledge in Switzerland. His proposals were implemented, and within a year improvements in performance were visible, within three years the merged company (Swiss Corporation for Microelectronics and Watch Making, known as SMH) was showing a profit. Hayek's consulting firm was quite successful, and he was searching for investments when a major banker suggested he invest in SMH. Hayek assembled an investment group and eventually bought 51% of the company. As originator of the group, he arranged to have the major leadership role in SMH and in 1986 he became president and operations manager. The market value of the company began to climb.

A major product of SMH at the time of the merger was the Swatch—an inexpensive plastic watch, produced in different colors, which was becoming a fashion accessory. The Swatch had been developed by two company engineers under the guidance of Ernst Thomke. It was produced in fully automated production lines and was very successful in the low price segment of the global watch market with many models under $100. When Hayek assumed his leadership position, he became the Swatch champion and nurtured its further development and marketing. He consulted with designers and increased the advertising budget in the United States and Europe. The Swatch became a lifestyle product, and Hayek hired celebrities to promote the watch—including Jack Nicholson, Cindy Crawford, Andy Warhol, and actors portraying James Bond. Advertisements emphasized fun activities, and new Swatch collections were launched each year. SMH skipped distributors and shipped the watches directly to retailers. In the first five years over 250 Swatch models were produced and by 1992, production had exceeded 100 million. The Swatch eventually created billions in revenue for the company. Hayek presented himself as Father of the Swatch and held a huge party to celebrate its success. His business acumen had certainly helped promote, distribute, and expand the production of the Swatch, but he did not originate the concept or begin its development and production. Ernst Thomke later gave credit to the creative engineers who originated the Swatch idea, but received only small bonuses for their extra efforts.

Another successful watch brand acquired by SMH in 1983 from a small watch company was the Rado, which sported scratch proof metal, a ceramic face, and sapphire crystal. It sold well in the middle to high priced market segment ($700 to $30,000) and was very well accepted in Middle Eastern countries. Hayek wanted to develop the Omega brand, the luxury line of watches produced by SMH, to challenge Rolex. Omega had been producing over 100 models with over 1,500 variations in all price brackets. The meaning of its brand had become unclear and it was losing its appeal to customers. Hayek asked Thomke to take control of Omega and restore its position in the luxury market. Thomke reduced the number of Omega models to fewer than 20 and reduced the staff to 33% of its former size. Production and sales increased and it began to be profitable. The same result occurred with the SMH Longine brand, which was a luxury watch just under Omega.

Hayek's strategic vision was to be strong in all segments of the watch market. He had an excellent management team with Ernst Thomke and other colleagues. Hayek set the strategy while Thomke and others carried it out. Thomke loved to start new projects and move on to other things; Hayek wanted to build his own business empire with all the recognition that went with it. Both were extremely talented, egocentric, combative, and reacted emotionally to unpleasant news. They were either loved or hated by employees. Hayek was a patriarchal leader who emphasized autocratic leadership over his employees. Although often blunt, he was a persuasive communicator and able to make people like him. He was approachable and people who worked with him indicated they learned tremendously from their experience. He was loyal to his people, although sometimes tough on his executive managers. Those who left the company were usually persona non grata. Eventually Hayek's tendencies to exert control of all activities became intolerable for Thomke, and he left to form his own companies. SMH was eventually renamed the Swatch Group and board members indicated that Hayek controlled the board of directors.

Hayek told interviewers from Harvard Business Review that his strategy demonstrated how high wage countries could manufacture high quality products for the mass market and be competitive. He did this not by decreasing wages, but by decreasing the proportion of labor costs to total costs through automation and increased efficiency. If mass production was shipped to other countries, he asserted that the United States and Europe risked losing key skills and the loss of these skills for low cost items endangered the production of high quality items. He lobbied Swiss and international labor organizations to allow for night work so the Swatch automated production facility could run around the clock. Throughout the 1990s he continued to expand through the purchase of small watch companies that focused on the extreme luxury market with brands such as Patek Phillipe, Blancpain, and Breguet. These watches sold primarily to collectors and royalty for $500,000 or more each. With these purchases he realized his vision of a major market presence in all segments of the global watch market. He also developed a relationship with Tiffany in the United States to produce luxury watches for their stores.

In the late 1990s, Hayek developed an interest in producing an eco-friendly hybrid powered car for European cities. He saw a similarity between watches and cars—both were consumer goods with strong emotional appeal. He partnered with Mercedes Benz to produce the car, planning to call it the Swatch Car. He helped promote the new car through clever publicity events and interviews. Although Hayek is credited for the original idea, the final result produced by Mercedes was called the Smart Car and was far from his planned creation. He eventually withdrew from the project due to its size and possible financial endangerment to his watch company. He did, however, establish a company to conduct research on clean power for cars and named actor George Clooney to the Board of Directors to help promote green projects in the United States.

Although Hayek professed no interest in politics, he often made controversial public statements that reflected his beliefs. He was an anti-militarist, opposed nuclear energy, and condemned extremely high executive salaries. Considering his great personal wealth, he was personally thrifty and believed management must consider all corporate stakeholders in making decisions—including stockholders, employees, and the public. He cultivated excellent relations with labor unions in the watch industry. He continued representing his company throughout his life, appearing as a torch bearer in the 1996 Olympics in Atlanta, Georgia, as the only business representative. From the mid-1990s he bought company stock and consolidated his holdings, while the Swatch Group remained debt free with a market value of $10–20 billion and over 24,000 employees mostly in Switzerland. He received numerous awards and honorary degrees and is viewed as a classic model of the modern entrepreneur/leader and savior of the Swiss watch industry. Hayek died of heart failure in his office in June 2010. His son is currently CEO and his daughter is Chairman of the Board of Directors of the Swatch Group.

Nicolas Hayek was a *visionary strategic leader* with excellent *communication skills*, as addressed by Transformational/Charismatic leadership models. He also excelled at *boundary spanning* by networking and representing his companies to important outsiders. This behavior pattern is addressed by the Multiple Linkage Model and Reformulated Path-Goal Theory. He was highly *directive* of followers in assigning them to carry out his decisions, although he was often authoritarian. This is described by Path-Goal Theory, Fiedler's Contingency Theory and Situational Leadership Theory. In decision making he was *autocratic* and *patriarchal* which are addressed in the Normative Decision Theory and Leadership Grid Model. He was *supportive* with his factory workers by maintaining high wages and avoiding layoffs whenever possible. This behavior is also included in Path-Goal Theory, Fiedler's Contingency Theory and Situational Leadership Theory. Hayek's *intelligence, determination,* and *self-confidence* are addressed by Trait Theories of leadership.

Discussion Questions

1. Was Nicolas Hayek's autocratic and directive leadership style necessary to save the Swiss watch making industry? Why or why not?
2. There were two major elements to Hayek's vision for the Swatch Group: preserving Swiss watch making skills in the country, and establishing a major presence in all the price segments of the global watch market. Was one of these elements more important than the other to his success? Why or why not?
3. How important were Hayek's boundary spanning efforts at networking and representing in building the Swatch Group's success?

4. What do you think of Hayek's practice of controlling the Board of Directors and making all major decisions himself?

References

Nicolas Hayek. (n.d.). In *Wikipedia*. Retrieved February 18, 2010, from http://en.wikipedia.org/wiki/Nicolas_Hayek

Swatch Group History (n.d.). Retrieved February 18, 2010, from http://www.swatch group.com/en/group_profile/history/yesterday

Wegelin, J. (2010). *Mister Swatch: Nicolas Hayek and the secret of his success*. London: Free Association Books.

Chapter 16

César Chávez
American Labor Leader

César Chávez is one of the most prominent labor leaders and civil rights activists in United States history. He fought tenaciously for improving the work and living conditions for farm workers in the United States. He cofounded and led the first truly successful Farm Workers Union which resulted in great improvements for farm laborers. He succeeded in spite of the migratory nature of these workers and tremendous opposition from powerful growers, politicians, legal officials, and another powerful union. He was a forceful advocate of nonviolence and he came to symbolize the history and collective spirit of farm workers in the United States.

César's grandparents emigrated from Mexico in the late 1800s before Arizona became a state. He was born in 1927 on the small family farm near Yuma, Arizona. When he was 11 years old, his family lost the farm and most of their possessions during the Great Depression and they moved to California to work as laborers in the fields. There was a long history of immigrant labor in the farm fields of California, dating back to the mid-1800s when the Gold Rush ended. At that time, large banks and industrialists bought up the valleys to produce food to be shipped all over the country by the new transcontinental railroad. They used mostly immigrant labor on the farms and the pay and working conditions were miserable. By the 1930s, most of the farm workers were Mexican or Filipino immigrants earning about $.60 for picking 100 pounds of cotton. Any efforts to gain better wages through strikes were met with violence from growers.

César's family with six children moved throughout California following the harvests. All members of the family worked in the fields and they lived with the poorest of the poor—often in tents with no running water or toilets available. César grew up amid this back breaking farm work and observed the injustices of low pay and poor working conditions. He volunteered for military service in World War II and returned to the fields after the war. He soon married Helen Fabela whose family was composed of farm workers and was familiar with the conditions in the fields. While they were living in a barrio (a poor neighborhood of Mexican Americans) in San Jose, he met a civil rights activist named Fred Ross. Ross worked for the Community Service Organization (CSO), which campaigned for the rights of Latin Americans and he recruited Chávez to help recruit Latinos for their cause. César learned from Ross how to organize and lead poor laborers. He also learned from Father Donald MacDonald who worked to obtain social justice for Latinos. In the 1950s, Latinos were still discriminated against in restaurants, parks, and theaters, and were usually paid considerably less than white farm workers for the same work.

Father MacDonald introduced César to writings by St. Francis of Assisi (an Italian monk who devoted himself to helping the poor) and Mohandas Gandhi who advocated nonviolence in his campaign against the British for Indian independence. César also studied the actions of Martin Luther King who followed Gandhi's guidance. César realized that to be a successful leader he must be a positive role model for followers and set an example of nonviolence. At first he worked in the fields during the day and at night he taught farm workers about their civil rights and registered them to vote. Later he became a full time organizer for CSO, earning $35 per week traveling around California fighting racial and economic discrimination against Latinos. From 1959 to 1962 he was the Executive Director of CSO where he gained the respect of farm workers by advising them about insurance, citizenship applications, translations, and other personal business. He sought out and gained endorsements of Catholic priests for his efforts which increased his legitimacy in the eyes of farm workers. But he became frustrated when the CSO membership refused to direct efforts to form a union for farm workers. So César resigned and moved his family to Delano in the San Joaquin Valley, the heart of California farm land. He rented the cheapest house he could find for his family, which eventually included eight children, dressed in work clothes, and began driving up and down the valley in his old station wagon talking to farm workers about their wages and working conditions.

He advised workers how to deal with supervisors in the fields and publicized growers' illegal tendency to hire *Braceros* instead of resident farm workers. *Braceros* were temporary farm workers from Mexico who first came to the United

States to fill in for resident laborers who were serving in World War II. The program was not discontinued when the war ended, and growers were supposed to use *Braceros* only when resident workers were unavailable. But they often hired them at lower wages and/or used them as strike breakers—replacing resident workers when they were striking for better wages and working conditions. This not only took the jobs of resident workers, it rendered their strikes ineffective. César convinced Dolores Huerta, a talented negotiator and organizer with the CSO, to join him in his efforts.

Chávez and Huerta worked in a garage turning out pamphlets and they traveled throughout the San Joaquin Valley signing up members for a farm workers union. César again gained the active support of Catholic priests in the area. After six months they held an organizing convention in Fresno, north of Delano, and in 1962 they formally adopted the name National Farm Workers Association (NFWA) with César as president and executive officer. Farm workers were not covered by the National Labor Relations Act which guaranteed for other workers the right to join a union and bargain collectively with employers. They agreed to focus on lobbying the governor for a $1.50 per hour minimum wage, unemployment insurance, the right to bargain collectively as a union, and to set up a credit union for members. César soon borrowed money against his brother's home to start the credit union. At first the credit union lost money, but his wife Helen took over and by the mid-1980s they had raised enough money to loan out over $5 million in small loans to farm workers.

César's wife and children continued to work in the fields to support the family, and farm workers often gave them food to live on. He started an underground newspaper that advocated for workers' rights and often used humorous cartoons that addressed farm worker issues which illiterate workers could understand. Early in its life, the NFWA supported several groups of unhappy workers who declared strikes although they had little success. He made all members promise they would be nonviolent in all dealings with growers and others. In 1964 he was offered a job by the Peace Corps as director for Latin America for $21,000 per year. He turned it down (promoting anger in his wife's family) to stay with his $50 a week job in the union which he also supplemented by working in the fields.

In 1965, Filipino grape workers went on strike over being paid less than other farm workers for the same work. César called an NFWA meeting and spoke in a calm but determined voice. He compared their struggle for fair treatment to Mexico's struggle for independence. He said they were struggling for the freedom and dignity denied to them by poverty. He convinced the members to join with the Filipinos in the strike and directed them to picket, which meant standing at the entrance of the largest grape grower's farm and trying to convince others not to enter the farm. He coached them on how to picket nonviolently. He contacted other unions, churches, and spoke at university campuses to generate support by sending food for the strikers. He invited them to come and see the conditions of the farm workers and activist students and clergymen began to appear at the strike. More farm workers and activists became involved. César's wife and 44 clergymen and strikers were arrested. César was speaking at the University of California at Berkeley and when he heard of the arrests, he took up a collection of $6,500 in donations for their release and they were released. César then directed NFWA members to follow the grapes from warehouses to shipping points and picket, resulting in unionized longshoremen in Oakland refusing to cross the picket line to load grapes on ships. Walter Reuther, President of the AFL-CIO (the powerful federation of dozens of national and international unions) marched with César and the NFWA and pledged financial support for the strikers. A United States Senate subcommittee on migratory labor held hearings in Delano on working conditions at the farms. Senator Robert Kennedy was a subcommittee member and he sided with the strikers, befriended Chávez, and marched with him on one of their picket lines.

Chávez then led a 300 mile march from Delano, up the San Joaquin Valley, to the state capital in Sacramento. The purpose was to dramatize the grape strike and lift the spirits of the union members. They started with around 100 people and much publicity from the press. César suffered bloody blisters, and a nurse recommended he ride the last part of the march. But after a rest, he limped all the way to the state capital and held a rally with over 10,000 supporters. Shortly before their arrival, the grower who they were striking agreed to recognize the NFWA and signed a labor agreement. At the rally, César demanded the governor call a special session of the legislature and enact a law which guaranteed farm workers the right to bargain collectively with growers. He then emphasized to the crowd the importance of their victory, but that they must show humility and remain dedicated to their cause.

Another large grower began negotiating with the union but threatened members when they tried to speak with their workers. César directed them to cut off negotiations and called for a boycott, which urged people not to buy the growers numerous products. He had a religious altar built on the back of a station wagon and parked it next to the grower's farm where people prayed for the workers. The altar became famous in the press, and publicity increased for the union. On very short notice, the grower announced an election to choose a union for their workers and a short time later announced that the Teamsters Union had won the right to represent their workers. The Teamsters had previously organized truck drivers and packers for agricultural products but not farm workers. César saw their action as a takeover of NFWA members and went to the farm advocating a strike. He was arrested and shackled but released the next day. News spread of his arrest and the Teamsters' actions. California Governor Ronald Reagan, Senator Robert Kennedy, and others urged the grower to hold a legitimate election. At this point, NFWA merged with another small farm workers union which was affiliated with the AFL-CIO with César made president. The grower allowed the new election, NFWA won, and other major growers of wine and juice grapes in California signed contracts with the union. The Teamsters then withdrew their efforts to organize the grape growers.

César then addressed growers of table grapes who refused to negotiate. He held a meeting of union members who voted for a strike. A large grower brought in strike breakers and obtained a court order opposing the strike. So César declared a boycott of the grower's grapes. When the grower shipped grapes under another name, César initiated a national boycott of all California table grapes which became the largest most successful boycott in United States history. Violence erupted between strikers and growers' employees and César worried about how to control his members. He confiscated guns, expelled union members who provoked violence, and began to fast until members recommitted themselves to nonviolence. The fasting idea came from his studies of Gandhi, who used the fast as an effective symbolic gesture. After fasting for 25 days, his health had declined dramatically, and members finally agreed to his nonviolent strategy. It also increased the members' dedication and unity to their cause. Robert Kennedy visited César to celebrate the end of his fast. Before the fast, union members described César as a leader and brother of the farm workers. After the fast, members attributed tremendous moral stature and authority to César. He had become famous and staffers hesitated to disagree with his ideas.

César sent people all over the country and to Canada to promote the boycott. President Nixon opposed the boycott, and Governor Reagan called it immoral. Both had received political support from major growers. Time magazine described the boycott, books were written about it, and in 1970 the major growers of table grapes eventually recognized the NFWA and signed contracts with the union. The grape strike and boycott had lasted five years, and 17 million Americans had refused to buy grapes until it was settled.

The same year, the Teamsters signed a secret deal with major salad growers in the Salinas Valley to represent their farm workers. When he learned of this, César led a 3,000 member march through Salinas and addressed the workers about the travesty of a few white men from the Teamsters and growers determining the destinies of Latinos and Filipinos in the California fields. He urged them to join the NFWA rather than the Teamsters. Many responded and César began lobbying the AFL-CIO and a Catholic Church fund for financial support during the strike. He also directed a lettuce boycott and began a fast, but soon learned the Teamsters had backed off from organizing lettuce workers. Other unions had supported the NFWA which negotiated much better wages and working conditions for their members than the Teamsters. Other large growers began meeting with César to avoid boycotts of their produce.

In 1971, the NFWA became the United Farm Workers Union (UFW) and was affiliated with the AFL-CIO. The lives of UFW members were much improved as they saved money, many bought modest homes and settled in one place, and their children finished school. They had toilets in the fields, drinking water, work breaks, pensions, seniority rights, medical insurance, opportunities for advancement, and respect. The Federal Bureau of Investigation (FBI) had observed César and the union for years when they were tipped by an anonymous informant that the union was affiliated with the Communist Party. They found no such affiliation, but continued to observe the battles in the fields. The FBI notified César of a plot to murder him in 1972, but the hired killer was arrested and convicted of an earlier murder.

In 1973, the Teamsters again tried to organize the grape workers in the San Joaquin Valley, and records show that President Nixon's administration sided with the Teamsters. Judges issued injunctions against picketing, and the Teamsters tried to incite violence with the UFW members who continued to picket the fields. César visited the picket lines, sought AFL-CIO strike funds, pursued lawsuits against the Teamsters and growers for conspiracy, and went to Washington, DC, to lobby for a federal investigation into violence against the farm workers. Always seeking to avoid violence, he rejected offers from the Seafarers Union for burly men to protect the UFW picketers. With the press present, he stood in front of huge insulting Teamsters and told them the UFW picketers would not leave. When two UFW picketers were killed, César called off the strike until federal officials would guarantee the safety and rights of picketers. In 1973, 3,500 farm workers were arrested and most were released when charges were declared unconstitutional.

César led another successful march of 130 miles to force a large winery and grower to hold union elections rather than signing secret agreements with the Teamsters. In 1975 he successfully lobbied the new governor, Jerry Brown, to help the legislature pass the Agricultural Labor Relations Act (ALRA) of California. It guaranteed the right for farm workers to organize and bargain collectively and set up an office to supervise union elections and to investigate violations. These are the same rights given to non-agricultural workers by the National Labor Relations Act of 1935. He then successfully fought growers' efforts in the state legislature to block funds to carry out the provisions of the ALRA. He carried out a fast for over three weeks to stop a grower-sponsored legal proposition to outlaw strikes and boycotts among agricultural workers which the voters of California eventually rejected. In 1977 he finally convinced the Teamster leadership to stop all organizing efforts of farm workers.

In the late 1970s he led other marches and strikes on lettuce growers resulting in significant increases in wages and benefits for UFW members. By the 1980s, union membership was around 100,000 and some farm workers under piece rate systems could earn up to $20 per hour. Union elections were common and workers usually selected the UFW. César became more directive and controlling during this time. He laid off many professional staffers and hired young people from farm worker families, believing that their commitment was greatest and they identified with the members. César kept the union highly centralized without local affiliates because so many farm workers were still migrants. By this time, he was viewed by many as a cultural icon, and few ventured to disagree with him. However, some began to question his leadership. César wanted the union to fund a Latino lobby to pursue the interests of all Mexican Americans but staffers and members insisted they continue their focus on farm workers.

César had opposed the use of pesticides for decades as more cancers and birth defects began to appear among farm worker. Governor Deukmejian, who succeeded Jerry Brown, vetoed a bill to help protect workers from pesticides and cut funding to the ALRA. César responded by making a short film titled *The Wrath of Grapes* that showed the damage pesticide use had on farm workers. The film was shown around the country and generated much support for the union against pesticides. At age 61, César began another fast to force growers to bargain regarding pesticide use. The fast lasted 36 days and was ended due to serious health concerns. He continued speaking out against pesticides over the next few years. In April 1993, César was weakened by the flu and died in his sleep of natural causes. In 2004 California passed a law controlling pesticide use, but it remains a controversial issue. The UFW is active today in 10 states and continues to campaign for farm workers' rights. Chávez was awarded the Presidential Medal of Freedom posthumously in 1994.

The leadership of César Chávez has been described as Charismatic/Transformational due to his *role modeling, risk taking,* and *inspirational speeches.* He became a *symbol* for farm workers who identified with his poor background, sacrifices, and his family's hard work in the fields. He was also highly *directive* of union members when quick response was necessary to the growers' efforts to avoid recognizing their union and to exploit their workers. He continuously *supported* farm workers through strike funding and participating in picket lines, marches, and lobbying efforts to improve their working conditions. These leader behaviors are described by Fiedler's Contingency Theory, Path-Goal Theory, Situational Leadership Theory and the Multiple Linkage Model. He was constantly active in *boundary spanning* by representing the Farm Workers Union to growers, different levels of government, law enforcement officials, Teamsters, and the public. This leader behavior is addressed by the Multiple Linkage Model and Reformulated Path-Goal Theory. His high *moral character, resilience, hope,* and *confidence* in the union cause combined with the trigger events of his early experience in the farm fields resulted in a type of Authentic Leadership that was dedicated to the improvement of the living and working conditions of farm workers. Although Chávez was five feet six inches tall and often quiet and inconspicuous, he demonstrated *determination, assertiveness, self-confidence, cognitive capacity,* and *integrity* which are described in Trait Theories of leadership.

Discussion Questions

1. What did César Chávez do to make the farm workers so devoted to him and the union?
2. Why was César's farm worker union so successful against the big growers and the powerful Teamsters union?
3. Do you think Chávez would have been equally successful in leading a profit making business organization? Why or why not?
4. Give one or two examples of César's actions that reflect the Authentic Leadership model.
5. Give one or two examples of César's actions that reflect Charismatic/Transformational leadership.

References

César Chávez. (n.d.). In *Wikipedia*. Retrieved February 2, 2010, from http://en.wikipedia.org/wiki/Cesar_Chavez

Ferriss, S. & Sandoval, R. (1997). *The fight in the fields: César Chávez and the farm workers movement*. New York: Harcourt Brace.

Griswold del Castillo, R. & Garcia, R. A. (1995). *César Chávez: A triumph of spirit*. Norman: University of Oklahoma Press.

Chapter 17

Konosuke Matsushita
Japanese Industrial Leader

Konosuke Matsushita was under 5 feet 5 inches tall, thin and sickly, not considered handsome, and seldom recognized. His youth was filled with tragedy and poverty. He was neither a good speaker, nor a good student, and was not considered extremely intelligent. But he motivated many thousands of employees to achieve socially worthwhile goals through his inspiring and caring leadership and his insight into the role of private business organizations in society. He supplied high quality household appliances to billions of people at affordable prices and was a key person in helping to rescue the Japanese economy after World War II. He started with nothing and created an organization with $42 billion in revenue at the time of his death. In Japan, he was more admired than movie stars and professional athletes and was considered a national hero.

Matsushita was born in 1894 in Wasamura, Japan, to a family of eight children. He was the youngest child, and his father was a relatively prosperous farm owner. His earliest years were very happy, but his father lost everything by speculating in commodities when Konosuke was 4 years old. The family was forced to move to the city where they lived in a three room apartment and tried to survive. His father failed at a small business, three siblings died in 1901, and Konosuke became the oldest living son with hopes that he would help rebuild the family's respect and fortune. At 9 years of age, after only four years of schooling, he was apprenticed to a charcoal heater maker in another city where he lived and worked with the owner's family and other apprentices. Three months later his employer downsized and no longer needed young Konosuke. His father found him another apprenticeship in a bicycle shop in Osaka (a larger city) where he lived and worked seven days a week with a stern boss who allowed no laziness. But his master cared for him and taught him his trade. He worked there until he was 15 and with encouragement and support from his master, he learned how to control costs, to buy and sell merchandise, and to care for customers.

In 1906 his father and two sisters died. In the same year, Matsushita became interested in electricity which was becoming widespread in Japan. He saw it as a technological breakthrough which signified the beginning of a new age. He left the bicycle shop and obtained a job in an electric light company to learn about electricity. He began as a wiring assistant but his openness to learning, curiosity, and ambition led to several promotions over the next few years. By the age of 19 he was supervising several large projects at one time. He tried returning to school part time but his writing was inadequate, he fell behind and quit. His self-confidence at work grew steadily and at one point he convinced a crew to work around the clock for three days to finish a project on time.

His mother died in 1913 and at 22 he entered into a marriage arranged by his sister. His wife, Mumeno, was 19, and she and Konosuke were not acquainted before the marriage. About this time, he designed a new light socket which he presented to his employer who showed no interest. Matsushita was hurt by this response and resolved to quit and start his own company to manufacture light sockets. His original design had several flaws which he eventually corrected and in 1917 he quit the light company and began his own business. He was 22, had little savings, a new wife, and 13 years of work experience. He began with four assistants—his wife, two previous coworkers, and his 14-year-old brother-in-law. None had a high school education. The business occupied a two room apartment, and Konosuke and his wife slept in the corner of one room. They had little money for supplies and only made a few items which they were unable to sell to wholesalers. Two employees eventually quit for other jobs to support themselves. Konosuke and his wife pawned their clothes and personal belongings to keep the business going. One wholesaler liked them and advised them to make 1,000 insulating plates for electric fans which were in demand. They did so, sold them immediately and received an order for another 2,000. This revenue allowed Konosuke to rent a larger house with more floor space where they made the plates, electric sockets, and another attachment plug which was needed in most Japanese houses that had only a single electric outlet. By emphasizing very low overhead and long work hours, he kept costs low and sold his products for 30% below the market price with good quality. All his products began to sell.

As demand increased, they worked 12 to 16 hour days and eventually hired more workers who specialized in different aspects of production. A distributor approached him for exclusive rights to sell the attachment plug. Konosuke then showed his shrewd negotiation skills. He agreed, in return for a loan to finance his further expansion. He began taking in young apprentices who lived with the Matsushitas and were fed by Mumeno. Konosuke was stern but paternalistic, and Mumeno became their surrogate mother. His overall business strategy which he adhered to during most of his life was to create improved versions of existing products, produce them at low cost with minimum overhead and long hours (which were common in Japan) and sell them at below market prices. This required close attention to detail during production and no-one in his organization worked harder than Konosuke. He was fiercely independent, optimistic, and determined to make his company prosper. He was also very willing to take risks.

In 1919 another sister died, and in 1921 his last sibling passed away. At 27, Konosuke was the only survivor of his family and continued to devote himself to his business. At first he did all his own product designs, later he hired others to work under time pressure to satisfy perceived customer needs. He opened an office in Tokyo in 1921 and built a larger plant in 1922 which was financed through a loan he negotiated from his contractor. Matsushita Electric now had modern equipment and 30 employees and was developing one or two new products every month. They developed a much improved battery powered bicycle lamp which he first sold through a creative marketing strategy in bicycle shops. The shop owners were not required to pay for the lamps until they were sold to satisfied customers. Lamp orders increased, more money flowed into the business, and they began making radio parts.

Matsushita was not considered a good public speaker but he was sincere, with infectious energy, and earned increasing credibility from his success in business. He began to devote his energies to training and developing his workers. He believed that a "collective wisdom" would make his company successful and this required empowering employees with the information they needed to continually improve performance and managers having faith in their employees' capabilities and development. These capabilities must be nurtured by leaders through a caring attitude, as well as an inspiring vision and mission that motivated them to meet and exceed goals. He modeled a strong work ethic for his employees as well as a willingness to experiment, learn continuously, and take risks as they developed new products. He urged his employees to do likewise. He created a Matsushita employee organization that sponsored cultural, recreational, and sporting events for employees.

Konosuke and Mumeno had two children born in the 1920s. Their daughter was healthy but the son died before his first birthday. This was a great tragedy for

Konosuke since sons were very important in Japan at that time. He continued to work incessantly and built a bigger plant in 1929 just as the world economy crashed into a depression and sales slumped. He refused to lay off workers, but decided to reduce them to half time while continuing to pay their full wages and eliminating all holidays. He asked all employees to try to sell the huge backlog of products when they were not working. They responded and sales increased, resulting in their plant returning to full time work only three months later. Radios were unreliable at that time. Matsushita built their radio business in the 1930s by buying a radio factory and working to improve their reliability while opening their own stores with qualified personnel who could repair the radios. In ten years they were the biggest radio producer in Japan. By 1931, Matsushita Electric produced over 200 products and continued to grow during the depression. Konosuke expected much of his employees but he showed concern and support for them by treating them well and with respect.

In an employee meeting in 1932, Konosuke presented his vision and mission for Matsushita Electric. He described their mission as creating useful household products that are as plentiful, inexpensive, and high quality as clear tap water. When they achieved this mission, his vision was a world in which poverty had vanished and his employees could enjoy their lives while benefitting future generations. He created ideal principles and asked employees to recite them together aloud each morning before beginning work. They included resolutions to serve the public, treat everyone with fairness, honesty, courtesy and humility, and emphasize teamwork and continuous improvement. At first, most employees saw the mission and ideals as very idealistic. But over time, as they recited them and saw how Konosuke and his managers modeled their behavior to fit these principles, employees began to see them as useful as general guides to their behavior. They also began to see their business as noble and just and to put more energy and dedication into their work.

Matsushita Electric was incorporated in 1935 and Konosuke immediately developed several plans to encourage employees to own stock in their company. He also reorganized the company into major product divisions that allowed him to delegate authority to each division to adapt to their market as needed. They began opening manufacturing plants in other countries. He constantly monitored financial and other reports, asked questions, and offered advice to his division managers. If a manager was reluctant to address a problem, Konosuke often yelled at the manager. If a manager failed to take action that was needed, he usually moved the manager to another position with a minimum of loss in pride and found a new manager. He opened a sales training institute in 1934 and a factory workers' training facility in 1936.

During World War II, Matsushita was required by the Japanese government to produce products to support the war. He complied and focused strictly on production while his marketing organization deteriorated. At the end of the war, he lost 39 foreign plants and 17 Japanese plants that the occupying forces required to be spun off into separate businesses. This was part of the occupational force's plan to restructure the Japanese economy and Matsushita Electric was selected as one of the large conglomerate businesses to be broken up. The major executives were required to leave their jobs and this included Konosuke, until a petition and repeated pleas by Matsushita employees changed the ruling for Konosuke. He was allowed to stay on as president.

He began rebuilding the company, and by 1951 it was profitable again. He then decided he needed to learn from more advanced countries such as the United States and Europe. He visited the United States, spent much time in New York, and returned to Japan with plans for their own research laboratory. This was built in 1953 and began developing new Matsushita technology for televisions, microwaves, mixers, recording equipment, refrigerators, rice cookers, and other household products. Their product sophistication grew and their reputation increased worldwide as they marketed products under several brand names including Panasonic.

In 1956 Konosuke told employees that Japan was behind the United States and Europe in standard of living. He wanted all Japanese homes to have washing machines and other labor saving devices at a reasonable cost. So he set the goal of quadrupling their sales in five years. Employees thought he was crazy, but they adopted techniques such as statistical quality control and product development teams and reached the goal in four years. In 1960 he told them in five years he wanted to reduce their work week to five days (from the traditional six days) and keep wages at the same level. This was to catch up with United States living standards and let workers enjoy their prosperity. Again the managers thought he was crazy, but they worked at developing more efficient work methods and automating plants, to become the most efficient organization in Japan. By 1972, Matsushita employee salaries were approximately equal to those in the United States and exceeded those in Europe.

In 1977, Konosuke was 82 years old and he promoted an independent and creative product manager to be president of Matsushita Electric. The new president adopted his predecessor's technique of challenging managers with high goals that reflected humanitarian values and giving them independence to act on these goals. Konosuke spent more time with the Institute for Peace, Happiness and Prosperity, which he founded in 1946. Its purpose was to prevent Japan from ever repeating the mistakes that led to World War II. He wrote and published books about private business organizations being "public trusts" with broad social responsibilities. He wrote that a humble person was not arrogant or reckless, kept a focus on the mission, always listened to others, and did what was right. He repeatedly emphasized the collective wisdom of people working together toward goals that benefitted society and the importance of leaders who created inspiring missions that motivated people to place all their efforts to achieve the mission. He also created the Matsushita Institute of Government and Management to promote government leaders for the twenty-first century. In April 1979, Konosuke Matsushita died of a lung infection at age 94.

Konosuke Matsushita's leadership style reflects several popular leadership models. His *supportiveness* and *concern* for employee development and prosperity reflect Fiedler's Contingency Theory, the Leadership Grid, Path-Goal Theory, Situational Leadership Theory, and the Multiple Linkage Model. His challenging goal statements and insistence on efficient production also reflect *directive* leader behaviors discussed in these theories. His *inspirational vision, mission statements* and *role modeling* are discussed extensively in Charismatic/Transformational Leadership theories. His negotiation skills and information gathering abroad are part of *boundary spanning* discussed in Reformulated Path-Goal Theory and Multiple Linkage Model. His *reward behavior* with employees in allowing them to own stock in his successful company and in raising their wages also reflects these theories. His continued *hope, self-confidence* and *optimism* coupled with a *supportive organizational climate* exemplify the Authentic Leadership Model. Matsushita's *determination* and *drive, self-confidence, integrity,* and *cognitive insight* reflect Trait Theories of Leadership.

Discussion Questions

1. In what ways do you think Matsushita's leadership style reflected his culture and personal experiences during his childhood and youth?
2. No one who knew Matsushita described him as especially intelligent or a good speaker. So how do you explain his inspirational effects on his employees?
3. Which of his leadership behaviors do you believe was most important in motivating his employees to work so hard and be committed to his goals?
4. Why was Matsushita able to remain effective for so long while society and the world went through many changes?
5. Do you believe his leadership approach would be effective today in highly developed economies?

References

Konosuke Matsushita. (n.d.). In *Wikipedia*. Retrieved April 5, 2010, from http://en.wikipedia.org/wiki/Konosuke_Matsushita

Kotter, J. P. (1997). *Matsushita leadership: Lessons from the 20th century's most remarkable entrepreneur.* New York: The Free Press.

Chapter 18

Bill Wilson

*Cofounder and Leader
of Alcoholics Anonymous*

William (Bill) Griffith Wilson was cofounder with Dr. Robert Smith of Alcoholics Anonymous (AA), the self-help organization of over 100,000 groups around the world. AA is composed of recovering alcoholics who dedicate themselves to staying sober and helping other alcoholics stay sober. Bill Wilson led AA from its inception in the late 1930s until 1955, dedicating his life to staying sober by working with other alcoholics to help them battle their addiction. He worked very hard to remain anonymous and humble by turning down a paid position as an alcoholic therapist when he badly needed money, offers of honorary degrees from distinguished universities, and an invitation to appear on the cover of *Time* magazine. He never saw himself as a role model for other alcoholics. He maintained he was an ordinary man who became an alcoholic and experienced a spiritual epiphany, which led him and Bob Smith to discover a set of steps that has helped many alcoholics stay sober.

Bill Wilson was born in rural Vermont on November 26, 1895. His father left ostensibly on a business trip when Bill was 10 years old and never returned. His mother left shortly thereafter to study osteopathic medicine, leaving Bill and his sister to live with their grandparents. These experiences resulted in Bill's first bouts with depression, which plagued him throughout much of his life. He read incessantly, played the violin, and eventually achieved success in athletics at school. Emerging from his depression, he fell in love with a young woman who was a classmate. Life began to look promising, but she died a short time later during surgery. Bill was 17 and his depression returned. He spent time with his mother outside Boston, did poorly in school, and failed the entrance exam for Massachusetts Institute of Technology. Although he had not graduated from high school, he had enough credits to enroll in nearby Norwich University—a military school.

During the summer he met Lois Burnham whose family was wealthy, from New York, and spent summers in Vermont. The family all liked Bill, and Lois pulled him out of his latest depression. In 1917, all students at Norwich were automatically enlisted in the United States reserve forces. Bill received officer's training and was commissioned a second lieutenant. While in the military, he took his first drink, which relieved him of being self-conscious and anxious when around people of high status. He became talkative and popular with a magnetic personality and he loved the feeling. He and Lois were married in January 1918 before he was shipped to France. He never experienced combat since the war was winding down by then, but he did enjoy drinking French wine with the local people where he was stationed.

When he returned to New York after the war ended, he had a drinking problem. He worked doing investigations for an insurance firm and studied law part-time but his drinking caused him to put off picking up his degree and he never graduated. He began investigating industrial firms for investment groups and became successful as an astute investor and investment advisor. He and Lois were prosperous until the stock market crash of 1929 but he maintained his job as an advisor until his drinking caused him to be fired. His drinking had become progressively worse—he was unreliable, abused people he worked with, and disappeared for two or three days to be found passed out in the street. He and Lois moved in with her parents in Brooklyn, New York.

In 1933 his sister's husband paid for Bill to enter the Towns Hospital for detoxification of alcoholics. Bill was admitted to this hospital three times between 1933 and 1934 and while there he learned of the Oxford Group—a quasi-religious organization dedicated to moral renewal of its members. It included alcoholics and other addicts and had helped an old drinking pal of Bill's reach sobriety. Its program included confession through sharing one's experiences, religious commitment, strict instructions in all aspects of one's life, and the obligation by those who were helped to "pass it on" by helping other addicts. During his last stay in Towns, he prayed for help with his addiction and experienced a spiritual epiphany, which convinced him he was cured. His doctor indicated that recovery was often brought on by an intense religious experience, and he and Lois both agreed that Bill looked different after this experience. He never took another drink.

He returned to their home in Brooklyn and began attending Oxford Group meetings. He slowly realized that talking with other alcoholics helped him stay sober. He visited Towns Hospital and talked with alcoholics about his own and their addiction. The Oxford Group dedicated itself primarily to highly educated elites who became uncomfortable when alcoholic members were unruly. The alcoholics began approaching Bill who they saw as nonjudgmental and patient, had experienced their addiction, was a great listener with empathy, and had an inspirational appeal when speaking. He told them his life story and his belief that a spiritual epiphany and surrender of rationality was needed to defeat alcoholism. They became a group of alcoholics within the Oxford Group, but Bill noticed they only stayed sober for a short time before they relapsed. He spoke with his doctor at Towns hospital and he told Bill to stop preaching and to talk with them about the disease of alcoholism.

In 1935, Bill and Lois needed money so Bill took a group of investors to Akron, Ohio, to attempt to take control of a small machine tool company. After several days, it appeared they had failed and the investors returned to New York, leaving Bill to try to salvage some type of deal. He was discouraged and paced back and forth in the hotel lobby just outside the bar. To avoid drinking, he phoned a local church to try to find an alcoholic to talk with. Eventually he contacted Dr. Robert (Bob) Smith, a physician and member of the local Oxford Group whose struggle with alcoholism was ruining his medical practice. Bill told Bob he needed his support to keep from drinking. The two met that evening and both were changed forever. They shared their life stories, and Bob was inspired by Bill's ideas about how to become sober. He had read everything available on alcoholism, and they discussed what they had learned far into the night. Bill and Lois moved in with Bob and his wife while they worked on a plan for their lives without alcohol. Bob relapsed one time on a business trip but Bill and Bob's wife took him home and dried him out in time for a scheduled surgery two days later. Bob never drank again. They developed an approach on how to counsel alcoholics and Bill and Lois returned to Brooklyn.

After meeting Bob, Bill became more confident in his speaking ability and was able to describe alcoholism and its effects with a disturbing vividness that touched every listener. He realized that no alcoholic wanted to hear s/he could not drink again, so he advocated "one day at a time." He still believed some type of spiritual epiphany was needed to defeat alcoholism, but he told alcoholics they should define God anyway they wanted—as a symbol, a group with Good Orderly Direction, or a Group Of Drunks. They needed to surrender their personal will and place their trust in their own conception of God. Lois's mother died and her father remarried, moved out and gave the house to them. Bill held regular meetings around the fireplace for his group of alcoholics, which varied in attendance. He began these meeting by saying "My name is Bill and I am an alcoholic" and this became the norm for each member. Their big house became a flophouse. Few could pay rent and eventually most of their personal belongings disappeared. At this point, he was offered a job at Towns Hospital as an alcoholic therapist, and the hospital owner offered to provide facilities and support for his work with the group of alcoholics. He was excited but when he described the offer to his group they said "No." They believed if he took money for what he was doing, it would cheapen his efforts and alcoholics would assume he was there for the money and lose faith in him. He took their advice and turned down the job. This consultation with the group became known as the "group conscience" and he used it as part of his regular practice. The will of the group had the final say in his decision making. Bill and his group were not comfortable with the Oxford Group's evangelism, strict rules, and focus on elite and highly educated membership, so in 1937 they split with Oxford. It eventually died out partly due to its founder's support of Adolf Hitler.

Bill and Bob met again to work on their approach with alcoholics. They became convinced they had the best method yet devised to overcome this addiction. They combined the members' conception of trust in God and group conscience with complete anonymity of all members. They knew that no member wanted to reveal his entire name due to the stigma of being labeled an alcoholic and the risk of losing one's job. Humility was emphasized so no single member was featured above the group. Even Bill tried throughout his life to maintain this anonymity and his actions spoke of his humility. He made plans with Bob for fundraising, missionaries, education centers, leaflets, books and eventually hospitals that used their methods. But his group nixed all but the fund raising and approved of Bill writing a book about their approach for those who could not attend meetings. He worked on the book for two years, obtaining major input from several groups and other individuals and *Alcoholics Anonymous* was published in 1939 by a small publishing company they started with the loan from a friendly doctor. It included the now famous 12 steps for alcoholics to overcome their addiction and the only requirement for membership was the desire to stop drinking.

Through his brother-in-law, he made contact with the John D. Rockefeller organization. Rockefeller was a major philanthropist but he rejected their request for a grant for $50,000 and gave them an account for $5,000 with $30 per week salary for Bill and Bob each. He also authorized his advisors to help Bill set up an alcoholic foundation with a board of directors composed of alcoholics and non-alcoholics. Later Rockefeller's son gave a dinner for AA that resulted in several donations, although they still needed money. The same year the book was published, Bill and Lois lost their home to foreclosure. This began two years of living with various friends. Eventually they rented a converted stable for AA in New York and lived in two small upstairs rooms. Bill started feeling depressed again and was visited by a Jesuit priest who told him that saintly men like Bill were not happy and never would be. For some reason, this cheered Bill up. Not long after this, a recovering alcoholic in one of their groups sold them a home a short distance north of New York City. It included woodlands that reminded Bill of Vermont and they paid nothing down and $40 per month. They lived in this home for the rest of their lives.

In 1941 the editor of the *Saturday Evening Post* (which had over 3 million subscribers) commissioned a tough reporter to do an article on AA. Sensing a scam, the reporter visited the AA office and interviewed Bill about the program. Bill told the reporter his personal story and how AA started, then invited him to visit several AA groups in different cities. They did so and the reporter wrote a glowing article praising AA as the best method yet to overcome alcoholism. He pointed out it was not perfect but it was working for many alcoholics. Another complimentary article appeared in *Reader's Digest* a short time later. At their insistence, Bill and Bob's names were disguised in the articles. Within a few weeks, thousands of letters of interest poured into the AA office. Bill had previously answered all letters but this time he had to ask for volunteer help. The book began to sell and AA membership grew in 1941 from 1,500 to 8,000; in 1942 it reached 10,000 with almost 400 groups; in 1946 it had 30,000 members. Royalties on the book eventually eased Bill and Lois's financial problems.

When Pearl Harbor was attacked by the Japanese, Bill tried to enlist in the army, but his alcoholic past prevented him from being accepted. Sticking to AA's anonymity and humility guidelines, he had neglected to describe his key role as cofounder and leader of the increasingly successful AA organization. Disappointed, he and Lois began visiting AA groups across the country. He was famous at these groups and was always asked to speak. His stories ignited passion in the members and he continued these visits throughout his life. He gathered ideas from these groups about how they operated regarding money, leadership, anonymity, service and other issues. This later resulted in the 12 traditions he developed for groups to help them manage themselves. He used the word "traditions" to avoid the strictness implied by rules. He believed each alcoholic had his/her own story and path to recovery and he extended this idea of self-control to how the groups governed themselves.

Between 1944 and 1955 Bill experienced another major depression that sometimes made him incapable of work. Yet during this time he and his staff initiated a regular AA newsletter in which he often wrote articles about alcoholism, he developed and published the 12 traditions, and he developed an organizational plan for AA. The plan included a General Services Office with rotating trustees, a Board of Directors composed primarily of AA members, and a regular AA conference in which all groups were represented. All of these changes were developed with heavy input from AA members and groups. In 1951, Lois founded Al-Anon, a self-help group for relatives and friends of alcoholics. Bill continued his travel visiting and connecting with groups throughout the United States and Europe where AA was expanding. At the conference in 1955, he turned over the leadership of AA to the new Board of Directors and his depression disappeared.

Bill was always a caring individual and, when he had money, he sent checks to both of his parents and friends who needed help. When visiting AA groups, he described his vision of AA as a living whole that must survive to ensure the survival of each of its members. He believed God expressed his will through the "group conscience" and majority rule, which governed group decision making. He emphasized that all members who were helped by AA should try to help other alcoholics, that the core of AA was one drunk talking with another drunk about their addiction. In 1954 he was offered an honorary law degree by Yale University. He was excited and thought it would help promote the AA program. When he presented it to his foundation board, all were supportive except one member. That member was Archibald Roosevelt, son of Theodore Roosevelt. He stated that his father avoided all such honors (except the Nobel Peace Prize) because he feared they would feed his great attraction to power. Bill decided it would violate the principles of anonymity and humility, and asked if the degree could be given to the AA organization. Yale said "no" and he declined the degree. He also declined an offer to appear on the cover of *Time* magazine, even with only his back showing.

Bill knew he was weak in many ways. He was a chain smoker and eventually died in 1971 from emphysema and pneumonia. As he traveled visiting AA groups, he ignited passions in members and other admirers and apparently engaged in several extra marital affairs. His life was a constant struggle with depression, alcoholism, infidelity, smoking, and the desire for privacy after 1955. A friend once described Bill as being really good at struggling but not very good at being happy. His descriptions of his lifelong struggles probably made his communication with other alcoholics more genuine. He constantly tried to discourage the impression that he was a great leader or role model and insisted he had received much help in his battle against alcoholism. His struggles and striving for humility actually made him the role model other alcoholics needed to inspire them to stop drinking. In 2012, AA worldwide membership is over 2 million people.

First and foremost, Bill Wilson was a Servant Leader—providing for AA members' needs, *listening* with empathy, being *open* and *honest, humble,* and possessing *self-knowledge* with a clear *connection* to a higher power. His leadership was also *charismatic/transformational* and *participative.* His *inspirational speeches* to alcoholics, his *role model* as a struggling alcoholic and the *vision* he described for AA are all charismatic behaviors. He also transformed the lives of thousands of alcoholics through the program and organization he cofounded and led. These leader behaviors and impacts are described in Charismatic/Transformational Leadership theories. Not all charismatic/transformational leaders are participative, but Bill's participative leadership is shown in his emphasis on the "group conscience" of the AA groups he led. He regularly submitted his decisions to his groups for feedback and approval, and only went forward with decisions that they approved. Participative leadership is described in the Normative Decision Theory, Path-Goal Theory and the Multiple Linkage Model. Bill worked hard at *external boundary spanning* leadership by contacting various organizations where he could locate alcoholics to talk with, meeting with reporters to help build the image of AA, negotiating with possible financial donors to the AA program, and personally answering thousands of inquiries about the AA program. Late in his life, he also engaged in extensive *internal boundary spanning* as he visited AA groups throughout the United States and Europe to strengthen the AA organization and learn from its members. Many of these boundary spanning behaviors are described in the Multiple Linkage Model and Reformulated Path-Goal Theory of leadership. Bill was clearly a *considerate* and *supportive* leader as he went out of his way to try to help those suffering from alcoholism. These supportive leadership behaviors are described in the Servant Leadership model as well as Situational Leadership Theory, Path-Goal Theory and the Multiple Linkage Model of leadership. His *determination* and *integrity* to AA reflect Trait Theories of leadership.

Discussion Questions

1. Why was Bill Wilson able to connect so effectively with alcoholics who wanted to stop drinking?
2. Do you think that Bill's efforts to remain anonymous as leader of AA were effective? Or would it have been better to accept awards for his work and create publicity for their program?
3. Why was Bill's idea of the "group conscience" important for the AA program?

4. Do you think that Bill's "flaws" were important to his success as leader of AA? Why or why not?
5. Would Bill have been effective leading a high technology business organization or a professional sports team? Why or why not?

References

Cheever, S. (2004). *My name is Bill: Bill Wilson—His life and the creation of Alcoholics Anonymous*. New York: Simon and Schuster.
Raphael, M. J. (2000). *Bill W. and Mr. Wilson*. Amherst: University of Massachusetts Press.

Chapter 19

Mark Zuckerberg
Facebook Creator and CEO

Mark Zuckerberg was a Harvard sophomore who at 19 years old, created the premier social networking Internet service that is currently used by over one tenth of the world's population. He started Facebook in 2004 from his dorm suite with some help from his friends. Facebook began exclusively as a Harvard-based service, expanded to other colleges, to organizations, and eventually worldwide to everyone not less than 13 years of age. Facebook records more hours than users spend on email. A 2009 survey showed Facebook as one of the 10 most trusted companies in the United States, ahead of Apple, Google, and Microsoft. A recent investment in Facebook by Goldman and Sachs implies a market value of $50 billion for the company. Although this is likely inflated, Zuckerberg has rejected offers of $15 billion in the past. As CEO, Zuckerberg remains in control of Facebook, which continues to expand and reflect his own beliefs and philosophy about availability of information, transparency, and connectedness in the world.

Zuckerberg was born in 1984 in a small village in New York state within an hour of New York City. His mother is a psychiatrist and his father a dentist, he has three sisters, and his family has been supportive of him in spite of his "strong willed and relentless" nature. His father taught him BASIC computer programming at an early age and hired a special tutor to continue his programming development. Mark became a precocious computer programmer and developed an early computer network for their home when he was 12. He attended an elite private high school where he was a fencing star and was able to read and write several languages by the time he entered Harvard. He is medium height with curly hair and typically wears jeans, t-shirts, and flip flops. He looks directly at those he is speaking with, speaks quickly, and shows little body language while listening, making it difficult to read his reactions.

Harvard is filled with elite students who are ambitious, self-confident, and from well to do families. Unlike his portrayal in the recent film, *The Social Network*, Mark is very social with a quick smile, and was well liked by his three suite mates. Facebook biographer, David Kirkpatrick, indicates they became involved in each other's projects—especially Zuckerberg's. He liked to build computer projects and usually had several going at one time. He created Coursematch, which helped students select classes with people they liked or admired. Then he started Facemash, which sequentially compared Harvard students' faces, two at a time, and asked students to vote which was the hottest. These programs were made available on the web to all Harvard students and were very popular, although he was disciplined by the Harvard administration for violating privacy restrictions. Zuckerberg does not ask permission to do things and was not deterred. It became clear to those who knew him that his programs were attractive to students. Three other Harvard students asked him to help them develop a site that would profile Harvard students to be used as a dating service. Mark agreed but did little on their project while he worked on developing Facebook. Years later these students sued him, claiming he stole their idea and a financial settlement was reached.

Zuckerberg launched Facebook on February 4, 2004, as a communication tool to help individuals keep track of their friends at Harvard and what they were doing. Users were invited to build their own profiles of personal information including whatever information they wished. They were required to use their real identities (verified by their Harvard email addresses) and could invite any other users to be their friends and access their profile. Profiles included a picture of the user, could be updated at any time, and Facebook allowed users to send messages to one another. It was used for meeting people, arranging study groups and meetings, sharing preferences in movies, music and books and included a Coursematch connection for checking who enrolled in which classes. In one month 75% of Harvard students signed up and by May there were almost 100,000 users, including faculty and staff. Facebook appealed to the strong social needs of college students to be accepted, and a user's number of friends soon became a status symbol indicating one's popularity. It also appealed to one's vanity by letting others know about all the user's activities and accomplishments. The interest in Facebook also likely reflected an element of voyeurism.

As Facebook grew, Zuckerberg's roommates were inspired by his enthusiasm and success and he hired Dustin Moskovitz to help expand the number of users and Chris Hughes to act as spokesperson. He also gave his business savvy friend, Eduardo Saverin, part ownership of Facebook to match Zuckerberg's own investment of $1,000 and to develop Facebook as a business. Zuckerberg added more features to Facebook and slowly opened it up to other colleges as they added server capacity to assure users did not experience delays. Earlier social networking services had suffered major delays that aggravated users and caused them to decrease their usage. Saverin began selling ads to start generating revenue, registered Facebook as a limited liability company in Florida, and investors began calling. One set of investors offered Zuckerberg $10 million for Facebook, but he was not interested. He was more interested in his evolving vision for Facebook to make the world a more open and transparent place. He believes strongly that the level of trust in the world has declined, there is a trend toward decentralized power, and the amount of information has compounded so fast that people need help in dealing with these changes. He describes openness as having access to more information, and transparency as sharing things, increasing understanding, and having a voice in the world. He also describes Facebook as increasing connectedness by helping people stay in touch and empathize with one another. By promoting these processes, he believes he is making the world a better place.

During the summer of 2004, Mark rented a house in Palo Alto, near Stanford University. He and some of his roommates and friends moved there to develop Facebook and be part of the Internet industry of Silicon Valley. He encountered Sean Parker, a 24-year-old programmer and entrepreneur, who had helped start Napster (the popular music sharing program) and another Internet company. Parker described how his startups had been taken over by venture capitalists who eventually ejected him from the companies. Mark had met Parker in New York earlier and was impressed so he invited him to live in their house. Parker was very interested in Facebook, and soon Zuckerberg was describing him as president of the company. Saverin had stayed in New York, ostensibly to sell ads, and showed no interest in moving to California. Everyone at the rented house began work at mid-day and worked into the morning hours, increasing features and adding more colleges to their service. They wore t-shirts with jeans, pajama bottoms or basketball shorts, and flip flops. They partied on the weekends, and the house resembled a typical college party pad. All were very intelligent and committed to Mark's vision of Facebook as being the catalyst that would help change the world. Mark was always in charge. His excitement and vision were contagious and he kept pushing them all to add "cool" features to the service. He frequently directed them to stay with him at their computers on the dining room table to finish a feature they were working on regardless of the time or whether they had not eaten for hours. He used the term "lockdown" to describe this practice, and it became part of the Facebook terminology.

Parker eventually took over Saverin's role as business manager and incorporated the company in Delaware, which has favorable tax laws. Saverin was moved out of an active role in the company although he kept an ownership interest. Costs continued to climb as they added more server capacity to handle the rapid increase in users. Local networking sites were developing at colleges they were not serving so they used a "surround" strategy to outmaneuver these local sites. They opened Facebook to potential users at a target campus as well as all colleges in the vicinity, allowing students to communicate with their friends at nearby campuses. This strategy worked well to capture users and demonstrated Zuckerberg's competitive nature and his desire for Facebook to become the industry standard for social networking. Zuckerberg and his family invested $85,000 in Facebook during that summer, but the operation continued to need more money. Venture capital companies were ready to invest, but Parker had made Mark wary of venture capitalists. He located an individual Internet investor, Peter Theil, who had started PayPal, and invested $500,000 for about 10% of the company. Theil became a member of the Board of Directors, along with Parker and Zuckerberg, with two empty seats controlled by Mark who was CEO and in complete control.

Zuckerberg was building an organization and he was growing into his new job. Despite his firm directiveness when working on a Facebook project, his employees were his best friends and he socialized with them when not working. Eventually he came to support them by providing three meals per day, snacks, dry cleaning and a housing subsidy if they lived near the work site. At the end of summer, Zuckerberg and Moskovitz did not return to Harvard. The two were very close and Dustin had an incredible work ethic, maintaining the system while adding colleges, servers and an exploding number of users. By November 2004, they had 1 million users and Facebook was 10 months old. Large media companies started trying to buy Facebook for around $75 million. Mark met with their CEOs to learn, but he was not interested in selling. He and most of his employees believed they were making history and did not want to stop. Eventually, he did negotiate a very sweet deal with a venture capitalist Parker trusted for $13 million in exchange for 15% of Facebook. Mark was 20 years old, he maintained complete control of the company, which was then valued at $98 million, and he was building the organization.

Parker was very intelligent and an expert programmer, but he was a playboy and became erratic in his personal behavior. He had been valuable in helping Mark raise money while maintaining control of the business with new investors being added to the board. A problem occurred with a drug charge, and he became absent from work for long periods. Zuckerberg was pressured to get rid of Parker and he eventually did so although Parker maintained his ownership interest and signed his Board seat over to Zuckerberg. The staff was growing and they were adding more new features such as a photo option that allowed users to create albums on their Facebook site, comment on their own and other's photos, and identify individuals in the photos. Zuckerberg made it easy to page through a user's album, encouraging what they called the "Facebook Trance" that kept people clicking through pages on their service. The photo application became the most popular feature on Facebook and the most popular photo site on the Internet. By fall 2005, 85% of all American college students were on Facebook, their ad revenue was about $1 million per month, and they were spending $1.5 million per month.

Mark eventually held an offsite meeting with all their staff and described his long term vision. He explained his goal was to continue pushing change that reflected his beliefs in openness and transparency, to make Facebook a major force on the Internet, and not have it taken over by outsiders. He described his belief that by pushing society toward more openness, people would be made more responsible and empathetic. The staff was encouraged since they knew he had been meeting with CEOs who wanted to buy Facebook and were further inspired to be on the cutting edge of societal change. He continued to keep careful control over the type of ads on Facebook, directing that they must be helpful to users. His ad requirements limited their ad revenue and reflected his primary interest in growing and improving the service rather than making money.

Several of the features Zuckerberg added have aroused protests among users. One was Newsfeed, which periodically sent highlights of what was happening in users' lives to their Facebook friends. After widespread objections, Zuckerberg modified the feature to allow users more control over what was broadcast on Newsfeed. He had urged users to email him about Newsfeed and used this input to make it more acceptable. He did the same with a feature named Beacon that broadcast buying habits of users to their friends via Newsfeed. Huge objections and email caused Zuckerberg to increase user controls over this feature. His response to feedback included apologizing on his blog and inspired faith in Facebook by its users, but these features show Zuckerberg's bias toward sharing information. Although he maintains he is concerned about privacy, many new features urge users to reveal more about themselves. Facebook can be seductive and some users have trouble stopping themselves from compulsively revealing personal information. Once the information is on a user's profile, Facebook has it and it is available to all the user's friends. With little privacy there is little intimacy, and interpersonal relationships can be replaced by Facebook relationships which are usually at a low emotional level. Zuckerberg has been described as "blinkered" regarding his attitude toward privacy.

In 2006 he opened the service up to organizations and non-student adults. The response by organizations was slow but other adult users grew quickly. Zuckerberg then pushed his staff to make Facebook an Internet platform, a service where others could design and deploy their own software and deliver it to users through Facebook. Developers were not charged for using Facebook, and he allowed them to keep all the revenue they generated from their software. He saw this as another way to grow the number of Facebook users. He scheduled a launch event in May 2007 for the platform in San Francisco and invited the media. The crowd was amazed and the coverage was immediate. Zuckerberg and his programmers worked for the next 8 hours with application developers to help make their software work with Facebook and then retired to their hotel to turn on the platform. The next day they were overwhelmed with new applications and within six months there were 25,000 new pieces of software running on Facebook. Most were games at first and eventually they had to modify the acceptance criteria to avoid duplications and malfeasance. They opened up Facebook for international users in late 2007 and within a year Facebook had grown to 70 million users.

Providing service around the world was expensive and they needed to get serious about raising more money and increasing revenues. After a long negotiation, Microsoft who was a major advertiser on Facebook, invested $240 million for a 1.6% interest in the company (implying a valuation of $15 billion). In December 2007, Zuckerberg met Sheryl Sandberg, an extremely successful ad executive with Google, at a Christmas party. They began a conversation that lasted two months and he eventually hired her as chief operating officer for Facebook in March 2008. He then left for a one month trip around the world alone with only a back pack, apparently to give Sandberg a chance to establish herself at Facebook. She held a series of meetings with the executive staff (Facebook now had about 500 employees) and they explored ways to generate revenues consistent with Mark's vision of continued growth and improvement in their users' experience. When Mark returned, they had arrived on an approach that emphasized different types of advertising. They do not allow advertisers to see information about individual users, only aggregate data. But they provide a large menu of parameters for advertisers to select a very specific audience. They can thus target ads to people in specific age groups, who live in certain states and listen to music by specific entertainers. This made Facebook the most carefully targeted advertising medium in history.

Most of the key executives left Facebook over the next year. Several started their own Internet companies that work with Facebook, including Dustin Moskovitz, and they remain close to Zuckerberg. He moved the Facebook operation to a vacated manufacturing plant in 2009. Zuckerberg chose it because of its basic funky appearance, shunning locations that were more elaborate. He wants to keep employees from becoming complacent. Facebook allows groups of users to form around issues and garner support. One such group formed in Columbia against FARC, the revolutionary army that kidnaps citizens for ransom. Group members organized a huge demonstration that weakened FARC and apparently led to the release of some of their prisoners. Some executives find that they receive more honest feedback from employees through Facebook than when they talk face-to-face. Zuckerberg is excited about these uses of Facebook. Kirkpatrick describes him as fearless, competitive and very self-confident. His stockholding allows him to stay in control of his organization even after a possible public offering of their stock. He retains absolute authority in decision making (although he does listen to his board members) and apparently hopes to influence the evolving communication infrastructure of the world. Although they do not publicly reveal any information about individual users, their data set is larger and richer than the United States government and the Federal Bureau of Investigation has already shown an interest. Writers have pointed out that Mark will not control Facebook forever, and at some point it has potential to become a huge surveillance system. For now, his vision is to empower people to communicate more efficiently, to help them handle the information that is all around them, and to help prevent institutions from overwhelming people. His coworkers say he just wants to do the right thing.

Mark Zuckerberg may be best described as a Charismatic/Transformational leader due to his *vision* for Facebook, his ability to *inspire* employees and the media, and his *dedication* to use Facebook as an instrument of *change* in the world. He is also highly *directive* of his staff when he decides what features he wants to add to Facebook, and he is *supportive* of them by helping with their needs for housing and food (although these last items might also be viewed as a disguised means of control—keeping them at work for longer hours). These leader behavior patterns are described in Fiedler's Contingency Theory, Situational Leadership Theory, Path-Goal Theory, and the Leadership Grid. Mark has shown skill at *boundary spanning* leadership in effective *negotiations* with key investors and executives who seek to purchase Facebook. This leader behavior is described in the Multiple Linkage Model and Reformulated Path-Goal Theory. His behavior as CEO can also be described as Authentic Leadership by reflecting his extreme *self-confidence, optimism, resilience,* and his *moral belief* that Facebook is making the world a better place. Zuckerberg also likely fits the popular Implicit Leadership Theory of an Internet entrepreneur/CEO by being highly intelligent, intensely focused, and geekish in his demeanor. His *intelligence, self-confidence,* and *determination* also reflect Trait Theories of leadership.

Discussion Questions

1. What aspects of Mark Zuckerberg's leadership do you think were most important in building Facebook into a major Internet company?
2. Do you agree with Zuckerberg's practice of directing his employees to stay at work well into the morning hours ("lockdown") until they finished the Facebook feature they were working on?
3. Do you agree with Zuckerberg's vision that the world is becoming a more open and transparent place?
4. Do you think Mark would be an effective leader in a manufacturing or retail organization? Why or why not?

References

Grossman, L. (2010). 2010 person of the year: Mark Zuckerberg. *Time* magazine, January 3, 42–75.

Kirkpatrick, D. (2011). *The Facebook effect.* New York: Simon and Schuster.

Mark Zuckerberg. (n.d.). In *Wikipedia.* Retrieved November 12, 2010, from http://en.wikipedia.org/wiki/Mark_Zuckerberg

Chapter 20

Martin Luther King, Jr.
American Civil Rights Leader

Martin Luther King, Jr. was a Baptist minister who became the preeminent leader of the American Civil Rights movement in the 1950s and 1960s. Using the nonviolent methods of Mohandas Gandhi, he led boycotts, demonstrations, and marches that publicized in dramatic terms the practices and effects of racism and segregation in the United States. His efforts led to important legislation that changed the lives of millions of Blacks and minorities in the United States. Later in his career he expanded his activities to focus on obtaining social and economic justice for all poor and disadvantaged people. He also actively opposed the United States involvement in the Vietnam war. He received numerous awards for his activities and in 1964 he became the youngest recipient of the Nobel Peace Prize for his work to achieve the end of racial segregation and discrimination through nonviolent means.

King was born on January 15, 1929, in Atlanta, Georgia, to a comfortable middle-class family. His father was an autocratic Baptist minister who named his first son Michael, then later changed it to Martin Luther in honor of the German priest who began the Protestant Reformation. Martin was bright and precocious and became his father's favorite of three children. He learned to speak publically from the Baptist preachers who enthralled their congregations with their grand rhetoric and young Martin began to develop his own speaking skills. At about 5 years old, he learned about discrimination when he was slapped and called a "little nigger" in a department store by a White customer who claimed he stepped on her foot. He saw his father rebel vociferously at these affronts, and Martin quit his first job when his supervisor kept calling him "nigger." Biographers assert that these early experiences and his thoughtful moody nature combined to create the quiet, formal, and serious reserve he maintained in public throughout his life.

He skipped two grades in high school and entered Morehouse College, where he studied sociology, was an average student and a lady's man. He became fascinated by Thoreau's essay in Civil Disobedience that Gandhi had studied in his nonviolent revolt against British occupation of India. In his last year of college he decided to enter the ministry as a means of serving humanity. He studied philosophy, scripture, and the life of Gandhi at Crozer Theological Seminary, continued to practice his rhetorical skills, and was elected student body president and valedictorian for his graduating class. From there, he enrolled in Boston University, where he began developing socialist views with a Christian perspective, met and married Coretta Scott, and was granted a doctoral degree in theology. It was later found that he plagiarized parts of his dissertation. It was common practice for Baptist ministers to use past sermons and written material by others for their own sermons, and King often did this in his speaking and writing. In August 1954 he accepted a position as minister of a small church in a relatively prosperous area of Montgomery, Alabama. There, he rose at 6:00 a.m. and spent hours preparing and memorizing his sermons and practicing them before a mirror. His learned sermons and reserved nature were well suited for his congregation.

In the late afternoon of December 1, 1955 a tired 42-year-old seamstress named Rosa Parks boarded a bus in downtown Montgomery as she headed home after work. She sat toward the back in the section reserved for Blacks, but as the bus filled she was told by the driver to give up her seat for a White man. Other Blacks had complied, but Rosa repeatedly refused and was arrested. In the previous year the United States Supreme Court had held in *Brown versus Board of Education* that racial segregation in public schools was unconstitutional. Civil rights activists had been waiting for a situation to test this court decision in another context and they declared a boycott of the Montgomery bus system, which was the major means of transportation for Black citizens. They invited King to help support the boycott and asked him to address a large rally as their leader and spokesman. At first he was hesitant and unsure of his qualifications, but they saw him as new to their city, sympathetic, and highly skilled at public speaking. He spoke that evening in a large Black church that was packed with people and crowds were gathered outside where speakers were set up. His metaphorical rhetoric focused on the struggles of long oppressed people throughout history and inspired the human spirit in his listeners. He was startled by the mass cheering and shouting that interrupted him during the speech. He had struck the right chord for his audience.

The boycott lasted an entire year with car pool operations organized by the boycotters replacing the busses. Local officials suspected communists were behind the boycott and supporters were harassed and often arrested, including King. His vision for the boycott was a moral theater of direct confrontation that must appeal to America's conscience and the powers in Washington through the press. He emphasized nonviolence by boycotters to defeat physical force with moral or "soul" force and appealed to democratic principles contained in the Constitution. This 26-year-old Black minister, who spoke of loving the White oppressors to help redeem them from their evil ways, caught the fascination of the press. Thus began King's lifelong close relationship with the news media as television was just coming of age. During the boycott, he was constantly threatened with murder but turned to his faith through prayer for sustenance. His home was bombed and his front door shot gunned but no family members were hurt. A state court finally declared bus segregation unconstitutional and was supported by the Supreme Court, ending the boycott with a victory.

Publicity during the boycott made King the symbolic leader for the new civil rights movement in the South. He was written about in the *New York Times*, invited on television's *Meet the Press* show, and eventually featured on the cover of *Time* magazine. He directed the establishment of the Southern Christian Leadership Conference (SCLC) to facilitate a voter registration campaign for Blacks in the South to encourage them to vote and obtain representation in government. Bogus literacy tests and other forms of discrimination had long been used in the South to prevent Blacks from voting. He began traveling throughout the country giving speeches to huge crowds and attending fundraisers to finance the SCLC. He often gave three or four speeches per day, and worked with Stanley Levison (a New York attorney who became his ghost writer) on his first book about the Montgomery boycott. He traveled at least 25 days per month to appeal for support for their civil rights movement. During these trips, he was constantly expected to inspire the crowds who flocked to see and hear him speak, his life was frequently threatened, and he was stabbed in the chest by a deranged Black woman in New York.

King had attracted a group of capable lieutenants who had large egos, argued almost constantly and saw themselves as prophets. King often solicited their advice on his decisions, remaining calm and logical as he patiently listened and considered their views. Decisions were often made together with these individuals after long verbal battles. This participative approach exposed King to opinions that were different from his own, provided new information and ideas, and prevented him from becoming too inflexible in his approach. College students were increasingly involved in demonstrations against segregation, forming their own organization called the Student Nonviolent Coordinating Committee (SNCC). King encouraged their activities and was arrested with them at a demonstration in Georgia. He had forgotten he was on probation for a minor traffic violation and was shackled in the middle of the night, removed from jail, and taken to the violent Reidsville Penitentiary for four months of hard labor. His long time fear of lynching resurfaced and he despaired of leaving prison alive.

King was always careful when dealing with the federal government and avoided alignment with specific political parties. The United States Supreme Court had settled the Montgomery bus boycott so he endeavored not to offend federal officials. By not aligning with a specific party, he sought to keep his movement moral and spiritual rather than political. He was friendly with John and Robert Kennedy, who were impressed with King. When he was delivered to Reidsville Penitentiary, his wife Coretta phoned Attorney General Robert Kennedy who phoned the judge who had ordered King jailed and he was released.

J. Edgar Hoover headed the Federal Bureau of Investigation and began investigating King. Hoover suspected him of being controlled by communists due to his friendship with Stanley Levison, who did have communist connections. Hoover had ordered surveillance on numerous influential individuals, including congressional members and presidents. The Kennedy brothers knew Hoover had accumulated a file on President Kennedy's extramarital affairs and could use it to embarrass him, so they agreed to allow Hoover to bug King's phones and the motel rooms where he stayed. Hoover acquired hours of recordings of King's extramarital affairs and planned to use them to discredit King. However, when he presented the evidence to the Kennedy's, they took no action.

In 1963, Birmingham, Alabama, was a nucleus for racial segregation with cross burnings, abductions and mutilations of Blacks, and bombings of Black churches. King directed a full scale boycott of the Birmingham downtown merchants. He had had little success in converting local government officials so, based on input from his closest advisors, he reasoned he could pressure the powerful commercial interests into influencing the city government to end segregation and violent practices against Blacks. As usual, his goal was to create a dramatic confrontation to bring the national press and demonstrate on television the cruel racial practices of segregation in the South. He often stated that legislators can declare rights, but people must act to make those rights real. King violated a state court injunction against demonstrating and was jailed. He was careful not to violate any federal injunctions in order to allow federal officials to assist his movement whenever possible.

During his stay in jail, he composed what became known as his "Letter from Birmingham Jail." It was a response to several White ministers who publicly criticized the demonstration. King described how Blacks had experienced dehumanization in the United States for three centuries. He detailed the danger, fear and frustration of being Black in America and the ensuing sense of being "nobody." He thus explained why Blacks found it difficult to patiently wait for justice and equal rights in schools, employment and nearly all aspects of life. His letter was smuggled out of the jail in sections over several days and was eventually published nationwide. It became known as the best statement of the condition of Black America and the urgent need for change.

When he was released on bail, the boycott was weakening and they recruited Black high school students to march in support. This caused the local sheriff to turn fire hoses and a water cannon on the children which tore off their clothes, and snarling police dogs were used to terrify them. All this was caught on national television and broadcast to the entire country. Robert Kennedy responded to the violence and pressured the local government to negotiate with the Black leaders. An agreement was reached to desegregate department stores, lunch counters and all public facilities and to provide equal opportunities for all job applicants, regardless of race. King's strategy of staying on the good side of the federal government and addressing his boycott and demonstrations against commercial interests had worked. Hundreds of similar demonstrations began all over the country and President Kennedy proposed federal legislation guaranteeing access to all public facilities for all persons throughout the country.

In August 1963, shortly after the Birmingham boycott, King and his lieutenants organized a march on Washington, D.C. to generate support for Kennedy's public access legislation and demonstrate the size and vigor of the civil rights movement. The march resulted in a huge rally in front of the Lincoln Monument and concluded with King's "I Have a Dream" speech. Using his mastery of dramatic delivery and metaphorical language, he spoke of his vision of freedom and brotherhood among all races and religions. The crowd of over 250,000 was hushed during the speech and erupted in deafening applause when he concluded. President Kennedy congratulated King soon after, and the speech became known as one of the greatest public addresses in United States history. The public access legislation was eventually passed into law, but only after Kennedy was assassinated in November 1963.

Later that summer, a key civil rights leader was assassinated in Mississippi and a Black church was bombed in Birmingham, killing three young Black girls. Many in the civil rights movement sought violent reprisals. Malcolm X was a tall, charismatic leader in this movement who was highly skilled at rhetoric and described Whites as dogs or devils and integration with Whites as a weakness. He caused many in the movement to begin to question their nonviolent approach and this worried King. In 1964 a demonstration in St. Augustine, Florida, resulted in terrible violence against the demonstrators by local toughs with no efforts at protection by the local law enforcement. King managed to get the protestors into a church after the violence and, while King was contacting Washington authorities for assistance, his devoted lieutenant Ralph Abernathy reiterated King's spiritual nonviolent mission and vision to calm those who advocated violent reprisals. Later that year, while in the hospital with exhaustion and a fever, King was notified he had received the Nobel Peace Prize for his nonviolent actions to end segregation.

In late 1964 King joined with the SNCC in Selma, Alabama, in a voting rights campaign. The goal was to stop discriminatory voting practices that prevented most Blacks in the United States from voting. Their demonstration was met by the local sheriff with night sticks and electric cattle prods, which they used to herd the demonstrators out of town. King was jailed and a youth was shot to death trying to protect his mother. A subsequent march on the state capital was met with more terrible violence from state and local law enforcement and was observed by the media who showed the film on Sunday night television. It became known as "Bloody Sunday." President Johnson saw the film and denounced the violence in a subsequent press conference, promising to submit a bill to Congress to assure equal voting rights for all citizens. This legislation was eventually passed by Congress after another march on the capital of Alabama that began with 3,000 people and ended with over 25,000 marchers. The Public Accommodations Act and the Voting Rights Act eventually changed life for Blacks in the South and elsewhere in the United States. Within the next few years, restaurants, schools, stores, sports events, and theaters were integrated. Black voter registration increased exponentially and Black sheriffs, mayors, and congressional representatives became increasingly common.

King wanted to broaden his movement to achieve economic and social justice for all poor people. He was amazed to learn that most of the nation's poor were White. In 1967 he directed his followers to Chicago in a Poor People's Campaign to eliminate the slums where the poor were living amid squalor and violence. His efforts were disappointing when he confronted Mayor Richard Daly who ran a corrupt and powerful political machine in Chicago. Daly was clever and tough and agreed to everything they requested thus avoiding major confrontations. Later the agreed changes were lost in the morass of bureaucracy that was charged with implementation.

Major race riots erupted in Newark, Cleveland, and Detroit in 1966 and 1967, and violent elements of the civil rights movement were gaining power. King strove to straddle the line between violent tendencies of some groups (such as the

Black Panthers) and his own nonviolent mission. After seeing a photograph of a Vietnamese woman holding a baby that had been burned with napalm, he began a crusade to stop the Vietnam war. He declared the war was being waged for the wealthy on the backs of the poor. This assertion broke his connections with President Johnson. He announced that capitalism was not working and advocated a social democratic type of government (similar to Sweden) with assured jobs and a guaranteed annual income for everyone. He wanted to convince the voting public to pressure Congress for these changes. Many followers saw this as radical and dangerous, and he argued with them until he began suffering migraine headaches.

In March 1968 King traveled to Memphis to support a strike by sanitation workers when the mayor refused to recognize their union. He saw this as part of his Poor People's Campaign, but a planned march turned into a riot and King's followers spirited him away from the violence and out of town. J. Edgar Hoover had his agents spread rumors that King was responsible for the riot. King returned to Memphis four days later to address a church rally for the strikers. He delivered his famous last speech indicating he had climbed the mountain and seen the promised land they were striving for, but he might not be there when it was achieved. When finishing the speech, he fell back with exhaustion and was caught by his advisors during a deafening applause. The next evening he was shot to death by a sniper on his motel balcony. The killer was later caught and convicted of murder.

The civil rights movement was never the same after King's death. It seemed that King became a focal symbol and a leadership catalyst for a social movement that was wide and passionate enough to make a profound social transformation in the South. Although he had multiple affairs with different women, he explained to his lieutenants that they provided an escape from the stress. The inconsistency between his moral message of equal rights for all and his own personal behavior bothered King throughout his campaigns. He became guilt ridden and morose at times but did not change his behavior, and his wife seemed to ignore his indiscretions. Regardless of his private failings, he was effective in fulfilling his public leadership role as a symbol and spokesperson for the American Civil Rights movement and is remembered as a great leader.

Martin Luther King, Jr. is most often described as a Charismatic/Transformational Leader due to his outstanding *rhetorical skills* he used to describe his *vision* and *mission* of brotherhood and peace among all people. King's other behavioral characteristics that fit the charismatic/transformational leadership model include his *risk taking* during dangerous demonstrations and marches and his key role as a *living symbol* of the overall civil rights movement in the United States. King also excelled at external *boundary spanning* as he represented his movement to governmental organizations, funding sources, and the American people via the press. This leader behavior is described in the early Multiple Linkage Model and Reformulated Path-Goal Theory of leadership. He used *directive leadership* with followers as he guided them to demonstrations at key points and times in the South that were designed to assure the presence of the press. He also demonstrated sympathy and *supportiveness* for followers who were victimized by violence and discrimination throughout his career. These behaviors are described in Path-Goal Theory, Fiedler's Contingency Theory, Situational Leadership Theory, and the Leadership Grid. In strategic meetings with his closest advisors, he used *participative leadership* in gathering information from each of them, patiently listening and getting ideas, and mediating among them when they disagreed. This leadership behavior is best described by the Normative Decision Theory. King's *determination* and *cognitive* capacity reflect Trait Theories of leadership. King's leadership can also be addressed by the Servant Leadership Theory as well as Authentic Leadership since he was totally committed to his goal of a better America for all Americans.

Discussion Questions

1. Why did Martin Luther King, Jr. become so important for the civil rights movement in the United States?
2. How important were his boundary spanning activities with the press?
3. Why do you think the civil rights movement lost much momentum after King's death?
4. It was well known that King had many extra marital affairs. Do you believe a leader's personal behavior affects his/her effectiveness as a leader?

References

Frady, M. (2002). *Martin Luther King, Jr.* New York: Penguin Putnam.

Martin Luther King, Jr. (n.d.). In *Wikipedia*. Retrieved November 16, 2010, from http://en.wikipedia.org/wiki/Martin_Luther_King,_Jr

Nobelprize.org (n.d.). Biography Martin Luther King, Jr. Retrieved November 16, 2010, from http://nobelprize.org/nobel_prizes/peace/laureates/1964/king-bio.html

Chapter 21

George Washington
First President of the United States

George Washington was a Virginia militia leader and small plantation owner who led the Continental Army of the United States during the eight year revolutionary war against Great Britain. After the war, he emerged the hero of the revolution and was elected the first president of the United States. He served two terms as president and endured controversy, criticism, conspiracy, and threats of further war. During his presidency he led the new country from being a great political experiment in the ability of a people to govern themselves without an aristocracy, to a republic with established institutions that took its place in the world of nations. For his contributions to his country during its tumultuous formative years, Washington is often referred to in the United States as "the father of our country."

Washington was born in 1732 in northern Virginia, in an area that adjoined a large British land grant owned by Lord Thomas Fairfax whose family settled there and built a huge plantation. Although Washington's family was not wealthy, they associated with the Fairfaxes and other land holding families in the area. These families contained men who saw themselves as aristocratic and powerful, whose duty it was to lead others in this new land. George planned to attend school in England like his father and older brothers, but his father's death when George was 11 changed these plans. At that point the Fairfaxes became his mentors, and he began learning their view of the world and his place in it. He was sickly in his youth and spent much time riding for exercise. He had limited formal education but loved exploring the wilderness and became an excellent horseman. He developed an impressive physical appearance at 6 feet 2 inches in height, a muscular 175 pounds, blue gray eyes, dark hair, and pale skin. He had a deliberate manner, looked people full in the face when speaking, never drank heavily, and possessed a respectful pleasant voice.

At 17, Washington began working as a surveyor in the area surrounding his home and he started buying land. When George was 20, his older brother, Lawrence, died of tuberculosis. George leased and later purchased Mt. Vernon, the family plantation, from his brother's widow. Lawrence had been an officer in an American regiment of the British army and inspired George to seek a military career. Lawrence had also been appointed to train and lead the Virginia militia, so George sought this position and received an appointment. He had no military training but was given the rank of major and the responsibility for training men in military skills.

Over the next few years, he led militia men to confront the French who were occupying land in the Ohio Valley that the British colony of Virginia wanted to claim. He engaged in two battles with the French and Indian collaborators—one with his own troops and one with a British force. Both were disasters. He was accused of killing a French peace envoy in the first battle and was captured and released. Later he was the only surviving officer with the British force and supervised their retreat. He was promoted to colonel and returned with British and Virginian forces to attack the French Fort Duquesne, but found the fort abandoned by the French because their supply lines had been cut in the north. During these campaigns he demonstrated extreme courage in battle—actually enjoying the hiss of bullets in the air. Some thought him fool hearty as he exposed himself to extreme risks. But he had developed immense energy and stamina for long marches, he knew the wilderness better than any other officer, and he could garner supplies and use them wisely. He was hailed as a hero in Virginia for his efforts to defend the land and settlers against the French and Indians and was elected to the Virginia Assembly.

In 1759 he married a wealthy and agreeable Virginia widow. His wife, Martha, gave him a lifelong happy marriage and a significant increase in land holdings. At Mt. Vernon, he became increasingly frustrated with British agents in London who sold his cash crop, tobacco, at low prices or siphoned off proceeds for themselves. He began growing corn and wheat to be sold in local markets and stopped dealing with the British. England imposed a tax on the colonists to pay for the French and Indian war, but the Americans resisted. Britain imposed more restrictions and stationed more troops in the colonies, resulting in the Boston Tea Party. The British then blockaded Boston Harbor and Washington began to think of armed rebellion against Britain.

In 1774 he attended the first Continental Congress, spoke very little (he was not a gifted speaker), and helped approve commercial reprisals against Britain. Returning to Virginia, he began training militia forces. The second Continental Congress in 1775 was held after the battle of Lexington and Concord in Massachusetts. This was the first military engagement of colonial and British forces who were then in a standoff on the edges of Boston. At the Congress, John Adams argued forcefully for Washington to lead the Continental Army. He believed Washington could bring the southern colonies into the fight with England. George was embarrassed and left the room when Adams spoke in praise of his capabilities. Washington was selected to lead the army, though he stated he felt unequal to the task and refused any salary, asking only that his expenses be paid during the conflict.

Washington joined the Continental militiamen who remained in the standoff outside Boston. The British occupied the city, and Continental forces surrounded the city and harbor. He found his militia men poorly organized, disobedient, and grossly undersupplied. He set to work establishing strict discipline, demoted several continental officers, had soldiers flogged for cowardice under fire, and sent out requests for powder and shot. He quickly developed the respect of his army due to his discipline, supply efforts, impressive appearance and horsemanship, his total faith in the revolutionary cause, and the fact that he stayed with his men at the front. He enjoyed gambling with his junior officers, but he promoted men based solely on their merit. The standoff lasted for several months until Washington obtained cannons from the captured Fort Ticonderoga. He had them placed overnight in a strategic position overlooking Boston and its harbor, which was filled with British ships. Still short of powder, Washington held his fire and the British withdrew from the city without a battle.

Washington then moved his army to defend New York City, but was pushed back and escaped with his forces at night. Before retreating across New Jersey, he received a copy of the Declaration of Independence, which strengthened his resolve. He received little cooperation from other Continental generals in the north and he was discouraged when one of them was captured while sleeping with a pretty widow far from his troops. The British believed that most colonists sided with England and took supplies from civilians as they needed them. George refused to allow his troops to take from the colonists, resulting in tremendous hardships in winter, but they eventually received helpful support for his army from the people. The British withdrew most of their army to New York for the winter, leaving outposts manned heavily with mercenaries. Washington later described the revolution as a "war of posts" meaning the British would take territory and leave troops at different locations to maintain their gains. This eventually weakened the British forces and left them vulnerable.

On Christmas night, 1776, Washington directed his forces in crossing the ice filled Delaware River, marched with them 9 miles on frozen roads, and surprised the British outpost at Trenton. Washington led the attack, riding in front of his soldiers and overran the camp. He captured almost 900 Hessian mercenaries with only two of his own soldiers killed. His victory inspired his men, and his speech to them after the battle convinced many whose enlistments were expiring to stay with the army. A British force soon appeared, but Washington's army slipped away once more. He knew the wilderness better than any opposing officer, and his army of farmers and woodsmen traveled quickly with few supplies. They then attacked and overran three British regiments at Princeton, and George again led the charge against the enemy at the front of his troops.

France saw that the British were threatened in America and sent supplies to support the revolution. Washington attacked a major British force and was repulsed only to escape in the fog. George took his army to Valley Forge for the winter of 1777, and they suffered terribly for lack of clothing, shelter, and supplies. He stayed with his troops and shared in their suffering. After two months they completed cabins with plenty of firewood, and supplies arrived. In 1778 France recognized the United States as an independent nation and George planned another attack. As always, he consulted his council of war (major officers reporting to him) and they advised he wait for French help. He acquiesced (as he usually did when they disagreed with him), but other officers in the field objected; they wanted to attack. So Washington changed his mind. One of his generals requested to lead the attack but failed to carry out the plan and retreated. George stopped the retreat by his graceful and inspiring presence on horseback. He then directed his soldiers to turn and attack again, and they overran their pursuers. The British then withdrew to New York. Shortly thereafter eight states ratified the Articles of Confederation, creating a single unified country, and the French fleet appeared on the east coast.

Amazingly, the French fleet moored their ships and offloaded troops on an island near Rhode Island, but did not move. George met with the French commander but was unable to convince him to assist his army. Then Benedict Arnold (one of Washington's top generals) defected to the British, and Continental troops mutinied in Philadelphia and New Jersey due to lack of pay and supplies from the Continental Congress. Washington was discouraged but not deterred and, when pressured, the Congress responded and satisfied the troops. Washington then spread the word that he would attack New York. The British commander at Yorktown, Virginia, General Cornwallis, sent troops to reinforce

New York. George finally convinced the French to join him. They traveled quietly and laid siege to Yorktown with the French Navy in support. Cornwallis and 8,000 British soldiers and seamen finally surrendered. This was the beginning of the end of the Revolutionary War.

The Continental Congress had never supported the army adequately. The states refused to contribute money and supplies, and the Congress had no power to tax. Several officers including Alexander Hamilton, Washington's aid during the war, threatened a military takeover to impose a tax to pay the soldiers. They wanted George to lead the coup, but he called a meeting of his officers and spoke of his honesty, dedication and personal sacrifice during the war. In his own environment, he had become the best general on the continent and his candor was never challenged. This effectively stopped the coup and a peace treaty was signed with the British in September 1783. In December, Washington resigned his commission. After a tearful goodbye to his officers, he returned to Mount Vernon while continuing to advocate for the creation of a central government that could impose taxes to pay the military veterans and national debts.

Because he was forced to pay most of his own expenses and those of his officers during the war, he had lost a fortune. His plantation was a mess and he began selling and speculating in land to raise money. He started the Potomac Canal Company to facilitate transportation and commerce westward. This led to interstate conferences on waterways, and these conferences eventually became the Constitutional Convention in 1787. Washington and other Virginians drew up a plan for a federal government with separation of powers and a system of checks and balances. The constitution was eventually passed and Washington, the hero of the revolution, was elected first President of the United States of America in 1789.

During much of his presidency, Washington relied on Alexander Hamilton, a brilliant lawyer and politician, to help with his speeches. Not a natural speaker, Washington's hands and voice trembled when he gave his inaugural speech to Congress. John Adams was elected vice president to represent the northern states, but Washington, who never completely trusted northerners, exerted close control over the vice president's actions. Washington appointed men as cabinet members who he trusted and had been influential in the Continental Congress and war effort. Alexander Hamilton was Secretary of Treasury, Thomas Jefferson was Secretary of State, John Knox (George's close friend) remained as Secretary of War, and John Jay was Chief Justice of the Supreme Court and later governor of New York. James Madison, the primary author of the Constitution, became a Senator and trusted colleague of Washington.

From the beginning of his administration, Washington sought to avoid sectionalism that might split the nation. He made up agendas prior to meetings and disliked distractions and emotional displays. He came quickly to rely on Hamilton and Jefferson's competence and insight, although he misjudged their animosity toward one another. Both had lost their father when they were young and they saw Washington as a father figure. Hamilton was a doer, had a crisp military demeanor, dressed immaculately, was short, and favored a strong central government with a manufacturing and commerce based economy. Jefferson was a thinker, slouched and dressed sloppily, was tall, and opposed a strong central government in favor of states' rights and an agrarian based economy. Hamilton made his home in New York and Jefferson (like Washington) was from a plantation family in Virginia. They presented well-prepared opposing views on many subjects that Washington appreciated and endeavored to incorporate into his decisions. Most importantly, Hamilton favored closer commercial ties with Britain and Jefferson championed the French revolution and the new French Republic (Britain and France were inching close to war with one another). Washington generally discouraged private meetings and often did not reveal his thoughts until he announced a decision. Though he never let people push him around, he usually tried to strike a balance between the positions of his two major advisors. At all times during his presidency, he sought to maintain neutrality and avoid war. Washington obtained Hamilton, Jefferson and Madison's cooperation to pass legislation to repay war debts and establish a Bank of the United States to issue currency, service national debt, and make loans for large scale projects. The first session of the new Congress solidified the nation.

Since the end of the Revolutionary War, Britain had enacted punitive trade regulations against the United States and, with Spain, had incited Indians to attack U.S. settlers in the West. When Washington's first term ended, he stated he would not run for another term. He believed he had not united the government or the country. This exemplified his humble nature, although he seldom admitted mistakes or retracted statements. He believed his cabinet would stay on to provide continuity, but Jefferson threatened to resign. Fear spread that the new government would collapse without Washington, and in 1792 he allowed himself to be re-elected a second term without declaring himself a candidate.

The war between Britain and France split the United States population. Two major political parties had been formed. Hamilton had helped form the Federalist Party and Jefferson and Madison formed the Republican Party. Hamilton conspired with the British to establish diplomatic relations and favorable trade conditions, which Congress rejected. Jefferson cooperated with the French efforts to form an army in the United States and take over Louisiana from Spain, which Washington squashed. John Jay then negotiated a treaty with Britain to settle trade and other issues. After much controversy, Washington ratified the treaty though he hesitated to take sides on the British-French conflict. Before long, both Jefferson and Hamilton resigned and Washington lost the balanced input of two superb people. The other people available for their positions did not possess the insight and devotion to the country of these two men. Their replacements conspired against one another, continuing to make Washington's job difficult.

Hamilton helped Washington prepare his last address to Congress. This became a famous speech where George described the current state of the country, his efforts to build a government that would last, and warned that Congress must beware of those who served foreign causes. The British implemented the Jay treaty with tolerance, stopped supporting Indian attacks, and Spain opened up the Mississippi River to commerce. George spent more time at Mt. Vernon and did not take part in the presidential election of 1796. John Adams was elected the next president with Thomas Jefferson as vice president. During Adams' inauguration process, Washington received the largest applause from Congress. He stated his greatest reward from his lifetime of service was the love and respect of his fellow citizens. Washington's two terms as president became a tradition that lasted until Franklin Roosevelt was elected four times in the 20th century, and Congress later modified the constitution to prohibit more than two consecutive terms.

Returning to Mt. Vernon, Washington engaged in more land speculation to repay the huge debts he incurred as president and commander of the army. During his presidency, he had enjoyed Martha's tea parties that included men and women of influence. At Mt. Vernon, they had frequent visitors and socialized with those he referred to as "people of rank." He always sought to maintain consistency in thought and action and he had slowly come to oppose slavery as antithetical to the idea of liberty that was so basic to the revolution. He strongly believed abolition of slavery was needed to bind the nation together and he feared the country would be split between the north and south over the slavery issue. He tried to devise a way to free his slaves without setting them adrift in a society where they could not thrive or even survive. Always energetic, he spent six hours each day riding and walking on his plantation. He died in 1799 from a throat infection, though his illness was likely exacerbated by repeated bleedings by his doctors. He specified in his will that all his slaves were to be freed upon his wife's death and she freed them one year later. He left instructions to provide care and education of their freed slaves and children. His heirs' attempts to carry out these instructions were frustrated when a Virginia law was passed prohibiting the education of Blacks.

Washington was a *directive* leader during his military career (he still held a military commission at the time of his death) but he made every effort to *sup-*

port his soldiers as long as they followed orders. These basic leader behaviors are described in Fiedler's Contingency Theory, Situational Leadership Theory, and Path-Goal Theory. He also consulted frequently with his council of war composed of major officers under his command and often acquiesced with their wishes in his decisions. This type of *participative leadership* he continued during his presidency, and is addressed in the Normative Decision Theory. He was clearly viewed as *charismatic* by his followers, when he *inspired* them and *role modeled* an aggressive advance during battles, and his patriotic and *stimulating speeches* reminded them of the higher calling they were fighting to achieve. This leadership pattern is described in most Charismatic/Transformational Leadership theories. He spent considerable effort in *boundary spanning* when he represented his troops to the Continental Congress in trying to obtain supplies to support the army. This leadership behavior is described in the Multiple Linkage Model and the Reformulated Path-Goal Theory. Implicit Leadership Theory could also be used to describe Washington's leadership style as representative of the popular image of outstanding leadership at that time. Washington's *cognitive capacity, determination, integrity,* and *sociability* are described in Trait Theories of leadership.

Discussion Questions

1. In what ways was Washington a directive leader?
2. Describe the charismatic/transformational elements of Washington's leadership.
3. Why do you believe the army stuck with Washington during the eight long years of the Revolutionary War with very little support from the Continental Congress?
4. Describe the Implicit Leadership Theory (prototype) of an outstanding leader that likely existed at Washington's time. How does this leadership prototype differ from the prototype of an outstanding leader today? Would Washington fit the current prototype? Why or why not?

References

Fischer, D. H. (2004). *Washington's crossing.* New York: Oxford University Press.

Flexner, J. T. (1974). *Washington: The indispensable man.* Boston, MA: Little Brown.

Ford, P. L. (1970). *George Washington.* Port Washington, NY: Kennikat Press.

Chapter 22

Luiz Inácio Lula da Silva
President of Brazil

Luiz Inácio Lula da Silva is a labor union leader who served as 35th president of Brazil as it was transformed from a continually under-achieving economy to a major member of the global economic community. Lula, as he is known in Brazil, implemented social programs that pulled nearly 25 million people out of poverty and added almost 30 million people to the middle class—creating an enormous new domestic market for goods and services. He was first elected president in 2002 when Brazil received a $30 billion loan from the International Monetary Fund (IMF) to rescue its failing economy. When he left office in January 2011, Brazil had repaid its debt and was lending $5 billion to the IMF. Brazil's currency is now stable and income of the poorest 10% of the population has grown five times faster than income of the richest 10%. Unemployment is at a record low level, inflation is under control, and illiteracy is declining significantly. Brazil will host the World Cup of soccer in 2014 and the Olympic Games in 2016. Known as the working man's president, Lula began as a poor immigrant from rural Brazil with a fourth grade education. His name is now spoken with reverence by many Brazilians.

Lula was born on October 27, 1945, in a small town in northeastern Brazil, the seventh of eight children. His father left about the time of Lula's birth, ostensibly to work in Sao Paulo, a major sea port and the largest city in Brazil. Unknown to his wife and family, he started a new family in Sao Paulo with his wife's cousin and never returned to Lula's family. Like many Brazilians, Lula's family lived under very poor conditions, without running water or electricity, while his mother tried to support her children. When Lula was 7, his mother sold everything and took her children to Sao Paulo for a better life. The trip took several days in the back of a truck, and Lula saw his first bicycle and car at this time. They lived with his father's new family for a short time, but his father became an alcoholic and beat the children, so Lula's mother found a room at another location and moved with her children to avoid the beatings.

Lula became a streetwise kid, leaving school after the fourth grade and selling peanuts and fruit to help earn money for his mother. He worked different jobs as a youth and at 15 he began training as a lathe operator, eventually working in a screw factory and providing significant financial support for his mother and siblings. He worked in several factories over the next few years. He lost a finger in an industrial accident and had to wait for hours in extreme pain to get medical treatment. The experience left him with the realization that industrial safety and medical care were underprovided for poor and working people. His family moved around during this time and had little to eat but rice and potatoes when work was scarce. Sao Paulo was developing rapidly as a manufacturing center, and Lula observed several worker strikes that were sometimes violent. His brother, Frei Chico, became involved with the metalworker's union. He talked with Lula about how unregulated capitalists forced low wages on workers while requiring long hours and work on Saturdays. A military coup in 1964 had resulted in a dictatorial military president who increased censorship, arrested strikers, and repressed anyone the government saw as opposing its policies. The government also engaged in kidnapping, torture, and executions of many Brazilians who it viewed as radical and threatening.

Lula joined the metalworker's union in 1968 and was married in 1969. The same year, his brother Frei Chico apparently saw leadership potential in Lula and convinced him to become a member of the union's directorship. Lula agreed and worked hard for four years learning about union affairs and seeking answers to questions by union members. He empathized with the conditions of poor and working Brazilians. Also in 1969, the United States ambassador to Brazil was kidnapped by urban guerillas and the government had to release 13 political prisoners to obtain his release. This showed many Brazilians that the military government was not invincible. Brazil was growing economically with the support of the military government, but Lula saw the implications for workers of this unregulated growth—poor safety in factories, depressed living conditions, and government spies who saw to it that anyone who spoke out for workers' rights was fired and/or arrested. He lost several jobs during this period for speaking out on behalf of workers. He was wrongly suspected of being a communist, although the communist party was often influential in the Brazilian labor movement. He disliked the communists' sense of paranoia, secrecy and deceptive tactics.

In 1971 Lula's wife and baby died during childbirth. After mourning for several months, he began dating and fathered a child with a woman who he did not marry. A short time later he met and eventually married Marisa Letícia Casa, a school secretary who brought stability to his life. He adopted her young son and eventually had three children with Marisa, a strong supporter of his activities. In 1974 he was elected as a full-time officer in his union. Although he was shy of public speaking, he vigorously advocated progressive change and organized the first national metalworker's union conference in Brazil. He recruited hundreds of new members and was elected president of the Sao Paulo metalworkers in 1975. At his induction ceremony before 10,000 workers, he gave a carefully prepared speech about workers being crushed by the state in communist countries or being enslaved by capitalism, which deprived them of dignity by exploiting them with its mass production. This speech revealed his early vision of workers being caught between these two political/economic systems and indicated his socialistic beliefs that guided many of his later programs. The speech was well received by the workers.

Frei Chico was vice president of another factory workers union and was arrested in a government anti-communist sweep while Lula was at a conference in Tokyo. Against his colleagues' advice, Lula returned to Brazil immediately to try to gain his brother's release. Frei Chico was finally released after 78 days, during which he was tortured by government captors. Several others died during their imprisonment. This radicalized Lula, and he decided more strident action was needed to improve workers' rights. Brazil was borrowing money from international bankers to finance its development, but wages lagged behind the rapid inflation and the economic gap between rich and poor was increasing. An economic study showed the military government greatly understated inflation figures, which directly affected the official minimum wage. Lula visited factory gates and discussed working conditions and union policies with workers and he participated with other union officials in planning their strategies. He directed the circulation of a petition signed by over 40,000 workers claiming reinstatement of lost earnings from understated back wages but the government refused. In 1978 he was reelected president of his union and he announced to members that it was time to end the exploitation of workers in Brazil. Lula's confidence was increasing as Brazilian society was becoming more unhappy with their government, and he advocated a more confrontational strategy for their union.

He began networking with leaders of other unions to build bridges of cooperation and promote a freer labor movement. Although strikes were outlawed by the government, Lula was involved in directing a wave of strikes by the metalworkers. There were too many strikes nationwide for the government to stop them. Lula contacted a liberal army general and asked him to tell the union side of the story behind the strikes. The general told journalists that the strikes were generally peaceful, there was no evidence of subversive foreign influence, and police or soldiers could not force people back to work. The result was that several unions received wage increases and Lula became a national media figure with the unanimous backing of his union members. The Catholic Church increased its support of the workers' rights movement after a Catholic labor leader was shot dead at a factory gate during a strike.

In 1980 Lula and others began forming a Workers Party (PT) to put forth political candidates that supported wage increases, free worker representation in factories, rights to bargain collectively and strike, and the end to government strike breaking. He delegated much authority to other union leaders to assure strikes could continue if the top union leadership was arrested. A short time later, he was arrested with other union leaders and a Catholic Church representative during a non-violent strike in Sao Bernardo. He held a hunger strike while in prison and was released after 31 days. Almost immediately he was elected the president of the new Workers Party and became its charismatic symbol—a man of the people who was helping them confront the dictatorial military government and its exploitive policies toward workers. The population of Brazil was demanding basic services for the huge urban ghettos and expropriation of unused lands for the poor and landless. In the early 1980s, 71 million Brazilians were under nourished, hunger and malnutrition were responsible for 40% of infant deaths, and the minimum salary did not keep up with inflation. In 1983 Lula helped start a union for all Brazilian workers (CUT). Unions, the Catholic Church, and many professionals and politicians were demanding democracy and civic freedom for Brazilian people. Lula was no longer a shy speaker and was now a national figure inspiring crowds with his rhetoric.

In the early 1980s the government recognized that change was coming, granting amnesty to several activist leaders and relaxing some controls in order to keep power. But conservative shadow groups kidnapped, tortured, and bombed union activists to sabotage the relaxation strategy. Lula described the problem as a division in Brazilian society between the exploiters and the workers who were exploited, and he said only socialism would solve this problem. Inflation soared and the government held the first popular elections for state government positions since 1966 when they had been suspended by the military government. Lula ran for his state governorship as a worker candidate in the largest Brazilian state but voters expected someone with more education and he lost. He then supported a petroleum workers' strike, which was squelched by the government. This was followed by a national workers' strike, which the government suppressed with violence. Lula then began advocating a popular direct election for the Brazilian presidency. Since the military coup of 1964, the president had been ostensibly selected by the congress but it was prearranged by a meeting of military leaders who made sure their candidate would win. In 1984 Lula inspired demonstrations of over a million people who demanded popular elections. In 1985 the national congress established direct elections for president, granted 20 million illiterates the right to vote, and called for a constitutional assembly to rewrite the constitution. Lula was a delegate to the assembly and although he opposed some of its provisions, he supported its passage, which provided for a single term president.

In 1987 Lula was selected as the PT's presidential candidate. The economy was declining again. He visited Cuba and Nicaragua where he was further convinced that extreme leftist governments created poorer conditions for the people. While campaigning, he called for renouncing Brazil's international debt (which he saw as exploitive) and beginning major land reform for the landless. This apparently frightened the middle and upper classes and he lost the election. As its paid president, Lula worked to build the PT, traveling around the country and speaking for PT candidates. His strategy was always inclusive and participatory, advocating workers' councils in factories and participative budgeting in cities where the city's budget was open to citizens to argue their preferred priorities and vote on the budget. Corruption charges and continued inflation resulted in impeachment of the elected president in 1992. The vice president assumed the presidency and tried to broaden his support with labor leaders. Lula offered the new president a national plan for nutrition improvement and hunger elimination that later became Lula's successful Zero Hunger program. He began meeting with bankers and industrialists to build his networks for support in future elections. The new president appointed a financial minister, Fernando Cardoso, who was a professor turned politician. This minister initiated an economic plan that began to decrease inflation, increase productivity, and improve the purchasing power and consumption of the population. In 1994 the economy dominated the presidential election and Lula was defeated by Cardoso.

Lula was especially discouraged by his defeat in 1994. There was a worldwide surge in private enterprise by the mid-1990s including China, India, South Africa, Argentina, Chile, and the United States. Lula was caught between socialistic militants in the PT and the global trends. He focused on hunger, poverty, and global investors that penalized and exploited developing countries. Money flowed into Brazil and fostered continued deforestation, resulting in $5 billion in sales of soy exports while Brazil paid $7.5 Billion to import rice, corn, and beans—all typical Brazilian products. In 1997, congress approved a constitutional amendment allowing for two presidential terms. In 1998 Cardoso won the presidential election for a second term by claiming Lula's socialistic party would result in chaos.

Lula was determined to try a fourth time for the presidency by forming alliances and compromises where necessary. Cardoso's government struggled with a declining economy, increased crime, and increasing unemployment. Whenever he spoke, Lula described his vision and program called Zero Hunger, which was designed to ensure no family in Brazil would go hungry. He supported private property rights for all Brazilians and selected a self-made millionaire businessman for his running mate. These compromises apparently satisfied middle and upper class voters and he won the presidency in 2002.

He was inducted in early 2003 as the worker president from a poor background with little formal education, analogous to Abraham Lincoln. He interpreted his win as a mandate to address Brazil's social and economic inequalities. Almost immediately, he directed the creation of his Zero Hunger program that included the establishment of food banks and cooperatives for the poor, improved access to social security benefits, minimum income guarantees, increased minimum wage, and incentives for children to attend school. Some of these programs had been started on a smaller scale by the previous administration, but Lula expanded the programs and made them more effective. Zero Hunger became the defining program for his first term. He then directed his financial minister and head of the central bank to announce that Brazil would honor all foreign debt and focus on a sound currency, create an export surplus, and achieve economic stability. He worked hard to balance socialistic forces in the PT with the need for Brazil to get along with other nations by cooperating with the IMF and potential foreign investors. This calmed international concerns over Brazil's economic and political situation and growth resumed with increased exports, increased employment, and increased gross national product.

Lula concentrated on building alliances with former political opponents by forming commissions with wide representation to address social problems and appointing members of other political parties to government positions. Some appointees were accused of accepting bribes without Lula's knowledge. He disliked bureaucratic administrative matters and likely delegated freely without adequate controls in some situations. He also worked to increase Brazil's role in international relations by forming several trade organizations with other countries and striving to obtain a permanent seat for Brazil at the United Nations. He directed the creation of Bolsa Familia, a social program that overcame problems with Zero Hunger, provided welfare payments to the poorest families, expanded a school meal program, and increased the number of years of required education to keep children in school. He also directed the creation of a ministry for racial equality, a major program to improve housing for the poor, a program to provide government land for the landless, and expanded the national health service to make it more accessible to the poor. He avoided the nepotism that was common in Brazil and was careful not to alienate the governments of large developed countries. During his first term as president, Brazil paid off its loans from the IMF, became self-sufficient in oil products, improved health care for all, and decreased infant and maternal mortality rates.

He won reelection in 2006 using his ability to communicate with the common people of Brazil. He continued boundary spanning with other countries and international organizations such as the G8, G20, United Nations, and the World Social Forum to build Brazil's image and influence as a geo-political leader in South America and a world player economically. Lula is not an intellectual, but an instinctive leader with empathy for the poor who believes in inclusion and participative approaches to policy making. His speeches about his early life and his apologies to African governments for Brazil's involvement in the 18th and 19th century slave trade, often made listeners cry. His rise from poverty provides a wonderful role model for young Brazilians. He spent an hour or more each day in his office meeting with all visitors who wished to see him. His compassion and support for his countrymen are clearly shown in his social programs. Lula's impact on the Brazilian people is enormous and is shown by his 87% approval rating when he left office in January 2011.

Lula's leadership can be described as highly charismatic/transformational due to his *inspiring rhetoric*, his *vision* for eliminating hunger and starvation and improving the lives of all Brazilians, and his *role modeling* for young people regardless of their socio-economic status. These leader behaviors are addressed by theories of Charismatic/Transformational Leadership. He clearly began a major transformation in the lives of millions of his people. Through his career, he also became a master at *boundary spanning* by representing his union members in negotiations with employers and the government, networking and alliance building with influential groups in Brazil, and representing his country in international forums. This leader behavior is described in early versions of the Multiple Linkage Model of leadership and Reformulated Path-Goal Theory. Lula was also *directive* in his leadership as he established programs to carry out his mission to end poverty and hunger in Brazil, and he was *participative* by including a wide representation of Brazilians in the design of his programs. He was clearly a compassionate and *supportive* leader as shown by his empathy for the poor and working people and the programs he created to improve their lives. One or more of these three leadership patterns are described in the Leadership Grid, Path-Goal Theory, Normative Decision Theory, Fiedler's Contingency Theory and Situational Leadership Theory. The Servant Leadership Model is also relevant to Lula's leadership as he placed his highest priority on providing for his constituents' needs, listening, and reflecting on his own poor background as a youth. Lula's *determination, sociability,* and *integrity* as a leader are described in Trait Theories of leadership.

Discussion Questions

1. What leader behaviors were most important to Lula during his tenure as a union leader? What behaviors were most important during his presidency of Brazil?
2. In many Latin American countries, participative leadership is not considered effective. Why do you think Lula's inclusive participative approach has worked in Brazil?
3. Do you think a person with a fourth grade education could be elected as President of the United States? If so, could s/he be effective? Why or why not?
4. Why did Lula modify his early socialistic beliefs during his pursuit of the Presidency of Brazil?

References

Bourne, R. (2008). *Lula of Brazil*. Berkeley: University of California Press.
Luiz Inácio Lula da Silva. (n.d.). In *Wikipedia*. Retrieved January 22, 2011, from http://en.wikipedia.org/wiki/Luiz_Inacio_Lula_da_Silva

Chapter 23

Mohandas Gandhi
Indian Political and Spiritual Leader

Mohandas Gandhi is frequently known as the father of the Indian nation and is often referred to as "Mahatma" meaning Great Soul. He was the most influential Indian leader of the movement that freed India from almost 200 years of British rule. His humorous, cheerful, and optimistic manner made him easy to like, although his tactics were often difficult to understand. He emphasized human rights and suffering as the basis of his movement and he consistently taught and modeled nonviolent civil disobedience as the correct path for Indian independence.

Gandhi was born on October 2, 1869, in Porbandar, India. He was the sixth child of a father who was a skilled provincial administrator and a very religious mother. He began learning negotiating skills at an early age by observing his father and spent much time helping the sick and poor with his mother. At 13 he was married to Kasturbai Makhanji in an arranged marriage, as was the custom, and when Mohandas was 15 his first child and his father both died. He was expected to be successful and help support the family. After one year in college, a family friend suggested he study law in England. Mohandas' brother raised the money, and he spent the next three years in London completing his legal studies. While in England, he showed early signs of the asceticism that characterized his later life by not drinking alcohol, eating only vegetarian foods, and rigorously studying religious and philosophical texts. It seems counterintuitive that he also became a dandy wearing fancy British clothes and frequenting high-status social engagements.

Upon returning to India, he learned his mother had died. He opened a law practice, but it did not flourish. When he tried to intervene in a dispute for his brother, he experienced his first major insult by a British administrator he knew from London. The administrator had Mohandas pushed out of his office. Shortly thereafter he was offered a lucrative contract by an Indian company doing business in South Africa. In 1893 he traveled there alone and was thrown off a train for being a "colored" riding in a first class compartment, even though he had purchased a first class ticket. Later, he was prevented from riding in a stagecoach until other passengers intervened. Prior to this he had attributed prejudice and discrimination to individuals, now he experienced these insults as part of an institutionalized legal system. Indians had been brought to South Africa as contract labor to work in the mines. When Gandhi arrived in South Africa, there were sections of the country where Indians needed a special pass to walk on the street after 9:00 p.m., they could not own land or engage in business, they were forced to pay a resident tax and live in slums, and were forbidden from using public facilities such as sidewalks.

He began studying and informing Indian residents of the government practices and advising them of their legal rights. When he successfully settled the major legal case he had been assigned by his employer, he was persuaded to stay and help fight further discriminatory legislation aimed at Indians in South Africa. He directed volunteers to obtain signatures for a petition to repeal a new law depriving Indians of their voting rights and he sent the petition to all newspapers in the British Empire. Although major newspapers agreed with the petition, the law was eventually passed. Gandhi then founded the Natal Indian Congress of South Africa to pressure the government for Indian civil rights, to help train Indians in how to organize themselves, and to serve as a political party. He ran the Congress by collecting dues, keeping records, publishing newsletters, and raising funds. In 1896 he returned to India for his family, which now included his wife and four sons, and discovered he had become a symbol of Indian suffering overseas. Upon returning to South Africa, he was assaulted and beaten by a mob but refused to press charges—blaming the government discriminatory policies for the mob's actions.

Until 1900, pictures of Gandhi show a well-dressed professional lawyer in stylish British suits who is very image-conscious as an advocate for Indian rights. Sometime in 1900 he began what he later called his "transformation" to an ascetic celibate lifestyle, eventually rejecting all symbols of wealth and wearing simple clothing of the poor. He began volunteering two hours a day in a Christian mission to help nurse the sick and took leprous people into his home for care. His changes were undoubtedly difficult for his family members. He insisted his entire family do menial tasks cheerfully, including cleaning the chamber pots for those staying in their home. His wife was unaccustomed to this chore, and when he saw her frowning while carrying a chamber pot, he screamed at her. She reacted, and he dragged her out of the house and started to push her into the street. Her weeping question of how he had forgotten himself made him hesitate, and he realized how his anger had taken control of his actions. He began cutting his own hair, washed and ironed his clothes, and refused to allow his sons to attend a local European run school. He planned to teach them himself, even though he had little time, and they later regretted their lack of schooling. Gandhi studied home-based medicine, diets and fasting for healing and used them to treat himself and family members. He later organized and led an ambulance corps during the British military campaigns against the Zulus and Boers. In 1908 he decided to return to India and insisted his entire family donate their valuable jewelry, which they had received as gifts, to a fund for the needy. His wife objected, but he demanded that she comply.

Soon after arriving in India, he attended the All-India National Congress. Originally organized by a British civil servant, the Indian Congress was a political party, a platform for Indian public opinion, and a vehicle for social reform that eventually became instrumental in gaining Indian independence. At the Congress meeting Gandhi became a protégé of G. K. Gokhale, a famous Indian political leader, and opened a law practice in Bombay near his tutor and the center of political activity in India. He was called back to South Africa to meet with the British Colonial Secretary to press for Indian rights. After a disappointing meeting, he decided to stay again in South Africa to lead the fight for Indian rights. He helped start an Indian newspaper to express their political views, set up a hospital for plague victims in a Johannesburg ghetto, and wrote his brother that he and his siblings would not receive any more financial support from Mohandas. His brother viewed this as selfish and ungrateful. Gandhi then led a resistance campaign against a proposal to require fingerprinting and registration for all Indians. He had carefully studied Henry David Thoreau's *Essay on Civil Disobedience* and he planned his campaign accordingly. He called a mass meeting and delivered an inspirational speech advocating death rather than compliance with the proposal—but the resistance must be nonviolent. This passive resistance became his trademark tactic and was known as *satyagraha*—meaning "insistence on truth" or "soul force."

The registration act passed and Mohandas began directing a campaign to oppose its implementation. He used his newspaper to issue directives to followers and to notify government officials of his actions, he organized peaceful picketing of registration offices, burning of registration cards, and sent a representative to India to generate world opinion for their cause. Gandhi went to England for the same purpose. Returning to South Africa, he was arrested and jailed for a short time, which boosted morale for Indian protestors. He was then given the opportunity to negotiate with the governor of their district, who agreed to repeal the law but did not carry through. Gandhi opposed other legislation that provided legal recognition for only Christian marriages—effectively making non-Christian wives concubines. He directed strikes and long protest marches resulting in beatings of protestors by police and thousands of arrests, Gandhi among them. The British and Indian press expressed outraged, resulting in a British investigative commission coming to South Africa. Gandhi was released and negotiated with the governor, resulting in repeal of the marriage and registration laws and the resident tax on Indians.

Returning to India, he soon gave an invited address at a new Hindu University and surprised wealthy VIPs and benefactors by directing them to quit their high paying positions and begin working in the villages of India to serve the poor. He also told them to commit to massive civil disobedience against the British colonial government and to work toward an independent India. He began role modeling his directives, wearing the clothing of the Indian poor as he walked and spoke through most of India in his first year back from South Africa. Wherever he went he nursed the sick, opened primary schools, persuaded doctors to visit rural villages and clinics, and tried to prepare Indians for home rule. He used donations to start a commune (*ashram*), as he had in South Africa, to help poor families through subsistence farming. He advocated for the elimination of "untouchables"—the lowest members of the Hindu caste system who were prohibited from participation in many aspects of Indian society. He investigated injustices to share croppers from British landowners and was arrested. A huge crowd gathered and he was released—demonstrating the power of peaceful civil resistance to the peasant farmers. He was called to negotiate a major dispute between textile workers and their employers and fasted to obtain workers' compliance with his position.

When the British government implemented widespread censorship of the press and limits on free speech and assembly to quell the movement for Indian independence, Gandhi called for a general strike. Violence ensued between strikers and the police and Gandhi began a fast to protest the violence. British troops fired on an unarmed crowd at a meeting, killing over 350 and wounding over 1,000. Mohandas met with the Indian National Congress and proclaimed independence as their goal. He traveled with Muslim leaders throughout India advocating peaceful civil disobedience and refusal to pay taxes to pressure Great Britain for Indian independence. He directed Indians to burn all foreign made clothing and to use spinning wheels to make homemade fabric for their clothing. He used drama by beginning each speech asking everyone to strip off all foreign made clothing, to make a large pile and burn it. He had adopted a popular goal in India, independence from Britain and home rule, and made it the core of his vision for the country. But his vision also included elimination of untouchables and a unified India with all religious groups living together in peace. His mission to achieve the vision featured nonviolent civil disobedience in the form of protests, strikes, boycotts, and noncompliance with unfair laws and taxes. Gandhi's sincerity and self-sacrifice along with his good humor and optimism resulted in a flow of donations to his cause. His followers were beaten with metal tipped sticks when they protested a sham British investigation of India's readiness for home rule. Gandhi directed Indians to refuse to pay a 22% increase in taxes. Donations flooded in to support the resistance, and the tax was withdrawn.

The British held a monopoly on salt processing and sales in India and imposed a significant tax on salt sales. This had long been a source of irritation for Indians as the poor often used more salt than the wealthy, due to their hard physical labor and the warm climate, which increased perspiration. In 1930, when Gandhi was 60 years old, he began a 240 mile salt march to the Arabian Sea, the source of high quality salt for India. The march began with 78 members from his *ashram* (he provided the British government with all their names before they began) and gained thousands of additional followers as they marched. When he arrived at the sea, he picked up a piece of sea salt, and Indians all over the country began gathering, processing, and selling their own salt. Gandhi directed demonstrations, strikes, and boycotts related to salt resulting in 60,000 arrests and some killings among the primarily nonviolent demonstrators. He then informed the government that he would march to and raid a major British salt works in another city, resulting in his arrest. The raid was carried out by his followers who were unmercifully beaten and seriously injured by police with metal tipped sticks. Waves of protestors came forward for several days to be beaten without even raising their hands in defense. Gandhi had publicized the march, and the world watched through the eyes of journalists who witnessed the beatings. World opinion was mounting against British control of India. Gandhi directed Indians to boycott British shipping, insurance, and banking organizations, and many Indians stopped paying taxes. Britain could no longer maintain law and order and their revenues were declining in India. The government decided to negotiate with Gandhi and they eventually agreed to allow Indians to produce salt, to release all nonviolent prisoners, to return confiscated properties, and to allow the boycott of foreign cloth.

Shortly thereafter, Mohandas was invited to attend a conference in London, where he lived in poor areas and spoke to many working-class groups. He told them that one fifth of the world population in India was on the edge of starvation. His optimism, sincerity, and sense of humor made him popular wherever he went, even to textile plants that were hurt by the Indian boycott of foreign cloth. He returned to India after three months and was again arrested and jailed by the new viceroy (governor general of India) who planned to crush the Indian National Congress Party. More civil disobedience, violence, and arrests occurred. The British planned separate elections for untouchables, separating the electorate from other Hindus and Muslims. Gandhi objected and started a "fast to death" to eliminate the designation of "untouchable" from Indian society. He became ill very quickly and a hasty conference of different voting groups was held, a compromise was reached and approved by the British in London, and Gandhi stopped his fast. Over the next several years, he was in and out of jail and fasted frequently as an example of willing suffering and a means of influence to keep his followers nonviolent. He traveled throughout India and shook hands with untouchables in violation of age old traditions. He built a small hut for himself with no electricity that would be his home for the remainder of his life.

In 1939, Great Britain declared war on Germany and the British Viceroy did the same for India without consulting any Indians. Gandhi advocated nonviolent civil disobedience against the Nazis and he actually urged voluntary sacrifice by Jews, homosexuals, and gypsies who were being murdered in German gas chambers. At first he opposed continued civil disobedience against the British in India while they fought the Germans, not wishing to take unfair advantage of their misfortune. When the Indian National Congress offered to fight the Nazis in return for independence, Winston Churchill (British Prime Minister) refused and the Congress asked Gandhi to take charge. He realized Japan, which had invaded the Asian continent, was a threat to India and believed Indian independence was essential in order to defeat the Japanese. So he directed more civil disobedience, was arrested, and riots erupted with fires, destruction of railroads and telegraphs, and killings of both British and Indians. In 1943 a famine in Bengali killed over 1.5 million people and while in prison, Gandhi began another fast, announcing that the British were willing to die for their freedom but would not grant India its freedom. He quickly became ill but recovered with his wife's nursing only to have his long time secretary, as well as his wife, both die a short time later. He later contracted malaria and was released after almost two years of imprisonment.

By this time, most of Britain had decided trying to control India was too expensive and probably no longer possible. Gandhi wanted a unified India free from prejudice with equality and justice for all citizens. But Muslims feared being dominated by the Hindu majority and wanted their own country to be called Pakistan. In 1945 a new prime minister in Britain announced support of self-governance for India. Terrible violence erupted in India between Hindus and Muslims when Britain announced that two countries were unrealistic. Gandhi traveled extensively in India preaching peace between Hindus and Muslims. He founded hospitals and schools with the help of his followers and generally restored peace wherever he visited. The Muslim leader, Mohammed Ali Jinnah, then announced in London that they would wash the Indian continent in blood if a separate Muslim state were not created soon. Weary of the struggle and violence, Jawaharlal Nehru, then head of the Indian National Congress, and other elected officials decided to agree to the creation of a separate Muslim nation. In spite of achieving Indian independence that he had fought for so long, Gandhi felt he was totally defeated and refused to attend Indian Independence Day celebrations on August 15, 1947.

The government of the new India had originally promised to pay Pakistan a share of the Indian treasury but later decided not to follow through on their promise. As Muslims traveled to their new country of Pakistan and Hindus traveled to their new India, violence was rampant and over half a million died. Gandhi traveled to help quell the violence and started his last "fast to death" in January 1948 at 78 years of age. As he weakened, the new Indian cabinet agreed to pay Pakistan. The violence decreased when Hindu and Muslim leaders pledged to stop the fighting and Gandhi stopped his fast. He announced his next peace journey would be to Pakistan, but on January 20 his prayer meeting was interrupted by a bomb. Ten days later he was shot to death by a member of a radical Hindu organization that advocated military conquest of Pakistan and elimination of all Muslims from India. Through his dedication and unusual tactics, Gandhi achieved one of his two major goals—the independence of India from British colonial governance. But his other goal of a unified India with equality and justice for all and without prejudice had eluded him. In later years, his leadership became a model for other great leaders—including Nelson Mandela and Martin Luther King.

Gandhi's leadership is probably best described by Charismatic/Transformational and Servant Leadership theories with a strong emphasis on *boundary spanning.* His charismatic leadership is shown by his *inspirational rhetoric* and a *clear vision* and *mission* for Indian independence. He also exhibited *self-sacrificial behavior* in the form of repeated fasts, arrest and imprisonment and a poor lifestyle as well as continued *role modeling* of nonviolent civil disobedience. His Servant Leadership is shown by his lifelong *concern* and *service* to the poor, *providing for followers' needs* through giving away worldly possessions and establishment and *support* of ashrams, as well as his *empathy, openness, humility,* and *optimism.* His boundary spanning behaviors are demonstrated by his successful *negotiations* with governing officials in South Africa and India, his effective *use of the media* to publicize to the world the condition of his followers, and his amazing success at *fund raising* for his campaigns. These behaviors are described in the Multiple Linkage Model and the Reformulated Path-Goal Theories of leadership. He also clearly used *directive leadership* in organizing and conducting campaigns of civil disobedience, strikes, marches and boycotts. He was *supportive* of his followers financially and spiritually throughout his life. These behaviors are described in several leadership models including Path-Goal Theory, Situational Leadership Theory, the Leadership Grid and Fiedler's Contingency Theory. His *determination, sociability,* and *cognitive capacity* are addressed in Trait Theories of leadership.

Discussion Questions

1. Why was Gandhi successful in gaining Indian independence when Indians had longed for freedom from British domination for so long before Gandhi's time?
2. What was the purpose of Gandhi's fasting and why was it important for his leadership?
3. Do you believe Gandhi's type of leadership can be used in other organizational contexts, such as business or educational organizations?
4. What can you learn from Gandhi's leadership that you can use as a leader?

References

Kytle, C. (1982). *Gandhi: Soldier of nonviolence.* Washington, DC: Seven Locks Press.
Mohandas Karamchand Gandhi. (n.d.). In *Wikipedia.* Retrieved May 25, 2010, from http://en.wikipedia.org/wiki/Mohandas_%22Mahatma%22_Gandhi
Severance, J. B. (1997). *Gandhi: Great soul.* New York: Clarion Books.

Chapter 24

Sitting Bull
Sioux War Chief

Sitting Bull was born near the Missouri River in 1831 and served as war chief and holy man for the Hunkpapa tribe in the Sioux federation of plains Indians. He later became Supreme Chief over all the Sioux tribes and led their resistance to White peoples' incursions into their traditional domain in what eventually became North and South Dakota, and parts of Montana and Wyoming. He epitomized the four Sioux virtues of a Sioux man—bravery, fortitude, generosity, and wisdom. He was feared and respected by all plains Indians and admired by all the Sioux. One of his opponents, General Nelson Miles, described Sitting Bull as a thinking, reasoning leader who was a strong warrior with great influence. Journalists who interviewed him described him as a powerful leader whose leadership came from wisdom with unshakable principles and conviction. His words were repeated throughout the Sioux camps, and he continued to fight for Indian rights throughout his life.

Sitting Bull's father and uncles were Hunkpapa chiefs. He spent much time with them learning to ride, hunt buffalo, and use weapons against their long-term enemies including the Crow and Ree tribes. The Sioux culture centered around the buffalo hunt and war on their enemies. It included regular sharing with extended families that included adopted members. The Sioux virtue of bravery was shown by counting coup (first touch of an enemy) in battle; fortitude was demonstrated by enduring pain, as well as dignity and reserve; generosity reflected giving property and food to the needy; and wisdom included age/maturity and a spiritual life that provided insight and good judgment in war, hunting, and tribal affairs. These virtues resulted in honor, respect, and influence in the tribe. Leadership was based on example, wisdom, and a tribal council of elders who governed by consensus, not majority rule—often leading to factions and inaction.

Sitting Bull killed his first buffalo when he was 10 and gave it to the poor. He counted his first coup by downing a Crow enemy when he was 14. He was admitted to prestigious fraternal societies that provided tribal police (*akicita*) at an early age. Any warrior could organize a war expedition against enemies of the Sioux to gain horses and scalps, and Sitting Bull led many such expeditions that often went looking for targets. He became expert with bow and arrow, tomahawk, and war club and was very good with firearms—acquiring many horses, belongings and praise from his tribe. He wore yellow and red paint in battle and, at 25, during their annual sun dance, he hung suspended with skewers piercing the muscles of his chest and back, staring at the sun until they tore loose. At 26 he was made war chief for the Hunkpapas and part of the tribal council. He was a dreamer and saw visions of his people that had spiritual meaning and allowed him to predict future events involving war and the hunt. He became a holy man (*wichasha waken*) and performed sacred rituals, composed and sang songs of tribute and lament, and practiced medicine for his people. He was called on to mediate disputes among factions and between his tribe and other tribes. He usually dressed simply, interacted as an equal with other Sioux, listened carefully and never interrupted, and spoke slowly and quietly with dignity. At 26 his first wife died in child birth and his young son died four years later. He then adopted his nephew, One Bull, who became his companion and supporter all his life.

Over the next five years, the Sioux began facing the biggest threat in their history as White immigrants headed for Oregon and the California gold fields by traveling through their domain. The United States government held a council with the Indians at Fort Laramie and promised to protect the Indians from Whites. The government also committed to providing payment and goods for 50 years in exchange for safe roads and military posts through Sioux land, although they later reduced the compensation to 15. Chiefs who "touched the pen" (signed) to the treaty likely did not understand its contents and could not control young warriors' attacks on enemy tribes that spilled over onto Whites. Factions developed among the Sioux with older men wanting peace with the Whites and to accept their presents, while young warriors wanted the honors, status, and rank from war that their fathers had achieved. Sitting Bull was one of these young warriors with much influence on his people.

In 1854 a young U.S. Army officer precipitated armed conflict with the Sioux when his group opened fire on a Sioux village and was completely over run by Sioux warriors. More soldiers appeared who killed and captured Sioux women and children. General William Harney convened a council and made demands the chiefs could not meet—such as Indians not "lurking" near roads used by Whites. He appointed new "head chiefs" who were not recognized by the tribes but were used by the government to obtain signatures on treaties and to help distribute goods to buy Indian cooperation. One of these head chiefs was murdered by enemy Indians inside a U.S. fort when he went there for discussions with the soldiers. Eastern Sioux in Minnesota attacked White settlers surrounding their reservation and were defeated by soldiers, with survivors fleeing west to obtain shelter and protection from Sitting Bull's Hunkpapas and their neighboring tribes. Soldiers followed and more conflict developed with the Sioux being routed by soldiers with long range rifles and artillery. Soldiers then retaliated against a war party that killed an Army engineer by killing the war party and placing their heads on poles on a nearby hill. The Sioux consolidated their forces and confronted a large Army force, only to be driven off and their village, belongings, and supplies all burned. This became the pattern for much of the conflict between plains Indians and White soldiers for the next 15 years. Soldiers would attack villages, often just before dawn in mid-winter with below zero temperatures, shooting and killing indiscriminately. The surviving Indians would scatter with what they could carry while babies froze in their mothers' arms and their attackers burned everything in the village.

As war chief, Sitting Bull was pushed by young warriors to resist the White incursions and lead the attack against them. In 1865 in Colorado, a village of Southern Cheyenne (who were friends with the Sioux) was brutally attacked by a group of militia at Sand Creek. Again, survivors fled to the Sioux for protection. Sitting Bull led repeated attacks against soldiers that further built his reputation, but more forts appeared. The government initiated another treaty to clear Indians from the overland route west. Red Cloud, chief of the Oglala Sioux who had fought hard against the Whites, reached an agreement with the government whereby Whites would abandon the Bozeman Trail through his country in return for his surrender and leading his people to a reservation. The "Great Sioux Reservation" was formed containing all of what would eventually become South Dakota with "ceded territory" to its west for Indian bands that wished to live off the buffalo and not on the reservation. The government planned for the extinction of the buffalo herds that would eventually force the "hunting bands" onto the reservation. Reservation Indians were expected to stop war against other tribes and Whites, give up the buffalo hunt, obey Indian agents' regulations, and dress and live like "good Christian farmers."

Indian treaties were often fantasies of White government administrators who dictated terms in language the Indians did not understand. Sitting Bull and other Indian chiefs repeatedly stated their conditions for peace—the Whites were to leave their territory and let the Indians pursue their life according to the old ways. In 1869, Sioux chiefs made Sitting Bull the Supreme Chief of all the Sioux federation with final authority over war and peace. This was an unprecedented title and was designed to address the fractures among the different Sioux groups about the Whites. At this time, he formed a close friendship with Crazy Horse, the great Oglala Sioux warrior. Crazy Horse supported Sitting Bull's policy of continued resistance and pursuit of the buffalo in the ceded territory with minimal contact with the Whites. Sitting Bull managed to hold together a coalition of Sioux tribes that stood against the Whites for seven years in the ceded territory.

Soon the railroad began moving west with surveyors coming through Sioux territory. The railroad frightened the buffalo, split the herds, and brought more Whites with hunters who slaughtered the animals and left them to rot. In 1872, the government expected war with the Sioux over the railroad but the government was not prepared, so they authorized extra rations for Indians to keep as many as quiet as possible while they prepared for war. Sitting Bull resented government rations, but his people needed them to survive the winter. The same year, Sioux warriors seeking enemy Crows ran across a force of soldiers and the youngest warriors attacked without their chiefs' permission. The chiefs then followed the young men to provide support in the attack. This was a common occurrence among the plains Indians because they fought as individuals and only followed a particular leader into battle if he inspired them with his bravery or wisdom. During the fight, while the two forces faced one another across an open valley, Sitting Bull took his pipe and tobacco, bow and arrow, and rifle and walked out in between the two forces in full view of the soldiers. They continued shooting at him as he calmly sat on the ground and invited other Indians to join him. Several accepted his invitation and they calmly smoked his pipe with bullets whistling all around them. When the tobacco was finished, Sitting Bull cleaned his pipe, picked up his things and walked calmly back to his comrades. Sioux valued bravery in battle above all else and they viewed this as the greatest exhibition of bravery that was possible. This solidified his authority as Supreme Chief and his reputation among the Whites continued to grow.

The Black Hills were included as part of the Great Sioux Reservation. They were viewed with mystical significance and as a "meat pack" by the Sioux. They knew that game and firewood were plentiful and they could always retreat to the Black Hills and survive during hard times. But in 1874, White miners viewed the Hills as potential gold country, and General George Custer led a "surveying expedition" into the Hills accompanied by miners and newspaper writers.

The result was the discovery of gold, and miners flocked to the Hills, violating the treaty agreement. In 1875, Sitting Bull contacted the Cheyenne to solidify their long-term cooperation in resisting the White incursion. He organized a sun dance where he performed a highly symbolic dance that represented Sioux and Cheyenne unity. Meanwhile the government sought ways to extinguish Indian title to the Black Hills and approached Sitting Bull wanting to buy the Hills. He along with Crazy Horse and other Sioux chiefs refused and Sitting Bull declared he would fight Whites whenever he encountered them. President Grant then decided the government would not try to stop miners and others from entering the Black Hills and they would force the hunting bands to give up the ceded territory and move onto the remaining reservation lands. The government overstated the severity of Sioux raids on reservation Crows and Whites, and decided to "whip" the Sioux into subjection.

The war against the hunting bands was orchestrated by Civil War General Phillip Sheridan from his office in Chicago, with Generals George Crook and Alfred Terry carrying out the operation. In March 1876, they invaded and burned a Cheyenne and Sioux village in an ice fog at 40 degrees below zero, driving the survivors into the cold. They stumbled into Crazy Horse's camp, and he took them to Sitting Bull where they were fed and comforted. The leaders held a chiefs' council and agreed to fight the Whites together. A Cheyenne later described Sitting Bull as having good medicine, a brave and kind heart, and strong in Indian religion as shown by frequent prayer, fasting, and whipping his own flesh. He was considered the wisest chief and he held them together, believing their numbers would frighten the soldiers away and they could return to their old ways.

It became clear the soldiers were targeting their attacks on non-reservation Indians, not protecting roads and the railroad as promised. The Indians began to combine their camps for defensive purposes. As more bands joined Sitting Bull's camp, it had to move every two to three days to provide food and firewood. In late May 1876, Sitting Bull went to a hilltop near his village and had a dream of their village being invaded by a huge storm of soldiers, with the storm falling to pieces and the village remaining together and serene. He later described his dream to the other chiefs and its significance of an upcoming successful battle with the soldiers. He prayed to their great mystery (*Wakantanka*) and held a sun dance where 100 pieces of flesh were torn from his arms as a sacrifice. Then he danced, stared at the sun, and had another vision of many soldiers falling upside-down into their village, signifying the soldiers' death. By late June his camp numbered about 3,000 people with 800 fighting men.

Generals Crook and Terry slowly moved their large forces in search of the Sioux and began having brief contacts with Indian hunting parties. The Indian chiefs decided not to fight unless attacked, but young warriors again took the initiative and attacked Crook's force. The chiefs again supported the attack and Crook was impressed by the Indian force, retreating to his camp to await reinforcement. Sitting Bull moved their village the next day to the Little Bighorn River where they were joined by more Indians including many from the reservation who joined the summer hunt. The village then numbered 3,000 to 7,000 Indians with between 800 and 1,800 fighting men. Another sun dance was held celebrating the fight with Crook and Sitting Bull again retreated to a hilltop. His concern from his early life was for his peoples' welfare and he prayed for the protection of his people.

General George Custer had been searching for Sitting Bull's village with a force of 750 men since mid-May. The Sioux knew "Long Hair" (their name for Custer) as leader of the Black Hills incursion and other battles. Custer planned to destroy Sitting Bull's village and followed its signs for several days. He apparently was confused at the jumble of signs from their recent camps, where the latest group of Indians had arrived at the village. On the morning of June 25, 1876, from the top of the Wolf Mountains, Custer's Crow and Ree scouts spotted Sitting Bull's village in the distance and informed Custer. He misjudged its size and decided to advance and attack that same day. As Custer approached on the warm afternoon, the Indians worried about an attack by Crook. The village was alarmed to the attack as soldiers crossed the river and moved toward the village in the open space beyond. The entire village exploded in activity as men rushed to move their families to safety, painted for battle, and prepared their ponies. Meanwhile, Custer had split his force, sending a battalion under Captain Frederick Benteen to scout the area south of the village, and another battalion under Major Marcus Reno to attack the village from the south. Custer led Reno to assume he would receive support in his attack, but instead Custer led his remaining group of 210 soldiers along a ridge above the riverside village and attacked from the north.

Reno's attack opened the battle and Sitting Bull's Hunkpapa tribe was the first group they encountered. Warriors from throughout the village began massing in defense. Sitting Bull was mounted on his horse gathering the warriors together and shouting encouragement—"Brave up! Brave up!" Reno's charge stalled, and the soldiers dismounted. After about 15 minutes, they retreated into a stand of timber where they were surrounded and continuously assaulted by Indians, including Sitting Bull and his adopted son, White Bull. Crazy Horse and his Oglalas then arrived, adding more force to the Indians. Warriors began entering the timber to fight, and the soldiers started retreating across an open area to the river and hills beyond. Indians pursued them, and at least 40 soldiers were killed before they reached a flat hilltop that they could defend. Many soldiers had been injured and some left in the timber. Sitting Bull took his horse to another hilltop, where he advised the warriors to let the remaining soldiers go so they could tell others of their defeat. Then word spread that another attack was coming from the north, and the Indians left Reno's hill, swarming to defend against Custer's attack at the other end of the village. They surrounded Custer's force from all sides. The Indians had superior numbers and many had excellent rifles taken from fallen soldiers. Custer and his force of around 210 soldiers were killed within about half an hour.

The next day Sitting Bull again counseled to let Reno's remaining force go to tell other soldiers of the Indians' victory. He also told them other soldiers were coming, which was true, so they abandoned the siege on Reno's troops and moved the village. Four days later they held a victory dance—it was the biggest Sioux and Cheyenne victory they ever experienced with over 250 soldiers killed and many wounded. The victory fulfilled Sitting Bull's vision. The importance of Sitting Bull's leadership against the Custer attack lay in keeping together a coalition of several tribes to resist the expected attack and inspiring them to fight and resist the onslaught. Unfortunately for the Indians, their victory stunned the United States population and government into a revenge mentality and more money, troops, and authority were committed to end the "Sioux problem" for good.

Shortly after the Little Bighorn battle, the Indians scattered to hunt buffalo and some returned to the reservation. General Crook tried to follow them but gave up and started returning for supplies, when he ran across a large village containing Sitting Bull and other chiefs. With his men exhausted, Crook attacked and burned the village with little loss of life, and then retreated. The United States Congress stopped all rations to the Indians and insisted on reservation chiefs signing over title to the Black Hills and giving up the ceded territory where the hunting bands lived. These chiefs did not even live in these areas, and the government ignored the earlier treaty requirement that 75% of adult males must agree. With the signatures of reservation chiefs, the government declared Indian title "extinguished" to these areas, and General Sherman plotted total war against the hunting bands. He had all reservation Cheyennes disarmed and dismounted and planned to occupy the buffalo lands and harass the Sioux until they surrendered and entered the reservation.

In October 1876 Sitting Bull was confronted by General Nelson Miles and a large force. They conferred for two days with no agreement. Miles then attacked with little damage, and the Indians scattered. Soon after the Miniconjous and Sans Arc tribes (who were allies of the Sioux), along with Sitting Bull's nephew White Bull, surrendered to the soldiers. Sitting Bull could see his coalition of tribes was coming apart. The winter of 1876–77 was terrible for the hunting bands—with soldiers occupying their hunting lands and attacking and burning their villages at every opportunity. Surrender meant giving up their guns and horses and moving onto the reservation—the end of their culture, which was based on the hunt and war with enemy tribes. Sitting Bull could not give up their entire way of life. In December, five chiefs approached General Miles to talk and were shot down by Crow Army scouts. In May 1877, Crazy Horse and his Oglala Sioux surrendered in Nebraska along with 300 Sioux. That May, Sitting Bull and his group crossed into Canada.

The Sioux were well received by the newly established Canadian Mounted Police. Major James Walsh met with Sitting Bull and apparently had compassion for their poor treatment in the United States. Although the United States government advocated their return, Sitting Bull refused and planned to stay in Canada. Things went well for them at first, but, in September 1877, Crazy Horse was killed in a dispute while in the custody of soldiers. His 2,000 followers left the reservation and joined Sitting Bull in Canada, followed by Nez Perce Indians in 1878. His camp then numbered about 5,000 with 1,500 warriors. Between 1877 and 1881 hide hunters decimated the buffalo herds to near extinction. Intertribal conflicts developed between Canadian tribes and the newly arrived Indians, who faced starvation while the Canadian government tried to provide resources and keep the peace.

Although Sitting Bull made peace with neighboring tribes, young braves raided reservation Indians and Whites in the United States. Other Sioux, including Sitting Bull, crossed the border to hunt. General Miles advanced along with a group of Crow scouts to drive them back to Canada. During a conflict, one large Crow warrior boasted he would kill Sitting Bull, who answered his challenge. In full view of both groups of Indians, he killed the Crow in single combat and, after taking his scalp and magnificent horse, the Sioux returned to Canada. In 1879 the Canadian government decided to pressure the Sioux to return to the United States. Major Walsh was replaced by another mounted police officer who began undermining Sitting Bull's authority with the Indians. He did not acknowledge him as chief and treated him without respect. The Mounties began breaking off small groups of Indians and convincing them that they would fare better on the United States reservations. These groups began returning to the United States until Sitting Bull's band was reduced to mostly women, children, and older men. Finally, a trader he trusted convinced Sitting Bull he must return and supplied and accompanied him across the border to surrender at Fort Buford in July 1881. His people were starving, and their clothing was in pieces; some Indians were completely naked.

His band was immediately put aboard a steamship and headed down the Missouri River to Bismarck, North Dakota, which had become a bustling city. There people flocked to see the great Sioux Chief Sitting Bull. He was allowed to leave the ship and was thronged with onlookers. He maintained his typical dignity and good humor; having learned to write his name, he signed autographs and learned he could earn between $2 and $5 per autograph (although they were free for women). He marveled at the city and was entertained with other chiefs at a large banquet. The Sioux reboarded the steamer and were taken to Fort Yates at the Standing Rock Reservation in North Dakota where other Sioux were kept. Sitting Bull had been told he could live at Standing Rock with relatives and old friends, but government officials changed their minds and moved him to Fort Randall in South Dakota, where he was kept as a prisoner of war for 19 months. In early 1882, Robert Lincoln, son of President Abraham Lincoln, was Secretary of War and was informed of Sitting Bull's status. He took action to allow him to return to Standing Rock and live with his people.

Sitting Bull continued to view himself as supreme leader and holy man for his people. But the Indian agent at Standing Rock, James McLaughlin, was a condescending and authoritarian individual who was determined to change all the Sioux into "civilized farmers." Sitting Bull sought to maintain as many of the old Sioux ways as possible, although he considered all government measures and approved of some and not others. His position placed him in opposition to McLaughlin, who was determined to undermine his authority with the Indians. The government coveted more of the Great Sioux Reservation, having already extinguished Indian title to the Black Hills. Proposals were made to the chiefs that individual title would be given for smaller plots to each family and the remainder, "surplus Sioux lands," would be opened up to homesteaders. Sitting Bull and other chiefs actively opposed this at meetings with government officials, and he was viciously insulted by a government representative. In 1889, this government land grab eventually succeeded when officials exploited factions they created within the Sioux and gained enough signatures to take more of their land. The government immediately reduced food rations for the Indians.

Meanwhile, McLaughlin exploited Sitting Bull's popularity and status by taking him to celebrations and public gatherings. He was allowed to participate in road shows for two years (including one with Buffalo Bill Cody, who became a friend) and his popularity continued. At first McLaughlin felt the exposure to the White world would win over the chief to their ways, but Sitting Bull maintained his devotion to the Sioux ways and McLaughlin refused to allow his participation in the shows to continue.

The government policies and programs were completely destroying the traditional Sioux culture. In 1889 they heard of a savior in the west who could help restore their old ways and rid their lands of all Whites and soldiers. The Sioux sent representatives to investigate and they returned convinced the savior was genuine. He was a Piute Indian named Wovoka and he preached a combination of traditional Indian and Christian religions. Central to his mystical teaching was a Ghost Dance that all the people participated in. Sitting Bull was apparently skeptical of Wovoka, but as the Sioux wanted to hold the Ghost Dance, he approved. It became very popular, and McLaughlin and others worried that it meant a Sioux uprising. They asked Sitting Bull to stop the dance, but he resisted, pointing out that Indians should be free to practice their own religion just as White people did.

McLaughlin and military officers developed a plan to have Sitting Bull arrested and moved to another location so they could eliminate the Ghost Dance. He told the Indian police that under no condition should Sitting Bull be allowed to escape. On December 15, 1890, the police were sent in the early morning to the log home on the reservation where Sitting Bull lived with his family. They broke in and handled him roughly, finally allowing him to dress before he left with them. He provided no resistance and agreed to go. But a crowd gathered and became raucous. Shooting broke out and two Indian policemen immediately shot Sitting Bull. He died instantly. Others were shot on both sides, and the Indian police barricaded themselves in Sitting Bull's log house. There they discovered his young son, Crowfoot, hiding under some blankets. They beat him with a rifle butt and shot him to death. The police were rescued soon after by soldiers. McLaughlin later had Sitting Bull buried in a pauper's grave on the reservation. When Major James Walsh, the Canadian Mounted Police officer who had befriended Sitting Bull heard of his death, he described him as the Mohammed of his people, the law and kingmaker of the Sioux.

Sitting Bull was probably first and foremost a Servant Leader for his people—the Hunkpapas and other Sioux tribes. In his visions, negotiations, decisions, and actions as a chief, he *devoted himself to the safety and preservation of his people* and their way of life. Even before he became a chief, he was known for his generosity in meeting the needs of the less fortunate members of his tribe. He can also be viewed from Implicit Leadership Theory as meeting the criteria of an ideal Sioux male—reflecting the four cardinal virtues of bravery, fortitude, generosity, and wisdom. His excellence in these virtues qualified him as a great leader to be emulated by other Sioux males. He was clearly a Charismatic Leader through his *inspiration* of followers by setting an example of bravery and *risk taking* in battle, by having *visions* that predicted important future events for his people, via repeated *personal sacrifices* in sun dance ceremonies, and his consistent (though unsuccessful) *mission* of driving the Whites from Sioux territory. He exhibited *supportive leadership* by generosity to the poor and needy as well as decisions that he believed would benefit his people. This leader behavior is described in Fiedler's Contingency Theory, Situational Leadership Theory, and Path-Goal Theory. He demonstrated *boundary spanning* in his leadership by forming alliances with other tribes and maintaining a coalition of tribes for many years to resist the white invasion. This behavior is described in the Multiple Linkage Model and Reformulated Path-Goal Theories. He showed *participative leadership* during much of his time as chief by working with village councils to make consensus decisions that benefitted their people. This leadership behavior is described in the Normative Decision Theory. Finally, Sitting Bull's overall leadership can be criticized from a contingency theory perspective in that he never modified his overall objectives for his people (driving the Whites from Sioux territory), even when it became clear that they could not defeat the White soldiers. His *determination* and *integrity* reflect Trait Theories of leadership.

Discussion Questions

1. How does the Implicit Leadership Theory (ILT) for a Sioux war chief during Sitting Bull's time differ from an ILT for a military leader in the United States Army at that time? How does it differ from a military leader in today's army or in a business today?
2. Do you believe Sitting Bull was an effective Servant Leader? Why or why not?
3. A well-known western historian has described Sitting Bull as an American patriot. Do you agree and why or why not?
4. In what ways could Sitting Bull have been a more effective leader of the Sioux?

References

Sitting Bull. (n.d.). In *Wikipedia*. Retrieved May 24, 2010, from http://en.wikipedia.org/wiki/Sitting_Bull

Utley, R. M. (1993). *Sitting Bull: The life and times of an American patriot*. New York: Henry Holt.

Chapter 25

Indra Nooyi
CEO of PepsiCo

Indra Nooyi is chief executive officer and chairperson of PepsiCo Incorporated—the largest manufacturer, distributor and marketer of soft drinks and snacks in the United States. PepsiCo major brands include Pepsi, Frito-Lay, Tropicana, Gatorade, and Quaker Oats. It operates in over 200 countries, generated over $60 billion in revenues in 2011, and earns almost half of its revenue outside the United States. Nooyi has been CEO of PepsiCo since 2006 and she has directed a major strategic shift in direction that has diversified the company to overcome poor conditions in specific markets and to emphasize healthy products for an increasingly health conscious world. Her leadership has resulted in significant increases in corporate revenues and profits and is creating a more sustainable and socially responsible company. She is a United States citizen and was rated by Fortune magazine as the number one most powerful woman in business in 2009 and 2010.

Indra Nooyi was born in a middle-class family on the southeast coast of India on October 28, 1955. As a youth she was unusual, playing in an all-girl rock band and a women's cricket team. She received a bachelor's degree from Madras Christian College and an MBA from the Indian Institute of Management in 1976. After graduating, she held jobs in India as a product manager at Johnson and Johnson and a textile firm. Seeing an advertisement for the Yale School of Management, she applied and was accepted in 1978. After obtaining permission from her parents (who believed her immigration would make her completely unmarriageable), she left for the United States and worked nights as a dorm receptionist to earn a master's degree in public and private management at Yale in 1980. She then joined the Boston Consulting Group and worked on international strategy projects until 1986, moved to Motorola for four years where she directed corporate strategy and planning, and then worked for Asea Brown Boveri until 1994 as senior vice president of corporate strategy and marketing. In 1994 she began at PepsiCo as senior vice president of corporate strategy and development and held this position until 2001 when she was named president and chief financial officer.

As chief strategist at PepsiCo, she worked to make the company's products both profitable and healthy. She pushed then CEO Roger Enrico to spin off its struggling fast food restaurant division of Kentucky Fried Chicken, Pizza Hut, and Taco Bell in 1997. She saw more future in healthier product lines with beverages and packaged foods. In 1999 she engineered and directed the $3 billion acquisition of Tropicana and in 2001 the $14 billion takeover of Quaker Oats, maker of Gatorade. She led the negotiation team for Quaker Oats and she was described as disciplined, focused, and very firm in her approach. The morning the acquisition was announced, she went to the Hindu temple and prayed. These acquisitions greatly enhanced the company's offerings of functional healthy foods and earnings rose quickly. She also directed the removal of trans fats from PepsiCo products well before other companies.

Howard Schultz, president and CEO of Starbucks, has worked with Nooyi. He has been especially impressed with her willingness to do the right thing for her customers and employees. He further described her as welcoming input from others who disagree with her, but she is single-minded about following the path she believes is best for the company. Another observer described her as a deeply caring and considerate person who communicates well with people on the front line as well as the board room. When Nooyi was selected for the CEO position, she immediately flew to visit with the other finalist who was the top operations manager for PepsiCo. They had worked together for a long time and she appealed to him to stay and help her continue creating her vision of the company. She told him she would do whatever was needed to keep him. She then enlisted three other company executives to help her convince the board to increase his salary to almost match her own and he stayed, resulting in what one writer called her team of rivals. This personal approach is characteristic of her leadership style, taking the time to listen to people who need to speak with her regardless of whether they agree with her.

Nooyi allows her culture to affect her leadership and behavior at work and often wears a sari to official functions. In traditional Indian culture, mothers are often highly involved in their children's lives. After her promotion at PepsiCo,

Indra (who is married with two children) visited her mother in India where they entertained many family friends. Indra noticed the visitors paid the most attention to her mother, congratulating her on doing such a fine job raising such a successful daughter. Indra remembered this and began writing thank you notes to the mothers of her major executives. She thanked them for doing such a wonderful job raising their child and how their son or daughter was doing an outstanding job for PepsiCo. The mothers were delighted and the executives appreciated her notes.

Shortly after becoming CEO, she announced her corporate mission for PepsiCo, which she calls "performance with purpose." Its intent is to combine financial performance with social responsibility with each element reinforcing the other. She describes her vision for the company as having three pillars that support the mission. The first element is human sustainability—providing products that include healthy choices such as low sugar and low calorie drinks for health conscious consumers. The second pillar is environmental sustainability—helping maintain the planet through increasingly efficient use of water, energy, and biodegradable packaging for all its products. The third element is sustainability of talent—attracting, training, and retaining the best people by providing a supportive healthy workplace where people can have a life in addition to their work. She encourages people to have fun at work, as she occasionally sings in the hallways, goes barefoot in the office, and sings karaoke at home and at corporate retreats.

With a market capitalization of nearly $100 billion, she notes that PepsiCo is larger than many countries and has tremendous influence in the world. She states repeatedly that the company must be a constructive member of the global society by encouraging a healthier future for people and the planet. She believes only this approach will assure sustainable growth for the company. Nooyi is an inspirational speaker on behalf of her vision. She has pledged that half of PepsiCo's revenue from the United States will come from healthful products such as oatmeal and Gatorade, they will seek to replace fossil fuels with wind and solar power, and they will actively campaign against obesity.

She describes herself as a workaholic and her position as more than a job. She often seeks help and information from colleagues and maintains close contact with several former CEOs. She has very high goals for herself and others and gives negative feedback when needed, often combining it with humor. She pushes people to solve problems until they find a solution, such as finding a replacement for unhealthy palm oil that was used in PepsiCo's products (rice bran oil was the replacement). She is a strong believer in the importance of boundary spanning as a leader of her company. She works to stay connected with important organizations and people in business and government. She often does this through service on boards, foundations, councils and international business forums that promote the arts, universities, world economic development, and other humanitarian causes. She believes leaders must work with governments and nongovernmental organizations to understand their perspective and avoid becoming adversaries. She describes much of her job as traveling to different areas of the world to meet employees and customers and spending quality time in these locations to learn the needs, desires and cultural influences on the consumers of their products. She recently committed to invest $140 million in a new beverage plant in Russia, which is the tenth PepsiCo plant in Russia. She strongly believes that organizations today must think and act with a global perspective and strives to emphasize this at PepsiCo. Nooyi's socially responsible agenda for PepsiCo is reflected in her own plans for the future. She has stated that after her time at PepsiCo, she hopes to continue her service in Washington D.C.

Indra Nooyi's leadership can be described as *charismatic/transformational* due to her clear *vision* and *mission* to change the focus of PepsiCo toward more healthy products and socially responsible actions. While PepsiCo was doing well when she became CEO, she was determined to push her mission of human, environmental and talent sustainability to assure the company is a good global citizen and continues to prosper in the future. In addition, her excellent *communication skills, willingness to listen,* and *considerate supportive style* inspire people to join in her efforts to transform the company. These leader behaviors are addressed in models of Charismatic/Transformational Leadership and *considerate/supportiveness* is described in several other leadership models including Fiedler's Contingency Theory, Situational Leadership Theory, and Path-Goal Theory. Nooyi clearly emphasizes *boundary spanning* behavior in her leadership as she serves on numerous boards and foundations to build networks and travels throughout the world to connect with consumers and producers of PepsiCo products. This behavior pattern is described in the Multiple Linkage Model and Reformulated Path-Goal Theories of leadership. She is also a highly *directive* leader when she determines to pursue a course of action. She focuses on specific issues and assures that her staff members contribute toward the goals she sets. This leader behavior is also described in Fiedler's Contingency Theory, Situational Leadership Theory and Path-Goal Theory. When facing big decisions, she often consults with others who are informed about the issue and exhibits some *participative leadership* in these situations. The Normative Decision Theory describes this behavior pattern. Nooyi's *cognitive capacity, determination, self-confident, sociability,* and *integrity* reflect most elements of Trait Theories of leadership.

Discussion Questions

1. Why has the vision and mission for PepsiCo outlined by Indra Nooyi been so well received by customers and employees?
2. Why does Nooyi believe she must spend much of her time boundary spanning (especially networking and representing) for PepsiCo?
3. Why did Indra Nooyi believe she needed to change the strategic focus of PepsiCo?
4. Do you believe Nooyi's charismatic/transformational and supportive leadership style will be effective if she enters government service in Washington D.C.? Why or why not?

References

Halpern, T. (n.d.). Indra K. Nooyi. Reference for Business: Business Biographies. Retrieved on October 19, 2010, from http://www.referenceforbusiness.com/biography/M-R/Nooyi-Indra-K-1955.html

Indra Nooyi. (n.d.). In *Wikipedia*. Retrieved October 19, 2010, from http://en.wikipedia.org/wiki/Indra_Nooyi

PepsiCo. (n.d.). Indra K. Nooyi-Chairman and chief executive officer. Retrieved October 21, 2010, from http://pepsico.com/Company/Leadership.aspx

The Boston Consulting Group. (n.d.). Performance with purpose: Indra K. Nooyi. Retrieved October 21, 2010, from http://www.leadership.bcg.com/americas/nooyi.aspx

Withrow, S. (April 13, 2010). Tuesday Tip Indra Nooyi 11 April 2010. *Mountain Lakes International*. Retrieved from http://www.mountainlakesinternational.com/?tag=indra-nooyi

Chapter 26

Horatio Nelson
*Vice Admiral of the British
Royal Navy*

Horatio Nelson was probably the most famous naval leader in British history. In 1805, after years of daring and largely successful naval battles in which he did not always obey orders, Nelson led a force of 27 warships against 33 French and Spanish ships in the Battle of Trafalgar. Nelson's force destroyed the French and Spanish navy and thus eliminated the possibility of Napoleon invading England with his army, which was one of his major objectives. Although he was killed at Trafalgar, Nelson was a master of naval leadership and, during his life, he gained the respect and adoration of the British people and much of Europe.

Nelson was born in Norfolk, near the eastern coast of England, on September 29, 1758. He was the sixth of eleven children and his mother died when he was nine. His father, Reverend Edmund Nelson, was a kind and caring individual who was not especially practical. Reverend Nelson did not remarry, choosing to raise his large family and care for his congregation and surrounding land on his own. Young Nelson had to compete for attention in his large family. He attended boarding school and learned to rely on himself with older and larger boys; he was a small boy and only five feet six inches tall in adulthood. At 12 he convinced his uncle, who was a naval captain, to take him to sea and he was appointed a midshipman on his uncle's warship.

When his uncle was transferred, Horatio served as an ordinary seaman on a merchant vessel to the West Indies (the Caribbean Sea and islands) where he learned that how an officer treats his men directly affects their attitude and reactions to the officer. A year later he was back on his uncle's warship learning navigation and piloting his uncle to and from shore. His uncle made sure Horatio had the necessary introductions and opportunities, but Horatio was highly self-confident, anxious to learn, and willing to push himself forward. At 14, he accompanied an expedition to the North Pole and gained valuable experience with a well-organized captain. He then served on several different warships and learned the importance of using one's authority in order to have it recognized and the damage that can accrue to young officers when they are mistreated. He contracted malaria in the East Indies (India and Southeast Asia) and experienced his first bout of depression on his trip home to England. He managed to pull himself out and resolved to be a hero for his country and to face any danger that he confronted. The remainder of his professional life he persisted in living up to this image—brave, decisive, unflinching in battle, constantly aware of the example he set for other officers and men, and anxious to attack and destroy the enemies of his country.

In April 1777 he passed his lieutenant's examination and received his commission. He was assigned to the HMS *Lowestoffe* under Captain William Locker and sailed for Jamaica. While in the West Indies, he helped capture several American and French ships, was promoted to post-captain in 1779 (at 20 years of age) and given a 28 gun frigate to command. After helping capture several more American ships and supporting a ground attack to capture Spanish colonies in Nicaragua, he had a recurrence of malaria and returned to England to recuperate. Within a year he was commanding another frigate accompanying convoys in the North Sea and North Atlantic. At one point he was confronted by three larger French warships and a French frigate. With no chance in battle, he retreated and used the advice of a captured American and his own piloting skill to enter shallow water where the larger French ships could not follow. He then turned on the French frigate, clearly showing desire to fight, and the French ship fled. With gratitude for the American's assistance, he released him and his vessel, only to have him return with gifts of fresh vegetables and meat for Nelson. He immediately shared these with his crew, who had been at sea for months without fresh food, thus demonstrating his spirit of fair play and support for his crew, which became part of his public image.

While in North America, Nelson demonstrated his susceptibility to the spell cast by pretty young women. Biographers record numerous women who captured his emotions even after his marriage. His extremely competent and exemplary behavior aboard ship was simply not matched by his repeated difficulties with women and money on land. Peace was signed with the Americans, and he was given another frigate and again sent to the West Indies to enforce the Navigation Act governing trade with the remaining British colonies in that region. He was dissatisfied that it was not a larger ship and there was no enemy to fight. But observers report his regular and careful attention to the young midshipmen who served on his ship. He taught them navigation, visited their class room, and raced them to the masthead. Midshipmen would repeat his phrases and commit them to memory. In 1787, he met and married a young widow named Francis "Fanny" Nisbet whose father had owned a plantation on the island of Nevis. He returned to England later that year and his wife soon followed with her five-year-old son, Josiah. Nelson was placed on half pay and spent the next five years on land.

This was not a happy time for Nelson. He was constantly wrangling with the admiralty for another ship and his new wife was not interested in society and hesitant to leave the home of Nelson's father, with whom they were living. Nelson also suffered from his limited income and made several requests to his uncle for money. Some captains became rich by capturing enemy vessels and having them sold or taken over by the Royal Navy for compensation ("prize money"). Nelson had not prospered in this manner. In early 1793 it was clear that the French revolutionary government was on a war footing on the European mainland and England began preparations for war. Nelson was given a 64 gun ship, the *Agamemnon*, and war was declared in February of the same year.

Horatio was 35, viewed as polite and agreeable, and assured that the needs of his crew were met by providing gifts of special foods while in port. He had learned that a well-fed crew was essential to a well-run ship. His stepson, Josiah, had gone to sea with Nelson since they could not afford his study for law. His wife, Fanny, retreated even further during his absence, and it began to be clear that she was a far second to his career. Early during this period, he met William Hamilton, the British ambassador to the kingdom of Naples, and his young and enchanting wife, Emma. France occupied Corsica, and England needed a naval base in that area. Nelson played a key role in successful land assaults on Corsica and was wounded in one eye when a shell hit his gun emplacement. He dismissed it as trivial at first but soon permanently lost the sight in that eye. In these actions, Nelson showed his abilities to cooperate with other military officers who did not avoid action, as well as the capacity to inspire and motivate his men to almost superhuman efforts in moving their ship's nine foot guns up mountains to support the land assaults. He also showed that given an objective, he conveyed it clearly to his men and they did everything possible to achieve it. Nelson did not receive the official credit he felt he deserved for these actions. It was not uncommon for some officers to take more credit than they deserve for successful actions. This frustrated and angered Nelson during much of his career. He expected full credit for his contributions and accomplishments and was generous in giving credit to his officers when they performed well. This active and continued support for awards and promotions for his junior officers added to his popularity.

In 1795 he severely damaged a much larger French ship (the *Ca Ira*) and played a key role in capturing that and another ship the following day. Nelson wanted to pursue the fleeing French, but his admiral declined. Nelson was vocal in his dissatisfaction with the admiral's decision and with the credit given to others for this action and capture. In late 1795 a different admiral was assigned to the Mediterranean who was more aggressive, and he instantly took to the charming and friendly Nelson. Horatio was 37, had experienced the horror of battle, but remained calm and confident. He was able to inspire his men to take pride in their ship and crew and to hate the enemy as he did. He was humane and considerate of his crew and aroused in them the belief that there was almost nothing they could not do. He showed an interest in his officers and men as individuals and encouraged, coached and disciplined them when necessary. He set and communicated high goals for his ship and demonstrated amazing physical and moral strength to persist longer than most captains in pursuing these goals. When his new admiral offered Nelson a larger warship, he declined and chose to stay with his smaller ship with its faithful team of officers and crew. He captured several small French vessels during the ensuing months and was promoted to commodore in 1796.

Later that year his ship was returned to England for repairs, and Nelson was assigned a larger ship, the 74 gun *Captain*, and instructed to blockade the French coast and intercept French shipping. Several key cities were lost to the French, forcing the British evacuation of the Mediterranean. During this process he captured a Spanish ship placing one of his best lieutenants in charge (the Spanish were now aligned with the French). He was soon confronted by a superior Spanish force of several ships. Nelson prepared for battle but his lieutenant sacrificed the captured ship, allowing himself to be captured and Nelson to flee. Shortly thereafter, Nelson helped arrange a prisoner exchange for his captured lieutenant, inspiring further loyalty from his crew.

Nelson's new admiral, Sir John Jervis, soon encountered the Spanish fleet off Cape St. Vincent and moved to engage. Nelson's ship was near the end of the battle line created to attack the Spanish. He realized that Jervis had misestimated his turning point to begin the attack, which left the British line vulnerable and might allow the heart of the Spanish fleet to escape. At the same time his friend, Captain Troubridge of the *Culloden,* who had led the attack, was heavily engaged. Nelson diverged from the battle plan, leaving the battle line and attacking two larger enemy ships near Troubridge. In 30 minutes Nelson and

Troubridge's ships were both badly damaged, but other British ships had finally arrived to help. Nelson's other friend, Captain Collingwood, severely damaged two other Spanish ships, passed between Nelson and his opponents issuing devastating broadsides to the two enemy ships, and moved on to engage the Spanish Admiral's flagship. Nelson had his ship crash into the nearest enemy. He then accompanied the boarding party wielding his sword and succeeded in capturing both Spanish ships that he had attacked. The result was a great victory for the British, and it was clear that Nelson's perceptiveness and creative interpretation of his admiral's unclear signals were the major difference in the battle. He was given much credit for the victory along with Troubridge and Collingwood. Always concerned about promoting his own image, he published his own account of the battle while giving credit to the other captains. Nelson was promoted to rear admiral and knighted after this battle.

Later that year Nelson was aboard the lead attack ship in a bombardment of the Spanish city of Cadiz. In repelling a Spanish counter attack, he jumped into his own boat and had his men row furiously directly at the enemy. In the ensuing man to man combat, Nelson's life was saved twice by one of his crewmen, who incurred serious injury. This personal involvement and risk in battle was a tremendous example to his men, although it was arguably unwise for a battle commander to risk his life unnecessarily with the possible loss of control of his forces if he was killed or seriously injured. Soon after, he planned an attack on Tenerife in the Spanish Canary Islands to seize a Spanish treasure ship. The Spaniards were well prepared and the attack was not successful. Nelson was shot in the arm as he personally led one of the attack battalions on shore. His stepson, Josiah, immediately placed a tourniquet on the gushing wound and probably saved Nelson's life. Returning to his ship, he refused assistance in boarding and immediately ordered the surgeon to remove his arm, which had a badly shattered bone. Shortly later he was again in command of the battle. Despite being defeated, Nelson's reputation for exemplary behavior continued to grow. He returned to England and received a hero's welcome. His wound and missing arm became a symbol of his sacrifice for England and added to his charisma in the public eye.

In 1798, Napoleon gathered the French forces in southern France. Nelson was recovered enough to take command of a new ship and sent to the Mediterranean. Napoleon sailed with his force for an unknown destination and Nelson was sent in pursuit. He finally found the French fleet in Abu Qir Bay, near Alexandria, Egypt, in the late afternoon of on August 1. Napoleon had disembarked his army and planned to take Egypt. The French were anchored in a defensive line in the bay, saw the British arrival, and assumed they would wait until morning to attack. They were anchored near a shallow sandbank to prevent the British from getting behind their battle line, and planned to fight with broadsides from one side of their ships. Lumber and other materials were stacked on the inland side. Nelson ordered an immediate attack, led by Captain Tom Foley. As Foley approached the French, he noticed that each French ship was using a single anchor and allowing their stern to swing with the tide. He recalled a Nelson phrase that if an enemy ship could swing, one of their own ships could take the advantage. He realized that he could navigate around the first French gunship and maneuver onto the other side of the French line where they were unprepared. He did so and was followed by several other British ships. Other British ships approached from outside of the French line and all anchored from their sterns and attacked the front of the French line from both sides. The result was devastating because other French ships down the line could not sail up against the wind to help. The battle raged into the night. Nelson, always on deck during a battle unless he was wounded, was hit by a piece of shrapnel in his forehead that tore off enough skin to cover his one good eye. At first Nelson thought he was killed, but his surgeon bandaged the flesh wound and Nelson resumed command. The French flagship *Orient* caught fire and completely exploded at about ten in the evening. By morning, few French ships were in condition to fight and only four escaped to the open sea. The French fleet in the Mediterranean was destroyed with no loss of British ships.

Nelson sailed his badly damaged ship to Naples, an independent kingdom at that time, and was greeted as a hero by the King and the British ambassador, Sir William Hamilton, who invited him to stay at his home. Numerous celebrations followed with honors for Nelson. He hoped to be made a viscount in England, but was made Baron of the Nile (a slightly lower level title). His stay in Naples began his infatuation with Emma Hamilton, the young wife of the British ambassador, and he was soon in love. Emma was incredibly beautiful and had been mistress to British noblemen, including Sir William, for five years before their marriage in 1791. He was 60 when they married; she was 24. Nelson spent the next two years trying to contain French expansion in the area. He helped evacuate and then reoccupy Naples, and he participated in the execution of several people who had cooperated with the French, but had been offered amnesty by the leader of the army of Naples. Nelson received public criticism for these actions. His relationship with Emma steadily grew during these years with little apparent concern by her husband, who seems to have admired Nelson as much as Emma. Emma became pregnant with Nelson's daughter, Horatia, during this time. He returned to England with the Hamiltons via land to applauding crowds—Nelson had become an icon of military valor. A few months earlier, Napoleon overthrew the French government and placed himself in charge.

Nelson had been gone from England for two years and his return was punctuated by public adoration and personal difficulties with his wife, Fanny. She accompanied him with the Hamiltons to several social events, but Emma's pregnancy was becoming obvious and Nelson's treatment of Fanny was neither affectionate nor kind. Nelson chose to spend Christmas with the Hamiltons rather than with Fanny and his father. Shortly thereafter, she left him, and he ignored her subsequent attempts for reconciliation.

In early 1801, Nelson was assigned as second in command to join a fleet to deal with an alliance of Russian, Danish, Swedish, and Prussian governments. The alliance was determined to break a British blockade of French merchant ships in the Baltic Sea that was interrupting their trade with France. Nelson generally demonstrated a very positive and likeable disposition. In route to the Baltic, however, he was alternately depressed and elated. Difficulties with Fanny, separation from Emma and his new daughter, and conflicts with his admiral, who he viewed as inferior, all probably contributed to his mental state. When they arrived off Copenhagen, his admiral decided to wait and let the combined alliance of fleets come to them but Nelson protested violently that they should attack Copenhagen harbor before the other fleets could arrive. He spent five hours with the admiral and other officers, and finally offered the admiral three choices of how they should attack. With other officers' help, he then maneuvered the admiral to choose the best option. The admiral offered to stay outside the well-defended Copenhagen harbor to prevent Danish ships from escaping. Nelson then realized he was really in command of the attack. He planned the attack and held his typical war council to clarify his plan and answer all questions. The attack was severe for both sides and after several hours, Nelson's admiral gave the signal to withdraw. Nelson raised his eye glass to his blind eye, said he did not see the signal, and continued the attack. After five hours, the Danes had lost nearly all their ships, but shore batteries kept firing. Nelson asked for a truce and was able to negotiate a complete cessation of fighting. The Danes agreed to leave their alliance which, with the timely death of the Russian czar, effectively ended the threat to the British blockade with no loss of British ships. Nelson had essentially won another battle and wasted no time in letting England know through letters and conversations with well-connected individuals.

Nelson then took charge of defending the English Channel to assure the French armies could not carry out their plans to invade England. He ordered a limited attack on the port of Boulogne using small boats at night to try to capture several gunboats, but the attack failed. Nelson took all responsibility for the failure and again became despondent and ill. He had often complained of illness at sea, especially during his depressed periods. The loss of eyesight in one eye and

fading sight in the other, his missing right arm that made eating and writing difficult, several other smaller wounds, problems with Fanny, missing Emma and
his new daughter, constant concerns over money when Emma spent money like
water, and worries about whether he had already experienced his greatest victory
all accumulated to create tremendous strain on the 43-year-old vice admiral. A
temporary peace was signed with France, and he returned to England for a year
with Emma and his daughter.

By 1803 it was clear that France had maintained her warlike policies and
England was in danger. England declared war, and Nelson was given command
of the Mediterranean fleet. He took his 100 gun ship *Victory* to join the blockade
of French ships at the French naval center at Toulon. While he was on patrol,
the French fleet escaped Toulon and departed for the West Indies with Nelson
in pursuit. Unknown to the English, Napoleon planned to lure Nelson away,
then hurry back to France to combine with several other French squadrons and
take control of the English channel for eight hours. This was enough time to get
Napoleon's troops over the channel to attack England. The French were engaged
by a British fleet under Sir Robert Calder and they went into a French port with
minor losses. Nelson returned to England and began planning a great battle with
the French, only to learn that the French and Spanish had joined forces and were
anchored at the Spanish port of Cadiz.

It was September, 1805, and Nelson said goodbye to Emma and went straight
to Cadiz to prepare his force for battle. He devised a tactic that would split his
force into two squadrons that would cut the enemy battle line into three sections. Similar to the Nile battle, this would allow Nelson's fleet to concentrate
their ships on portions of the enemy battle line while other enemy ships could
not come up against the wind to help. Unknown to the British, Napoleon had
temporarily postponed his invasion plans for England, and his French admiral
was hesitant to engage the British. But Napoleon decided to replace his admiral,
who took his fleet to sea before the new admiral could arrive. Nelson reminded
his officers that they were free to do their best as long as they understood and
adhered to his overall plan. He knew that once the battle started, things were
mostly out of his control. He therefore endeavored to be perfectly clear about his
battle plan and answered all questions as they arose.

At 4 a.m. on October 21, Nelson signaled his fleet to battle stations. He went
below and wrote his will, wrote a prayer, then returned to the deck. He had 27
ships to face 33 enemy ships, which Nelson considered good odds. He told his
captains he wanted to capture 20 enemy ships. As they approached the enemy
battle line, his fleet captain suggested he remove his admiral's coat as it would be
a target for enemy snipers. Nelson refused. Others suggested he move to another

ship to better observe the action and that a different ship should take the lead. Nelson refused. Leading the first line of attack, the *Victory* came under heavy fire very early. Nelson's secretary was killed as well as his replacement, the *Victory*'s wheel was shot away and she had to be steered from below decks. Her sails, masts, and the marine sharpshooters aloft were decimated. All this occurred before she entered the enemy line and went alongside the enemy admiral's flagship to begin her own firing. The British gunners were the best at sea, and the death and damage they created was horrible. Nelson and his captain continued to walk the deck, directing the firing and trying to keep as much order as possible.

French snipers in the enemy ships fired continuously at people on the *Victory*'s deck, and, in the early afternoon, Nelson was fatally wounded by a sniper on the French ship *Redoutable* and was taken below deck. The bullet had punctured his lung and lodged in his lower spine. He is said to have given a final order to a midshipman about guiding the ship as he was carried below. He knew he was dying but wanted to follow the battle. His captain and good friend, Hardy, came below somewhat later and reported that 12 or 14 enemy ships had surrendered and the battle was going well. The downwind enemy ships left the area, and the battle was won with 19 enemy ships eventually captured and no British ship lost. Nelson ordered Hardy to anchor the ship, asked that Emma and his daughter be cared for, and thanked God he had done his duty. He lived long enough to realize his great victory that had saved England from Napoleon's eventual invasion. His final victory, known as the Battle of Trafalgar, marked the beginning of 100 years of British dominance at sea. When the battle ended, the French *Redoutable* had suffered 522 (82%) of her crew killed or wounded. This was the final violent response of Nelson's crew to the ship that killed their beloved leader.

Nelson had characteristics of a classic Charismatic/Transformational leader. As his career developed, he acquired amazing referent power due to his achievements, his personal charm, and friendly personality, his positive and energetic discussions of naval engagements, his self-confidence, and commitment to his country, and his uncanny ability to make his listener feel special. His verbal skills were evident in his *inspiring* presentations to his officers as he described his *visionary plans* before a battle and exhortations to his officers and crew invoking their loyalty to their country. He thirsted for attention and honors all his life, demonstrating the *high self-image* characteristic of many charismatic leaders. Through his quiet seductive voice, he created a shared mental map of impending battles that allowed his captains and officers to use their ability, experience, training and knowledge to respond to situations while staying within the plan. This reflected the Substitutes for Leadership theory. He also reflected some *participative leadership* by using information from his captains, holding discussions of their ideas and concerns before a battle, and delegating them the authority to act as they saw fit during an attack. He demonstrated continued and active *support/consideration* for his officers and crews, and strong *directive leadership* aboard ship, which are described in Path-Goal Theory, Fiedler's Contingency Theory and the Situational Leadership Theory. He spent considerable time in *boundary spanning* on behalf of his officers and crew, pushing the naval authorities for promotions for deserving officers and adequate provisions for his crews. Boundary spanning is addressed by Reformulated Path-Goal Theory and the Multiple Linkage Model. His leadership also included *contingent reward behavior* for deserving officers, which is found in many of the above leadership theories. Nelson's leadership can also be viewed from an Authentic Leadership perspective in that he *lived the values* he espoused of giving everything for God and country in his professional activities. His experience made him conscious of the values, needs, and perspectives of his officers and crew, he was aware of the dangerous context in which they operated, and he exuded *confidence, optimism,* and *high moral conduct* in the Navy—all elements of the Authentic Leadership model. In his private life, however, Nelson's behavior left much to be desired. Nelson's leadership could also be described via Implicit Leadership Theory for a British Naval officer in 1800. As a professional naval officer, Nelson possessed *determination, cognitive capacity, self-confidence, sociability,* and *integrity*, all of which are addressed in Trait Theories of leadership.

Discussion Questions

1. Describe charismatic leadership behaviors shown by Horatio Nelson as an officer in the British Royal Navy.
2. In what ways did Nelson demonstrate supportive/consideration leadership behaviors with his officers and crew?
3. Do you think Nelson's childhood experience is related to his constant desire for awards and recognition as well as his leadership behavior as a naval officer? If so, explain.
4. In what ways does Nelson likely fit the predominant Implicit Leadership Theory for a British naval officer in 1800?
5. Did Vice Admiral Nelson make use of any other substitutes for leadership (in addition to the ability, experience, training, and knowledge of his captains) in leading his ship and fleet during battle?

References

Horatio Nelson, 1st Viscount Nelson. (n.d.). In *Wikipedia*. Retrieved May 25, 2009, from http://en.wikipedia.org/wiki/Horatio_Nelson

National Maritime Museum. (n.d.). Research Guide N1: Horatio Nelson. Retrieved on July 6, 2009, from http://www.nmm.ac.uk/researchers/library/research-guides/biographies-cook-and-nelson/research-guide-n1-horatio-nelson

Vincent, E. (2003). *Nelson: Love and fame.* New Haven, CT: Yale University Press.

Part III

Snapshots of Bad Leadership

Chapter 27

Adolf Hitler
Chancellor of Nazi Germany from 1933 to 1945

Adolf Hitler led Nazi Germany on the most destructive and violent military campaign in modern history. During the world depression of the 1930s, he transformed Germany into a totalitarian dictatorship using ruthless and violent tactics against many of his own countrymen. He originally gained support as leader of the National Socialist Workers Party through charismatic oratory advocating anti-Semitism, anti-communism, anti-capitalism, and ethnic purity with extensive use of propaganda and theatrics in his speeches. He pursued a policy of rebuilding the German military and eventually dominated Europe through military conquest. His territorial expansion began in the mid-1930s using political threats and lack of action by the international community and culminated in the invasion of Poland in 1939. In the next three years, he and his allies over-ran most of Europe and northern Africa, threatened invasion of England, and began a prolonged attack on the Soviet Union. His conquests and rule were filled with treachery, ruthless slaughter, and extermination of civilians. He was likely responsible for the deaths of 40 million people.

Adolf Hitler was born on April 20, 1889, in a small Austrian town near the German border. His father was a customs official, and the family lived at different times on both sides of the border. There were two older children in their family, one half-brother and one half-sister, and another boy and girl were born after Adolf. Their father was a strict authoritarian who expected his commands to be followed immediately. Adolf was closest to his mother and was apparently a happy prankish boy who did well in school and aspired to be an artist. He was outgoing, learned to enjoy argument at school, and became a ringleader among the other boys. In about 1899 Adolf's younger brother contracted measles and died. This tragedy apparently shocked Adolf and his demeanor and behavior changed abruptly. He became gloomy and sullen and his school work declined. His father refused to allow him to study art, causing Adolf to be more remote and rebellious at school. Finding magazines devoted to warfare in his father's small library, he became infatuated with organizing war games with other boys. He used his powers of persuasion and demanded obedience to his orders. He read fantasy stories of warriors fighting American Indians and became lost in a dream world in which he was an artist and a great military figure.

In 1903 his father died. In 1904 he was expelled from school. His mother enrolled him in school in a different town where he boarded with another student. One year later after a serious confrontation with school authorities and an illness, he left school never to return. He lived with his mother and sister in a larger city and read, attended opera, drew, painted, and lived on a small legacy from his father and pocket money from his mother. He was enthralled with an opera by Wagner and identified with his proud, great, and remote hero. When 18, he decided to move to Vienna to study at the Academy of Fine Arts. He relocated and prepared for the entrance examination but failed twice and spent the next several years living in dingy apartments and a poor-house, selling painted postcards and taking charitable donations for a meager living. He became interested in politics and often made frenzied speeches to other residents in the poor-house. He was erratic, he dominated conversations, and would often become sullen and leave. He consumed political writings that advocated the future of Europe ruled by Germany, the power of human will, and the supremacy of the Aryan race. In 1912 he visited his brother in England and was impressed with British engineering and industry. The following year he returned to Vienna, received another inheritance, and moved to Munich, Germany, to avoid military service in Austria.

At the outbreak of World War I, he joined the German army, serving as a runner delivering messages among military units. He was remembered by others as a solitary soldier who would occasionally jump up and begin yelling about some military or political issue. He was wounded and decorated before the war ended and was appalled at the punitive conditions imposed on Germany during her surrender at the Treaty of Versailles. He remained in the army for a short time doing menial tasks and later wrote that this was when he decided to become a politician and punish those who were responsible for Germany's defeat. The political and economic situation in his home state of Bavaria was in turmoil, and a communist group (whose leaders were Jewish) seized power for a short time. Hitler became an army undercover agent and informer, identifying communist sympathizers who were arrested and executed. He attended classes in Munich on political philosophy and delivered speeches on preserving German racial purity and attacking Jews who he associated with communists. He soon realized he had a gift for oratory, giving speeches with conviction on the spur of the moment with no preparation. He could hold his listeners' attention and sway an audience, and he became an instructor of indoctrination classes for returned prisoners of war. When he spoke against the Jewish people, he obtained a roar of approval from veterans who needed to blame someone for their defeat and poverty.

In 1919 Hitler was assigned to investigate a small political party (the German Workers Party) that advocated fierce nationalism and anti-Semitism. He attended their meeting and read a pamphlet by their leader that described a new socialist world order. It claimed the Jews were responsible for all of Germany's disasters and a savior was needed to sweep Jews and communists from Germany and preserve it for pure-blooded Germans. Hitler soon joined the party and began learning from its leader who apparently saw him as the German savior. He gave Hitler books to read, introduced him to society, taught him to dress with a military style that hinted of intimidation, loaned and gave him money. They shared the core belief that Germans represented the master race.

Hitler became the charismatic spokesperson for the party, and he drew growing audiences and attracted membership. He realized speeches are remembered when accompanied by violence so he encouraged interruptions and had his bodyguards initiate violent fights with objectors. He invented terrible visions of poverty and degradation of Germans and pounded his fist on tables before describing a future Germany as the most powerful country in the world, free of Jews and free of international financial obligations. He studied the acoustics and colors of the rooms before his speeches and he would always arrive late so the audience was tired and anxious to see and hear him. He would then enter from an unexpected direction, marching across the hall with a stern fixed expression and a wedge of bodyguards in front and behind. He often attacked the Berlin government, which suited his audiences, many of them believing it was filled with corruption. He wrote much of the party's platform that demanded all Germans be united into a single Germany, abrogation of peace treaties and reparation payments from World War I, denying Jews the right to German citizenship, and war against parliamentary government. In 1921 he engineered a coup of party leadership by threatening to leave the party. The executive committee knew his name had come to represent the party and reluctantly granted his demands for dictatorial power over all party affairs. He recognized the importance of strong recognizable symbols for influencing large groups of people and he developed the heavy black swastika in a white circle on a blood red field as the party symbol. It appeared oversized and menacing on posters, flags, and armbands of his bodyguards. He changed the name of the party to the National Socialist German Workers (Nazi) Party and invented a new title for himself—*Der Fuehrer* (the leader).

With his new title, he increased his violence including physical attacks on opposing party representatives. Hitler began organizing a private army with red arm bands and swastikas. They accompanied him when he spoke and marched in the streets of Munich often with small musical bands. He would bait those who opposed him into objecting to his exaggerated rhetoric. He had directed his troopers to attack the objectors on his signal—especially if they were suspected of being communists. This group of ruffians became known as Hitler's storm troopers, and their violence increased the drama of his speeches and his popularity grew. In 1923 he attempted a takeover of the Bavarian government with distinguished military figures from World War I and other right-wing groups that also had private armies. When they marched toward the capital, they were dispersed by Munich police who fired into the street. Ricocheting bullets killed several of the plotters and Hitler fled. He considered suicide while in hiding but was soon arrested and tried for high treason. He was given nearly unlimited time to speak in his defense and he claimed strong nationalistic motives for his attempted takeover. He thus became a nationally known political figure and was sentenced to five years in prison. He received favored treatment by prison authorities who were convinced of his nationalistic sentiments. He received unlimited visitors in prison and, with their help, wrote *Mein Kampf* (*My Struggle*), his autobiography and description of his political beliefs. Although sales of the book were good at first, they slumped after one year. However, by the end of World War II it had sold 10 million copies. He was released from prison after serving only one year of his sentence.

For a short period, his party was made illegal and he was banned from public speaking. When these bans were lifted, he took direct control of the party and resumed his theatrical speaking performances. He was always able to sway his audience by appealing to German national pride, which he claimed had been disrespected by the terms of the Treaty of Versailles and the huge reparation payments Germany was forced to pay. His revived storm troopers used violence against party rivals. His party leadership was totally centralized with subordinates appointed by him, not elected, and he demanded unquestioned obedience.

The post-World War I government of Germany had never been strong and was opposed by many groups, including the Nazis and communists. The depression, which began in the late 1920s, made economic conditions in a weakened Germany even worse. Hitler exploited these weaknesses in his speeches by blaming German Parliament and the existing government for the deteriorating conditions. An early election in 1930 gave Hitler's party 107 seats in Parliament to become the second most powerful party in government. In 1932 he ran for president by openly claiming Hindenburg, who was the incumbent president, an octogenarian and his major opponent, was senile and stupid. After a runoff election, Hindenburg won with 53% and Hitler was second with 37% of the vote. Mathematics was never Hitler's strength. He ignored Hindenburg's majority of the vote, and claimed that since a 51% majority was enough to govern and he had 37%, this entitled him to three fourths of the governing power and his opponents should have only one fourth. He refused the office of vice-chancellor and, after considerable pressure from German industrialists and bankers, Hindenburg appointed Hitler as Chancellor (equivalent to a prime minister) but gave his party only three other major positions in government. In that way, he hoped to minimize the influence of Hitler's National Socialist Party on governmental affairs. But Hitler now had power and he stated he would never relinquish his power while still alive.

Hitler proceeded to prevent all others from gaining a majority in Parliament, making governing nearly impossible. He then convinced Hindenburg to hold new elections but before they were held, Hitler apparently directed the Parliament building to be set on fire and he blamed the fire on a communist plot. He already had a list of 4,000 communists and directed that they be rounded up and placed in prison, removing the communist leaders as candidates in the new election. Hitler's party conveniently won a majority of parliamentary seats in the special election. He convinced the aged and confused Hindenburg to sign special decrees that supposedly would protect the people from communist violence. These decrees eliminated constitutionally guaranteed freedoms such as privacy in telephone and postal communications, freedom of assembly and press, rights to hold one's own opinions, and the right to avoid unlawful arrest. Hitler also managed to pass an Enabling Act that gave his cabinet powers to legislate new laws. With Hindenburg's mental and physical capacities failing, Hitler's government had become a dictatorship. He banned the other major political parties and his storm troopers ransacked trade union offices.

Many of Hitler's storm troopers were thugs and criminals, and he worried they might become too powerful and unruly. In 1934, he claimed their leader was plotting a government takeover and ordered their entire leadership arrested as well as opposing politicians, military officers, and clergy who had caused him problems. There were no trials and estimates are that 1,000 people were summarily executed by Hitler's select secret service at this time, most of them in a single day. Later that year President Hindenburg died and, ignoring the constitution, Hitler forced passage of a law transferring the powers of the president to him as leader and chancellor. He now had absolute power, and no one dared to oppose him. He was supreme commander of armed forces and he changed the loyalty oath for all sailors and soldiers to have them swear complete loyalty to him personally, not to an unnamed commander and chief. He claimed public support by describing himself as Germany's savior from the economic depression, the Versailles Treaty, Judeo-communists and other undesirables.

Hitler then began rebuilding Germany's economy by focusing on rearmament of the military using currency manipulation to fund his projects. He emphasized military spending ahead of unemployment relief and introduced universal military service. In 1935 and early 1936, his speeches emphasized how Germany wanted peace, and he manipulated several international agreements with this claim while he continued to build the German military. He signed non-aggression pacts with several European countries to gain time but had no intention of adhering to them. Violence against German Jews increased, and Hitler introduced laws banning sex and marriage between Aryan and Jewish Germans and denying Jews and other non-Aryans German citizenship. In 1936 his troops occupied the Rhineland, which had been a demilitarized zone since the Versailles Treaty. There was no international reaction. He spoke of the need for German "living space" and claimed that if Germany did not have the greatest military in the world then their country would be lost to communism. He signed a pact with Italian dictator Mussolini, jointly opposing international communism and began cooperative negotiations with Japan.

Hitler had increasingly complex ceremonies conducted in Germany to honor him as the sole hero of the German people. Parades, speeches in huge halls with thousands of swastika banners, music, and colored lights all flared as he stood in front of a large red and gold background. He stood behind a bulletproof lectern and shouted into the microphone displaying carefully choreographed violent emotions. Films of these events show the almost hypnotic emotion aroused in his audiences whose obedience was unquestionable. He claimed that Austria and Czechoslovakia were needed by Germany for "living space" and to save the German economy. He threatened Austria with invasion, and they reluctantly agreed to be annexed by Germany. He did the same with Czechoslovakia in 1939. He then prepared for the invasion of Poland while claiming he wanted peace, manipulating the German press, and bribing foreign newspapers to applaud his actions. Hitler kept demanding more concessions from other countries, secretly wanting them to refuse and allow him to justify a war. Poland finally said "No," and he manufactured a phony attack by Poles against a German radio station and directed his armies to invade that country in September 1939. He demanded his soldiers show extreme brutality to terrorize their opponents and the German *Blitzkrieg* (lightning fast war of movement) overran Poland in a short time. This was quickly followed by the mass murder of Polish military officers, priests, intellectuals, Jews, and aristocracy. He had negotiated a secret nonaggression pact with Stalin in the Soviet Union and gave the Soviets part of Polish territory he had acquired in the invasion. Two days after the invasion of Poland, Britain, and France declared war on Germany.

In 1939 Hitler was 50 years old, although he looked younger. He was fastidious and acted with extreme self-confidence, was widely read, and had an excellent memory. His speeches and writings were designed to excite his audience. In many small gatherings when threats were not needed, he would begin speaking in a quiet and reasonable voice that was very convincing. But he had mastered the art of lying. Hitler described himself in a speech to his generals shortly before the Polish invasion as the greatest personality in Europe, and there were no men of action who could oppose him. He believed everything depended on him. He ordered a plan of attack on France and Britain which his generals opposed claiming the army was not ready. They did not object to war, they merely wanted more time to prepare. At the same time, he began the systematic enslavement and murder of 10 to 15 million German Jews, communists, homosexuals, physically and mentally handicapped people, trade union members, psychiatric patients, and some religious groups. In 1941 he ordered mass exterminations by gas chambers. He stated that Jews should not simply die, they should die in agony. His ruthless hatred of these groups apparently had no limits.

Hitler had ignored the advice of his generals, who he viewed as weak and overly cautious, and ordered his armies to invade Denmark, Norway, Netherlands, Luxemburg, and Belgium in early 1940. Mussolini joined Hitler's war in the same year, and Winston Churchill became British Prime Minister and leader in the war against Germany. Hitler respected the British and knew Churchill was formidable. British troops had been sent to help defend Western Europe but could not resist the German onslaught. France was overrun in late June, and over 300,000 British and French troops were barely evacuated to England in an enormous flotilla of public and private boats. Hitler had insisted his troops stop their rapid advance, believing they were moving too fast. Overruling his generals was common for Hitler since he believed he possessed outstanding military knowledge and only he had the ruthlessness he believed he needed to continue his conquests. It was simply their duty to obey.

When France surrendered, Hitler toured occupied Paris early one morning and began planning a rebuilding of Berlin with huge avenues, fortress-style buildings, and his own office with a dome three times the size of the dome of St. Peter. He saw this as a symbol of his accomplishments. Meanwhile, Churchill vowed that England would continue fighting, and Hitler ordered bombing attacks on British air bases, radio stations and ports. When his air force failed to neutralize the British flyers, he ordered mass bombings on British cities. His submarine fleet was directed to sink so many British ships that they could not resist a German invasion. But German submarines were suffering large losses in the Atlantic. Hitler made an overture to Churchill for a negotiated peace, but Churchill knew how Hitler dealt with international agreements and rejected the offer. Churchill emphasized his answer by nightly bombing raids on German cities that produced tanks. This was soon followed by British bombing raids on Berlin, and they destroyed the German landing barges being prepared for the invasion of Britain. Hitler believed he was a great negotiator, but he lacked finesse and simply lied or threatened people into complying with his desires. He tried to convince the leaders of conquered countries to join him in an attack on England, but their leaders met him with silence or diversionary questions. After the British refused to surrender, German and Italian forces invaded Yugoslavia and Greece in early 1941. Ignoring his pact with Stalin, Hitler also began an invasion of the Soviet Union.

Soviet leaders were warned of the attack by their own Foreign Service, as well as by Britain and the United States, but they ignored the warnings and made no preparations. The Germans drove deep into Soviet territory in June 1941, and Hitler believed they would overrun Moscow by winter. He directed them to wage a war of annihilation, destroying cities and murdering the population. But he underestimated Soviet resistance, and their fighting retreat was costly on the Germans, especially when German soldiers were stopped just short of Moscow as the winter set in. The German army was not prepared for the Russian winter and suffered terribly. The same thing happened in their attack on Stalingrad. The Russians slowly drove them back from Moscow and surrounded the German force attacking Stalingrad where German soldiers were freezing, starving, and running out of ammunition. Hitler continued to overrule his generals and to make erratic and irrational decisions. He refused to allow German soldiers to retreat from Stalingrad. Over 100,000 German soldiers were killed and 180,000 were captured and marched to work camps in Siberia. About 6,000 of these survived the war. On December 7, the Japanese bombed Pearl Harbor and Hitler declared war on the United States, which was the world's largest industrial and financial power. He was also at war with Britain, which had the largest empire, and the Soviets, who had the largest army in the world. His generals had always advised against a two front war, but Hitler ignored their input. In late 1942,

Germany was also losing ground in North Africa. Hitler had spread his forces too thin and overruled his generals too often.

In 1943, Mussolini was deposed in Italy and his replacement surrendered to the Allied forces. The Russians continued to push German forces back from Moscow, and British, United States, and other Allied Forces landed in France in June 1944. Hitler aides had received warnings of the landing but ignored them. He was asleep when the landing began and his aides refused to wake him. The Allies established themselves on the beach and began to move forward. German generals then knew the war would be lost.

From the beginning of his invasion of the Soviet Union, Hitler had spent the war in various forest bunkers with his aides and summoned his generals to meet him at various times. He seldom appeared in Berlin from this point on and seemed alienated from the German people. He had been extremely generous to generals who were successful in the past—granting them houses, estates, and valuable gifts. He had also been quite considerate of his personal staff and office workers—celebrating their birthdays and keeping track of their families. But as the losses mounted, his hatred of the generals grew. He refused his greatest tank commander's advice to keep a strategic reserve of tanks, using them instead like soldiers to be sacrificed at his whim. The great German General Rommel told Hitler it was hopeless to continue fighting as the Allies pushed into France. Hitler exploded in fury, telling Rommel it was not his business to worry about the war, only his troops at the front. These outbursts became common as the losses mounted, and Rommel even decided to arrest or murder Hitler, but was prevented when Hitler left for Berlin. Rommel was later forced to commit suicide by Hitler's secret service. Toward the end when it became obvious Germany would fall, Hitler ordered the destruction of the entire German infrastructure—factories, supply depots, railways, bridges, electrical and water supplies, and communications facilities. Since the war was to be lost, he stated that Germany and its people had no right to exist. Since the remaining Germans were inferior people, they should all perish.

Several assassination attempts were made on Hitler's life by Germans during the war; most involved time bombs that did not detonate. In July 1944 one bomb did detonate at his forest bunker, Wolf's Lair. Hitler was launching into one of his long presentations that always dominated his meetings when the bomb went off, killing several German officers but inflicting only minor injuries on Hitler. He ordered the execution of the German officers who planned the attempt, as well as everyone else who might have been remotely involved. This resulted in about 2,000 executions.

As the Allies moved into Germany, Hitler retreated to his chancellery office and bunker in Berlin with his close staff, secret service officers, and his mistress, Eva Braun. He continued to insist that his troops must never retreat, resulting in enormous losses of German soldiers. He fantasized about the V-2 rockets he had used to terrorize England and his secret bomb that would change the course of the war. He screamed at people and ranted about his incompetent and traitorous generals. Some of his military advisors wondered why the German army kept fighting when they all knew they would lose. The answer was because Hitler ordered them to do so. To the end, Hitler seemed to believe that he was the only one who had maintained his honor, their losses were the result of errors by others, and his only fault was he was not ruthless enough. In fact, he had the secret service flood the Berlin subway tunnels to hinder the Russian advance, drowning several thousand Berliners who had used them as refuge. As Soviet forces invaded Berlin and advanced on his bunker, he made a last will and testament, married Eva Braun, and said goodbye to his staff. He and his wife retired to his bedroom. The staff expected him to commit suicide and began singing, playing records, and talking in loud voices, which they had never before done in Hitler's bunker. His secret service officers entertained several young women in their quarters. Hitler and his wife actually waited until the next day to end their lives. Hitler shot himself and Eva Braun took cyanide.

Hitler's leadership is often described as that of a "Dark Charismatic." He demonstrated many of the behaviors and personal characteristics of other charismatic leaders. His ability to address German frustrations with *inspirational speeches* that appealed to national pride was most notable. His rhetoric is said to have hypnotized his audiences and he made extensive use of *symbols* and *ceremony* that added to their effects. He clearly had a high *need for power* which characterizes most charismatic leaders. His excellent memory and wide reading gave the impression of a keen *intelligence* that impressed most followers and the media. Most leadership scholars do not consider Hitler a Transformational Leader because of his destructive tendencies and the disaster he brought on the German people and all of Europe. But his policy of rearmament did transform the German nation from an underemployed depressed economy into a single focused country with high employment and considerable unity of purpose. Many of Hitler's behaviors are described in Transformational/Charismatic Theories of leadership. His eventual impacts remind us that the power of charismatic leaders can be highly destructive.

Hitler was also extremely directive in his leadership. His authoritarian directions and punitive style necessitated complete obedience and represents an extremely severe form of *directive leadership*. He was very *considerate* and *supportive* of his personal staff and of the generals who were successful in military campaigns. He used *contingent reward behavior* with successful generals by granting them homes and estates and was highly *punitive* of those who were not successful. Several of these leadership behaviors are described in contingency theories of leadership including the Multiple Linkage Model, Path-Goal Theory, Situational Leadership Theory and Fiedler's Contingency Theory. Although Hitler believed he was an excellent *negotiator*, his typical strategy was to either threaten his negotiating partner to force his compliance or to lie and agree to terms that he had no intention of following. Eventually others learned of his duplicity and refused to cooperate with his threats and did not believe his lies. In the end, his external *boundary spanning* was not effective as others refused to comply with his demands in negotiations. Boundary spanning leadership is described in the Multiple Linkage Model and Reformulated Path-Goal Theory of Leadership.

Hitler's leadership can also be viewed from the perspective of Implicit Leadership Theory because he adhered to a prototype of German military leadership that was outdated. His style of requiring absolute obedience and using draconian punishment was typical of 18th century Prussian military leaders. It was no longer appropriate for 20th century military campaigns with separate armies that required general directives from the top and subordinate military leaders exercising considerable freedom in troop and munitions movements. His attempt at military leadership resulted in terrible losses of German military personnel and equipment that hampered the German war effort. Hitler's *determination* and *dominance*, as well as his *self-confidence*, reflect Trait Theories of leadership. His complete *lack of integrity, poor cognitive capacity* regarding strategic military issues, and his *erratic psychological/social behavior* included narcissistic and psychopathic elements which represent major flaws in his leadership traits.

Discussion Questions

1. Why was Adolf Hitler's vision of a future Germany so attractive to German citizens?
2. What do you think were Hitler's most important capabilities that made him able to attain so much power in Germany?
3. Why do you think some charismatic leaders become cruel and destructive of their followers and others, while other charismatic leaders are constructive and supportive of their followers?
4. Is it possible that another leader could attain the power and destructiveness of Hitler in today's world? If so, how can this be avoided?

References

Adolf Hitler. (n.d.). In *Wikipedia*. Retrieved February 15, 2011, from http://en.wikipedia. org/wiki/Adolf_Hitler

Megargee, G. (February 17, 2011). Hitler's leadership style. British Broadcasting Corporation-History. Retrieved from http://www.bbc.co.uk/history/worldwars/wwtwo/ hitler_commander_01.shtml

Payne, R. (1973). *The life and death of Adolf Hitler*. New York: Praegers.

Roberts, A. (February 17, 2011). Secrets of leadership: Hitler and Churchill. British Broadcasting Corporation-History. Retrieved from http://www.bbc.co.uk/history/ worldwars/wwtwo/hitler_churchill_01.shtml

Chapter 28

Albert Dunlap
Corporate Executive

Al Dunlap was an American corporate executive who became known for his ruthless downsizing and turnaround tactics based on layoffs, plant closings, and deceptive business practices. His career peaked in the 1990s when Wall Street fund managers and analysts became devoted to a management philosophy known as "shareholder value creation." This philosophy meant that corporate managers should pursue a single strategy—maximizing a corporation's stock price in the short term to add to stockholders' wealth. Dunlap carried this philosophy to extreme by sacrificing people and his companies' long-term welfare to benefit himself and his closest associates while making many fund managers and large investors wealthy. When his deceptive and fraudulent tactics became widely known, he was fired from his position as CEO of Sunbeam Corporation and prohibited by the Security Exchange Commission from serving as an officer or board member of any publicly held company in the United States.

Dunlap was born on July 26, 1937, in Hoboken, New Jersey. His middle-class family was loving and proud of their son who was pampered with nice clothes and supported in his school activities. He was athletic, muscular, and performed well in school and in sports. But he had a short temper and grew red with anger when things did not go his way. Later when describing his youth to reporters, he claimed he was a poor kid who had to fight his way out of poverty. This fabrication became typical of Al Dunlap. He attended the United States Military Academy at West Point where he was not happy but with family support and assistance from friends, he managed to graduate near the bottom of his class.

He served the required three years in the army in Maryland where he met and married his first wife in 1961. She was younger than Al and impressed with his military bearing and self-confidence. He demanded she dye her hair blond even though it irritated her scalp, he regularly inspected the house for dust, threatened to leave when she became pregnant, insisted the baby be kept in its room so as not to create a mess in their apartment, and did not provide enough money for her and their young son. She divorced him after two years, and a judge found Dunlap guilty of extreme cruelty. Although Dunlap became very wealthy in his career, he paid only $15 per week child support at first and later $150 per month until their son reached his 18th birthday, at which point he stopped all support for his son.

After his divorce, Dunlap left the army in 1963 and accepted a position in Wisconsin as management trainee with Kimberly-Clark Corporation that produced paper-based consumer products. He worked hard trying to learn all the jobs in the plant and was promoted to shift supervisor. He also met and married his second wife who accepted her subordinate role. In 1967 he landed a position as general manager of a small pulp and paper company that was having financial troubles. The elderly owner was a tough business person who developed a liking for Dunlap. Dunlap began laying off workers and cutting costs that resulted in threats on his life but also improved company profits. He did not seem to mind being hated. The owner died after seven years, and the company was sold. Dunlap then moved to American Can where he was placed in charge of two divisions. He closed plants, laid off workers, sold off assets, cut research and development shortly before company patents expired, and refused to increase production capacity even when plants were running at full capacity and the market was growing. He was brash and uncaring about his cutbacks and showed a complete lack of consideration or support for those who worked for him. His division profits improved quickly but subsequent managers were forced to reinvest and rebuild the two divisions that he had starved for resources.

He left American Can in 1982, worked for a short time at Manville Corporation, and then landed his first CEO position at Lily-Tulip, maker of paper cups and plates. The company was owned by investment bankers after a leveraged buyout and they wanted their investment to grow. Dunlap soon terminated most of the executives, half of the managers, and 20% of the staff. These actions added to the bottom line, and the company began showing a profit. He started attracting the attention of the Wall Street media as a corporate turnaround expert and was hired by Sir James Goldsmith, a financier who owned several companies and became Dunlap's mentor. Both men disdained traditional corporate managers who believed in considering multiple stakeholders in decision making, including employees, communities, customers, and suppliers as well as stockholders. Goldsmith rewarded Dunlap for cutting and slashing costs in his companies and eventually introduced him to a friend who owned a media empire in Australia. Dunlap worked for the media tycoon for two years, but their styles did not match and he left his position early and $40 million richer. He had made multiple millions from Lily-Tulip and Goldsmith so he returned to the United States a very rich man.

In 1994 Dunlap was hired as CEO of Scott Paper Company, a 100-plus-year-old producer of household paper products. Scott had been the victim of intense competition in recent years and its old line management seemed incapable of the changes needed to adapt to a new competitive environment. Within two months Dunlap announced layoffs of over 11,000 employees at all levels. He bragged to the press that he fired 9 of the 11 Scott executives in the first week—another fabrication. Although he claimed to employees and Wall Street analysts that he was building up the company, it soon became clear to insiders that he was pumping up short-term profits to sell the company. Similar to his actions in earlier positions, he stopped equipment maintenance, corporate charitable giving, community activities by managers, conferences with suppliers, hiring, and training. He also cut research and development by 60%, and sold everything Scott made until there was no finished goods inventory. He pushed sales people to increase sales by offering huge discounts (which were not shown on company books for several months) but booked the sales immediately at full price for reporting purposes. These tactics resulted in tremendous increases in reported profits, and Scott's share price moved up fast to the delight of investors and stock fund managers. He kept the managers he wanted by offering them rewards of huge stock options to convince them to stay with the company. Most of them understood that he planned to sell the company soon and they would be made rich.

Dunlap was now a favorite of Wall Street. He was interviewed many times on television and he published articles in top business publications on promoting shareholder value. He used clever sayings, short jokes, and well-rehearsed speeches to entertain potential investors and convince them to invest in Scott. Twenty months after joining Scott, when its stock was wildly inflated, he engineered its sale to Kimberly-Clark Corporation and left the company with $100 million for his efforts. Although many Scott executives were either fired or found other jobs during Dunlap's tenure, a sizeable number of those who remained became millionaires from their stockholdings. The sale was completed in late 1995, and Dunlap had projected $100 million in income for Scott in the last quarter of that year. When all the sales discounts became due, Scott actually lost about $60 million for that quarter.

Although very wealthy, Dunlap missed being a star on Wall Street. He had been labeled Chainsaw Al or Rambo in Pinstripes by the press and saw himself as a pirate captain—taking whatever he could and showing no compassion for his victims. In 1996 two investment fund managers had taken control of Sunbeam Corporation, maker of household appliances, and wanted a turnaround expert for a CEO to increase the value of their investment. They pressured members of the board of directors to hire Dunlap, who basically wrote his own contract with a $1 million salary and multiple millions in stock and stock options. He began firing executives and recruiting greedy and opportunistic managers who would do his bidding for the promise of riches. He told his associates they could increase corporate profits in one year, sell the company, and walk away rich. He hired Russell Kersh as vice-chairman and chief financial officer. Kersh had been with him at several other companies and did whatever Dunlap asked. Some managers in Sunbeam referred to Kersh as "Al's trained puppy" because he praised Dunlap at every opportunity and did not resist unreasonable demands. Dunlap called him a creative accountant.

Dunlap used a well-known consulting firm to plan his cutbacks. He never waited for their final reports before cutting personnel and only criticized them if their proposed cuts were too small. Shortly after joining Sunbeam, he bragged he would cut their 26 plants to four or five. Many of his plant closings made no economic sense and were done simply to impress Wall Street investors that he was maintaining his reputation as a cost cutter. He almost never fired anyone himself, preferring to have his lieutenants give the news to those being fired. In his first month he terminated three of the four top Sunbeam operating executives, who managed 90% of Sunbeam's revenue producing operations and had 40 years of company experience. Not long afterward he fired the fourth executive. He pressured his benefactors, the fund managers who had recruited him and who dominated the board of directors, to help him reconstitute the board with his handpicked friends and associates who would support his decisions. This resulted in Dunlap gaining total control of Sunbeam with no overall control of his actions by the board.

As CEO, he dominated the board and controlled the information they were allowed to see. No other CEOs served on the board and no members had extensive operational business experience. They were largely kept in the dark regarding his deceptive accounting and marketing tactics. His presentations to the board were described as similar to watching television with the volume turned on maximum. His words flowed in a constant stream without pause, as if he never took a breath. He constantly yelled at managers, berated and insulted them in front of their colleagues, and told them to "shut up" when they tried to answer his questions. He avoided detailed discussions of corporate strategy and operational problems by lapsing into stories of his successes at Scott and Lily-Tulip. He wore a bullet proof vest and began carrying a handgun, which increased the intimidation of his executives and managers. He grew red and threw things in meetings, pounded his fist and knocked water containers from tables, and kept a body guard close at hand. He apparently sexually harassed a young female employee who settled out of court in a lawsuit with Sunbeam.

At Sunbeam he cut headquarters staff from over 300 to 100, closed plants and regional offices, and moved their headquarters to a location near his home in Florida. He implemented a "buy and hold" policy whereby large customers like Wal-Mart, Kmart, and Target were offered huge discounts on merchandise to convince them to stockpile Sunbeam products for 20 to 30 months ahead but were allowed to delay payment until well after they took delivery. Sunbeam leased warehouses where these products were stored until the retailer needed them but Sunbeam booked these sales at full price when the "buy and hold" sales agreements were signed. Dunlap also sold Sunbeam's replacement parts inventories and accounts receivables—usually at large discounts—to increase cash flow. Budgets kept shrinking, new product development stopped in most of the company, and Sunbeam stopped paying its bills or resorted to partial payment. Sales commissions were withheld, increasingly generous credit terms were given to large customers, and other deceptive accounting practices were used to artificially increase sales and profit figures.

When Dunlap met with large retail customers, he showed no interest in their supply problems, lapsing again into exaggerated stories of his business success, and giving out signed copies of his book, *Mean Business*. This put off Sunbeam customers who later asked that Dunlap be excluded from their future meetings. Some Sunbeam executives began to resist Dunlap's poor decisions by delaying plant closings and not firing people or delaying their firing until their stock options were vested. Dunlap maintained his charisma when speaking to admiring stock analysts and financial reporters, touting new water and air filter products that were supposed to be available soon. These products were actually far from market ready and never worked as advertised. But Wall Street was still largely ignorant of Sunbeam's real status and saw Dunlap as a great turnaround CEO. Fifteen months after joining Sunbeam, the stock price was highly inflated and he was looking for a buyer for the company. With the inflated stock price and emerging information about possible losses at Scott Paper, no buyers were found.

Sunbeam executives knew that the deceptive tactics in their company would soon damage their financial picture and something must be done to save their enormous gains from the stock they had received from Dunlap. When no buyer was found for Sunbeam, Dunlap decided to acquire Coleman, maker of outdoor and camping equipment, Mr. Coffee, and smoke alarms. The inflated price of Sunbeam stock was expected to help pay for these acquisitions, and accounting adjustments involved with combining their operations would disguise the real financial condition of Sunbeam. When Dunlap met with the sophisticated financier who owned Coleman, Dunlap exploded and insulted the man when he insisted on a high price for Coleman's stock. Coleman's owner laughed at Dunlap's histrionics, and Dunlap stormed out. Eventually, Sunbeam executives excluded Dunlap from the negotiations and paid the high price to complete the acquisitions, although Sunbeam borrowed heavily to pay for Coleman. Dunlap later performed with his usual adeptness when describing the acquisitions to the admiring press.

During Dunlap's tenure at Sunbeam, several employees wanted to change or reveal the accounting and marketing tactics being used to pump up the stock price but their recommendations were squelched by executives. During the first quarter of 1998, Sunbeam executives could no longer hide the low sales results and Dunlap was forced to issue a press release that sales would be below expectations. Sunbeam's stock price began to fall. Sunbeam executives and managers were busy finding other jobs and the stock fell 25%. A few Wall Street analysts looked carefully at Sunbeam's operations and realized what was happening. One analyst published an article in a top level finance journal asserting that Sunbeam's 1997 earnings were the result of deceitful accounting. Fund managers began withdrawing their buy recommendations for Sunbeam's stock, and its price fell even more. One Sunbeam executive finally revealed Dunlap's deceptive tactics to the board of directors who immediately called a meeting with Dunlap and his vice-chairman—Russell Kersh. When they began to question Dunlap about the deceptive tactics and the real condition of Sunbeam, he became angry and threatened to leave the company and collect a large severance package. He ranted about not getting any support from the board, did not answer their questions, and walked out of the meeting saying he was going to London to promote his book. Soon after this meeting, on June 13, 1998, the board fired Dunlap via conference call. His vice-chairman was also dismissed.

The board then learned that sales were even worse than they expected and the company might default on $1.7 billion in loans that were obtained to finance the recent acquisitions. Sunbeam was also borrowing money through a revolving line of credit to meet its payroll. The Security and Exchange Commission (SEC) began an investigation of Sunbeam's operations, investors and bond holders began to file lawsuits against the company and Dunlap, and the stock price eventually fell to $5 per share from a high of over $50 per share. A new CEO was brought in to lead a recovery, but Sunbeam eventually filed for bankruptcy two years later and the remaining stockholders lost everything. The SEC charged Dunlap and his closest executives with fraudulent practices and each settled for fines of $500,000 or less. In the SEC settlement, Dunlap was prohibited from ever being an officer or director of any publicly held company in the United States. Dunlap settled the stockholder class action suits for $15 million. In the six months he worked for Sunbeam in 1998, he obtained almost $27 million and he wanted more. In a court judgment, he eventually collected another $5 million in severance pay and other benefits. His so-called turnarounds had been a smoke screen but his fame and hard-nosed style had fit Wall Street's image of an effective executive. He was later selected by Portfolio.com, a business news service, as one of the worst CEOs of all time.

Al Dunlap's leadership style was intimidating and demanding. His *directive behavior* relied on his formal authority and intimidating tactics to make others fear the consequences if they did not comply with his demands. He offered large salaries, stock grants, and favorable stock options as rewards to executives if they helped him in his deceptive practices, promising them huge riches when the stock price rose to new heights. He threatened them with firing and loss of their stock if they did not comply. His *reward* and *punishment behavior* was his major tool in keeping executives on board to maintain the deceptive tactics. When addressing large customers or other business people outside the company who were interested in doing business, he often disappointed and sometimes insulted them. He also alienated division managers and other executives inside the companies he led. His *negotiating skills* consisted of threats or the promise of huge riches through deceptive tactics. He was therefore very poor at *boundary spanning* and showed almost no *consideration* and *supportive behaviors* toward those who worked for him. Several of these leader behaviors are described in the Reformulated Path-Goal Theory, the Multiple Linkage Model, Fiedler's Contingency Theory and Situational Leadership Theory. Dunlap's relationships with other executives and managers could seldom be considered *close exchanges*, with the possible exception of his hand-picked vice-chairman. Most executives were *outgroup* members, as described in the Leader Member Exchange Theory. Al Dunlap's leadership style fit the Implicit Leadership Theory of many large investors, fund managers and Wall Street analysts during the 1990s, when their greedy quest for maximizing stockholder value drove stock prices to new heights using whatever tactics that worked. His *determination* and *self-confidence* are consistent with Trait Theories of leadership, but his *lack of integrity* and *poor social skills* with colleagues violate the recommendations of Trait Theories.

Discussion Questions

1. Why was Al Dunlap viewed as an effective turnaround specialist for so long?
2. What do you think of the interpretation of "stockholder value creation" that was popular on Wall Street in the 1990s?
3. Was Dunlap a charismatic/transformational leader? Why or why not?
4. What can we learn about corporate leadership from the Al Dunlap experience?

References

Albert J. Dunlap. (n.d.). In *Wikipedia*. Retrieved February 18, 2011, from http://wikipedia.org/wiki/Albert_J._Dunlap

Byrne, J. A. (1999). *Chainsaw: The notorious career of Al Dunlap in the era of profit-at-any-price*. New York: Harper Collins.

Chapter 29

Idi Amin

*President of Uganda
from 1971 to 1979*

Idi Amin was a Ugandan military officer who, in 1971, led a coup against the Ugandan government and had himself appointed president of that country. During his military career, Amin demonstrated brutality and cruelty towards prisoners and he continued this behavior as president. His administration became known for harassment, torture and murder of civilians and political opponents. His decisions were based on whim rather than logic and feasibility and he was eventually feared and hated by most of the Ugandan population. He was ousted from power in 1979 by Tanzanian and Ugandan rebel forces and died in 2003.

Idi Amin was born in a small remote village in northern Uganda near the Sudanese and Zaire/Congo border. He was part of the Kakwa tribe, which was not generally prosperous, and his poor family farmed for their food. He was raised in the Kakwa tradition that less fortunate individuals became servants of those who were successful. Little is known of his father, but Amin attended mission schools until the fifth or sixth grade where he learned to speak Swahili and English. He eventually grew to 6 feet, 3 inches tall and 230 pounds and was very athletic.

Uganda had been a British colony from the late 1800s, and the British army recruited young men in the northern provinces who had few opportunities and little education. In 1946 he joined a British military unit in Uganda named the King's African Rifles. Recruits received no political education; they were simply expected to carry out orders. Amin served in actions in several neighboring

colonies and became known for his obedience and respect for higher level officers, as well as his commitment and ferocity in carrying out orders. All of this
impressed British officers, and he was eventually promoted to second lieutenant.
He was described as cheerful, humorous, and energetic, but often brutal. He
was charged with cruelty for breaking limbs and killing some cattle thieves after
arresting them. Although the charges were squelched by higher level British officers, Amin used brutal wartime methods in every confrontation and this never
changed throughout his life. Although he performed his duty as a British officer,
he never gained the British sense of honor or loyalty to a civilian government.

When Britain granted independence to Uganda in 1962, Amin was one of
only two Ugandan commissioned military officers; both were promoted to captain and a year later to major. A military mutiny occurred in several African
countries in 1964 including Uganda, with African soldiers and officers demanding higher pay and the ouster of British officers from their army. Their demands
were granted making soldiers very well paid in their country. Amin was promoted to lieutenant colonel and given command of a battalion of soldiers. When
the southern Buganda tribe tried to oust Ugandan Prime Minister Obote, Amin
led an attack on the Buganda king's palace, killing several hundred Bugandans
and forcing their king to flee in exile. This action solidified Amin's relationship
with Prime Minister Obote. However, Amin had been implicated along with
Obote in illegal activities, involving the gold and ivory trade with Zaire/Congo.
Once again the charges were squelched and Amin was promoted by the prime
minister to army chief of staff. His rival Ugandan officer had connections with
the Bugandan tribe and was therefore isolated in a lower position.

Amin liked the power of his new military position. He enjoyed giving directives and having them obeyed without question. He often drank and joked with
his soldiers, which flattered them, and he became popular with his men. He
rewarded them to keep their loyalty—giving them extra rations, food items
for their families that were hard to obtain, imported clothing, and expensive
watches. Meanwhile, Obote humiliated the Bugandans and allowed his secret
police to harass, loot and assault Bugandans. Amin did not object to the Bugandans' treatment, but disliked the conflicts this created between southern and
northern tribal Ugandans in the armed forces. An unknown number of deaths
occurred within the army from these conflicts and Amin spent much time traveling quickly to the points of conflict to address them and restore discipline. He
spent the next five years expanding the Ugandan army by recruiting heavily in
the northern provinces and in southern Sudan, among tribesmen who were loyal
to him. He was gaining allies and they became a large part of the Ugandan army.
Over time, Prime Minister Obote's control of the country came to depend on the
army's backing, and Amin controlled the army.

In 1966, Obote had several of his government ministers and Amin's military rival arrested and jailed. He then gave Amin command of both the army and air force. Obote became president in 1967 under a new constitution and abolished the ancient kingdoms in Uganda that were the focus of the major tribes. Obote was badly injured by an assassin in 1969, and Amin was suspected, but he managed to block the investigation. Obote imposed a national emergency, dissolving all political parties except his own. He gave a free hand to the hated secret police to arrest and imprison suspected perpetrators, cut army wages, and divided the army into two segments with one made up of his own tribesmen who reported to him alone. Amin resented this division. Obote also began nationalizing banks, insurance companies, mines, and transportation companies with little promise of payment to the owners. Security declined in the country, criminal gangs increased their activities, and Obote clashed with Amin over many of these changes. Obote was concerned about Amin's growing power, but he could not have Amin arrested because Amin controlled much of the army. It appears that he developed a plan to have Amin replaced.

In early 1971, while Obote attended a conference in Singapore and the head of his secret service was in England, army soldiers apparently intercepted a call from Obote with instructions to have Amin arrested. The soldiers took action to prevent this and notified Amin, who took charge and carried out a coup, appointing himself head of the Ugandan government. Obote fled to Tanzania, and Amin released political prisoners from jail, with soldiers and many common people rejoicing. He stopped the nationalization of Ugandan industries and several western governments were delighted that the Ugandan trend toward socialism had been stopped.

At first, Amin appointed civilian and British-trained officials as his government ministers and listened to their advice. But he soon became bored because he did not understand them and felt they were wasting his time. Within a few months he was ignoring them and making decisions on his own without their input. He then required them all to join the army and take an oath to defend him as head of state and had himself promoted to the rank of general and president for five years. President Nyerere in neighboring Tanzania refused to recognize Amin as president of Uganda and supported training of troops loyal to Obote to overthrow Amin. Amin promised guerilla troops who opposed him that they would be pardoned and freed if they surrendered their weapons. He did not keep this promise and tribal conflicts increased in the army resulting in hundreds of deaths. Obote was a member of the Longi tribe. At the time Amin took power, about 40% of the army was Acholi and Longi tribesmen; one year later two thirds of these had been killed by troops loyal to Amin.

Amin began visiting heads of state in Israel and Britain asking for military aid to invade Tanzania. Israel, who had supported development in Uganda in the past, refused and Britain gave some aid but not the jet fighters and bombers he requested. Amin returned to Uganda without the military support he wanted only to confront a coup against his government, which claimed the lives of several of his loyal officers. Two American journalists investigating the coup were kidnapped and killed, apparently by army personnel. Although those responsible for the murders were identified, they were never punished and Amin paid some compensation to the journalists' families. He then began courting Arab leaders in southern Sudan, Egypt, Iraq, Saudi Arabia, and Libya for financial aid. Libya was rich in oil money, and Amin began claiming to be a devout Muslim and that Uganda was a Muslim nation, even though Christians far outnumbered Muslims in Uganda. He stopped all cooperation with Israel and supported the Palestinian cause, apparently to appeal to the preferences of Gaddafi, the Libyan head of state. Gaddafi responded with economic and military aid to Uganda.

The Ugandan people wanted lower taxes, lower cost of living, and increased security with an end to widespread robberies, arrests, kidnappings, and murders. The Ugandan treasury was empty, and money was owed to Israel that Amin refused to pay, so he could not afford to decrease taxes. If he decreased the cost of living, Ugandan peasant farmers would revolt. So he decided to eliminate the middlemen in Ugandan commerce, which was dominated by Asians whose families had come to Uganda during the colonial period and contributed to its commercial development. Asians had worked hard as store keepers and tradesmen, and had tried to preserve their ethnic identity. They were generally successful, many were doctors, accountants, and managers, and some had developed large agricultural holdings in Uganda. They were also resented in Uganda and other post-colonial African countries due to their reputation for taking economic advantage of native Africans and for staying aloof. Eventually, Amin expelled all Asians, claiming they hoarded wealth and Ugandan products and were harming the economy. Their expulsion was popular with many Ugandans who shared the belief that Asians had exploited them. Their businesses were confiscated and turned over to Ugandans who were often military officers. The new owners had little or no experience in commerce and no working capital with which to operate their business and most soon failed—leaving the Ugandan economy in worse condition than before the Asian expulsion.

Amin eliminated Obote's hated secret police and replaced them with two units of the police and army that carried out torture and murder of those suspected of threatening the government. They bore the harmless sounding names of the Public Safety Unit and the Bureau of State Research. Amin issued a directive that allowed soldiers to hunt down and arrest or kill bands of robbers. This gave soldiers, who often wore civilian clothes, the power to make and enforce the law with little or no accountability and many became robbers, rapists and car thieves themselves. Meanwhile, Amin continued to persecute previous supporters of Obote and many were executed in groups while in prison. Several escaped to Tanzania and publically reported the executions, which Amin denied. In 1972 he attended a conference of the Organization for African Unity and was quite popular at first as a new African nationalist leader whose anti-colonial policies included expelling the unpopular Asians and Israelis. Amin often used humor in speeches to disarm listeners and to disguise his cruelty. He entertained other attendees at the conference with humor and courtesy until he offered to show them how to suffocate a man with a handkerchief, explaining that he had often used the technique during his military days. They were not amused. He returned to Uganda to confront another attempted coup and had its leaders murdered, leaving 36 hours after his return to tour other Islamic countries for more aid.

A British diplomat met with Amin to object to the expulsion of Asians, many of whom held British passports. Amin was unresponsive and later admitted he understood almost nothing of what the diplomat said. Shortly thereafter all British military trainers were told to leave Uganda. The same day, Obote supporters invaded Uganda from Tanzania and were repulsed. During the battle, several British citizens including journalists were arrested and watched as other prisoners had their heads smashed with sledgehammers. Amin eventually severed all diplomatic relations with Britain. Amin had become a tyrant who had Obote associates and tribesmen hunted down and killed. This was followed by similar treatment of intellectuals with higher education. Amin felt threatened by their education because they saw through his deceptions. He directed the murders of the chief justice of Uganda's highest court, the vice-chancellor of Uganda's top university, the former president of the Bank of Uganda, and many military and political officials. He became sadistic in his treatment of prisoners, humiliating them in front of others before he had them murdered.

Amin loved to watch movies of wartime and apparently imitated the leaders he watched, but knew nothing of careful diplomacy. He considered himself anti-colonial and his vision was a Uganda controlled by Black Africans, but he knew nothing of public administration or what should replace a colonial government. He simply had power and no idea how to use it. He was only semi-literate so he found office work difficult, giving all his directives orally. He treated his government ministers like a dreaded drill sergeant treated raw recruits—slapping the face of one minister who brought him disappointing news. He was a one-man ruler whose ministers were prevented from objecting to his directives due to fear of retaliation. Consequently he made terrible mistakes in administration and international relations. He publically stated that Hitler was a great leader and that he and the Nazi party were correct in murdering six million Jews. The international community was stunned. Amin was a classic African "Big Man" who could be both charming with friends and visitors and ruthless with suspected enemies. He appealed to Ugandans at first because he came from a poor background and spoke to them on their own level, as well as being tough, humorous and uneducated with the courage to stand up to superpowers such as Britain and Israel.

Amin welcomed Palestinians and set aside 1,000 acres for their settlement. In 1976 when Palestinians hijacked an Air France passenger plane originating in Israel and brought it to Uganda, Amin welcomed them. He soon released passengers who were not Israelis, although the French crew and some others refused to leave, but detained the Israeli passengers. Finally a group of Israeli commandos rescued the hostages at Entebbe airport, although one Israeli hostage who was in the hospital was later murdered.

In 1977, religious leaders in Uganda wrote a letter to Amin complaining of the atrocities being committed by the army. Amin responded by accusing the Catholic archbishop of plotting against his government, which the archbishop denied. Amin had him arrested along with two other military officers and they were murdered while in custody. In 1978 the poor were not being helped by his government, only the military was benefitting. The economic infrastructure had collapsed due to neglect, incompetence and corruption. The population was increasingly unhappy and his supporters were dwindling. Mutinous Ugandan soldiers and some high level officials fled to Tanzania to join those opposing Amin. Amin accused Nyerere of helping the dissidents and invaded Tanzania. In 1979 Nyerere's army along with Ugandan dissidents counter attacked and drove Amin's army back to the Ugandan capital of Kampala. Amin then fled the country by helicopter to Libya. One year later he received sanctuary in Saudi Arabia, which gave him a generous subsidy in return for staying out of politics. He died of apparent kidney failure in Saudi Arabia in 2003. International agencies have estimated that Amin's government was responsible for the murder of as many as 500,000 people in Uganda.

Idi Amin was clearly an autocratic tyrant who held unlimited power in Uganda and was cruel and oppressive to anyone who challenged his government. His form of *directive leadership* was *authoritarian* and demanded absolute obedience with almost no freedom of action. This obedience was enforced by the constant *threat of severe punishment* for anyone who objected to his actions. But he generously *rewarded* those who cooperated with him by giving them businesses, land, food, clothing, jewelry, and money. Although Amin's form of these leader behaviors is not recommended by leadership scholars, these basic leader behaviors of directing, rewarding and punishing are described in the Reformulated Path-

Goal Theory and Multiple Linkage Models of leadership. Amin developed an *in-group* of people who were largely military officers. He relied on this in-group and they were loyal to him and his patronage, as described in the Leader-Member Exchange Theory. He fit the prototype of the African "Big Man," patterned after the legendary Zulu warrior Chief Shaka who was brave, cruel, and built a huge empire. The importance of leader prototypes is described in the Implicit Theory of Leadership. He made efforts at *external boundary spanning* with other countries to obtain military and economic aid, with limited success. He also had little success at *internal boundary spanning* by failing to resolve conflicts among different tribal members in the army and within his own government. This leader behavior is described in the Multiple Linkage Model and Reformulated Path-Goal Theory of leadership. He demonstrated *determination* and *drive* through his energy, initiative, perseverance and dominance. He was *self-confident* with high *self-esteem*—describing himself as a hero, prophet and the most powerful person in the world. He loved attention and was often very *sociable* and *friendly* with visitors, other heads of state and his army personnel. But he clearly *lacked the integrity* of a truthful and principled leader and did not possess the *cognitive capacity* to grasp the necessities of developing and leading a post-colonial government. Similar to Hitler, Amin's narcissistic and psychopathic behaviors were major defects in his leadership. This is addressed in Trait Theories of leadership.

Discussion Questions

1. In addition to the torture and murder of Ugandan citizens, in what other ways was Idi Amin a bad leader?
2. Did Idi Amin do anything that is characteristic of a good leader? If so, what actions of his were exemplary of good leadership?
3. How do you think current African citizens can overcome the leadership prototype of the African "Big Man?"
4. Are in-groups essential for a leader's success?

References

Idi Amin. (n.d.). In *Wikipedia*. Retrieved May 26, 2011, from http://en.wikipedia.org/wiki/Idi_Amin

Kyemba, H. (1977). *State of blood: The inside story of Idi Amin*. London: Corgi Books.

Listowel, J. (1973). *Amin*. Dublin: Irish University Press Books.

Melady, T. & Melady, M. (1977). *Idi Amin Dada: Hitler in Africa*. Mission, KS: Sheed, Andrews, and McMeel.

Chapter 30

David Koresh
Religious Cult Leader

David Koresh was born Vernon Howell (no relation to the author) in Houston, Texas, on August 17, 1959. His mother was 14 or 15 years old at that time and unmarried, although they lived with the father, Bobby Howell, for two years. After his father left, Vernon was passed back and forth between his grandparents and his mother and stepfather until his late teens. He was hyperactive and had a learning disability so he was difficult to handle and did not do well in school. He later stated he was mistreated by his stepfather and was sexually molested by other boys. He was eventually placed in a special needs class and called "Mr. Retardo" by other kids, an experience that shocked him and that he frequently mentioned in later life. His mother belonged to the Seventh Day Adventist (SDA) Church, and David attended this church from childhood. The Christian Bible fascinated him, and his mother reported that by the age of 14 he had memorized a major part of the New Testament. He dropped out of school in the 11th grade and began working as a carpenter and repairman, skills he apparently learned from his stepfather. At age 18, he began seeing a 16-year-old girl and moved in with her family. When she became pregnant, her father threw Vernon out. The relationship ended, and the girl later gave birth to Vernon's first daughter.

Two years later, he was attending an SDA church in Tyler, Texas, and impressed the congregation with his passion for the Bible and knowledge of scripture. When he announced that he had had a vision from God who told him he was to have the pastor's young daughter for his wife, the pastor banned him from seeing the girl. Undeterred, he continued seeing her, which resulted in two pregnancies that miscarried. Vernon also reported having other visions during this period; he believed God called on him to interpret the Bible as God's word for his people. He attended a series of seminars during this time dealing with the Book of Revelation—the last book in the Christian Bible—and it became a focus of his attention. Revelation describes images of beasts, sinister horsemen and natural disasters that are complex and often interpreted to represent a final confrontation between Heaven and Hell at the end of times as we know it. Many Christians believe it predicts future events shortly before the return of Jesus Christ and the restoration of a new Kingdom of God on earth. These events include much fire and suffering by believers before the new kingdom is created. The Book of Revelation is heavily emphasized in the SDA church, and Vernon claimed to have new insight to its teachings. He began to disrupt services in the church by ranting and raving about his visions and interpretations and this, combined with his relationship with the pastor's daughter, resulted in him being removed from the church roles and told not to return.

At age 22, Vernon had been alternately rejected by his father and grandparents, possibly sexually molested and/or beaten by his stepfather, called Mr. Retardo by other children, failed at school, and thrown out of the SDA church and the family he lived with. He also believed he had visions that showed his direct relationship with God. Soon after this, he visited Mount Carmel near Waco, Texas. This communal living facility was the home of the Branch Davidians, an offshoot of the SDA Church. He apparently had heard that their leader, Lois Rodin, was a living prophet of God. He studied their literature that emphasized Biblical scripture, began returning to do odd jobs for the group, and impressed them with his carpentry and mechanical skills. They were also amazed by his memory of the Bible and his speaking skills that inspired many members during the Bible studies he attended.

Vernon soon began having an affair with Lois Rodin, who was in her late 60s. Her late husband had led the Branch Davidians until his death and had emphasized preparations for establishing the new Kingdom of God in Israel. Lois had inherited his leadership position and in 1983 she supported Vernon in presenting a series of seminars at Mount Carmel describing what God had revealed to him. He titled his presentations the "Serpent's Root" studies and they established his position with Branch Davidian followers as an inspirational prophet with a true message from God. He visited Israel with Lois several times and became de facto co-leader of the Branch Davidians. This did not suit Lois's son, George, who was absent from Mount Carmel but had assumed he would become the leader after Lois's death. Hearing of the situation, George returned and listened to Vernon's presentations and the reaction they created among the followers. He promptly threatened Vernon, who wisely left the facility, taking with him a subgroup of Branch Davidians who were, by now, devoted to his teachings. They established their own primitive communal settlement about 40 miles from Mount Carmel with Vernon in charge.

Vernon wrote to George Rodin, explaining that he was the sickle wielding angel described in the Book of Revelation and he was to gather designated believers and lead them to Israel for the restored Kingdom of God. His vision was that he was God's spokesperson who would reveal the mysteries of God as told in Revelation. In 1984 he married Rachel Jones who was then 14 years old and the daughter of one of the most influential members of the Branch Davidians. He eventually fathered three children with Rachel. Vernon and Rachel returned to Israel in 1985 where he reported having another vision. Several Russian cosmonauts had reported seeing seven angelic beings while in space. The beings were flying toward earth, and Vernon claimed to have met with them near Mount Zion. He said these beings explained to him the final mysteries of Revelation. When they returned to the United States, he had renewed intensity and began to question Lois and George Rodin's leadership at Mount Carmel.

For the next two years, Vernon concentrated on spreading his message about the Bible and recruiting people inside and outside the United States to join his movement. His style was described as low key and conversational with a slow Texas drawl, and he was extremely confident in his message. In 1987 George Rodin, who had assumed leadership at Mount Carmel, challenged Vernon to a contest to see who could raise a person from the dead. George had exhumed a body of a Branch Davidian who had died years earlier and placed the body in the Mount Carmel chapel. Vernon went to the sheriff and placed a complaint of corpse abuse against George. The sheriff said he needed proof, so Vernon and some followers went to Mount Carmel and took pictures of the coffin. The sheriff needed further proof that there was a body in the coffin, so Vernon and seven followers returned to Mount Carmel armed and a gun battle began between George and Vernon's group. Apparently, they were poor marksmen because the battle lasted some time and all were arrested with only George having minor wounds. Vernon was soon released on bail and George began pestering the court with documents containing profane accusations about the law enforcement officers and courts. He was jailed for several weeks for contempt of court, and the eventual trial resulted in all Vernon's followers being found not guilty of attempted murder and a mistrial for Vernon. His charges were eventually dropped. George was subsequently released, but not long after he murdered a man and was committed to a mental institution where he died in 1998.

Lois Rodin had died, George was out of the way, and Mount Carmel was now vacant so Vernon raised money from his followers to pay off overdue taxes on the property and moved his followers in. He led his followers at Mount Carmel with authoritarian directives about their diet (mostly vegetarian), work tasks, and living conditions, which evolved over time. Only the communal kitchen had running water. He financed the group by establishing an automobile repair shop and a seamstress business, donations from wealthy members, and eventually a gun show booth where they bought and sold firearms and military-style survival gear. Members were expelled when they refused to follow his rules. Vernon spent considerable time in LaVerne, California, outside of Los Angeles, ostensibly as a base for recruiting new members and promoting his musical group. He also used this location to establish his claim to the right to have sexual relations with any woman he chose from the Branch Davidians. In 1989 he had announced his "New Light Vision" in which he was given the right to have sex with all unmarried Branch Davidian women, including some who were very young. In one case, he stated God had told him to have a child with his wife's 12-year-old sister. After much discussion, she and her family complied and she became pregnant at 13 and bore his child at 14. Later, he modified his New Light doctrine to allow him to have sex with married women in the Branch Davidians. He directed their husbands to have no further sexual contact with their wives and to become completely celibate. He convinced most of the members that it was part of God's plan. One member later reported Vernon had sex with at least 15 women and girls and fathered 17 children with them. He stated that his children would become the wise elders surrounding the king's throne in the new Kingdom. He sometimes described himself as a "sinful messiah" with a Biblical reference to a king who married virgins and had children who were princes.

While most members saw Vernon as sanctified by God and knowing God's will, almost divine, others rebelled at his sexual exploitation of young girls and women. One high level member left the Branch Davidians after he watched a 13-year-old girl report to Vernon's room and spend the night with him. This individual reported Vernon's exploits to authorities and alerted parents outside the group to the plight of their daughters in the "House of David," as his harem was described among members. Several law suits and custody battles resulted, and some women left the group to protect their children. He directed several unmarried men in the group to marry his women, probably to conceal the fatherhood of their children and possibly to prevent deportation of those from outside the United States. A representative from Child Protective Services visited Mount Carmel to investigate reports of child abuse with a wooden paddle used to discipline children, but no charges were brought. Vernon's sexual exploits continued, and he began to lose followers in Australia and California. He spoke metaphorically of being put to death because of his wives and claimed that Revelation predicted he and his followers would suffer a violent death.

In 1990 he changed his legal name to David Koresh to signify the Biblical Kingdom of David which they believed would be restored as the new Kingdom of God in Israel. Koresh apparently believed he would be the physical ruler of this new kingdom and Jesus Christ would be the spiritual ruler. Koresh was the Hebrew name for Cyrus, a Biblical leader who freed the people of Israel and encouraged rebuilding of the temple in Jerusalem. Koresh's confidence and narcissism never seemed to decrease and his near godly status was unmatched at Mount Carmel. His listeners were awed at his ability to string together seemingly disparate Biblical passages and make apparent sense of them. He told them that Revelation provided the code to interpret all of human history as recorded in the Bible and he was chosen to unlock that code for the people. His power over members clearly increased over time.

At some point, a delivery truck driver accidentally broke open a box addressed to Mount Carmel. Inside were a large number of hand grenades that had been disarmed. When delivering another load to the Branch Davidians, he noticed a shipment of explosive material that could be used to rearm the grenades. He reported this to authorities who began an investigation. They found a local gun dealer who had sold the Davidians well over 200 firearms and many were semi-automatics, meaning they fired once each time the trigger was pulled and released. Investigators also confirmed that Mount Carmel had received materials that could be used to convert these guns to fully automatic status, meaning the gun would continue firing repeatedly as long as the trigger was depressed. This is similar to the operation of a military machine gun. Possession of automatic firearms was legal as long as they were registered and a $200 fee was paid, but no such firearms had been registered by the Branch Davidians.

Koresh and the Branch Davidians knew they had attracted attention of the authorities and were being observed. Military-style helicopters frequently hovered over Mount Carmel and several new residents had moved in across the road from the compound. One of these, who was an undercover agent for the federal Bureau of Alcohol, Tobacco and Firearms (ATF), began visiting Mount Carmel masquerading as a potential recruit. Most members knew he was a government agent, but Koresh treated him well and began teaching him about his message. Meanwhile, custody suits were proceeding against Koresh with much damaging testimony from previous Branch Davidians and the media had become interested in Mount Carmel. Although in Texas it was legal for young girls to marry at 14 with their parents' permission, having sex with younger girls was statutory rape. Although Koresh may have addressed child abuse charges and dealt with the gun and explosive stockpiling in court, he undoubtedly knew he was guilty of child rape. He told members that "Babylon" would attack them soon and they must prepare. Babylon was a code name for what Koresh viewed as corrupt United States society and government. He began showing graphic war movies, required the children to watch, and they debated how the attack would come and whether the government would use tanks against them.

The ATF obtained warrants to search for illegal firearms and explosives. Surviving Branch Davidian members later claimed that the ATF falsified some of their evidence to obtain the warrants. There may be a basis for this claim, since the ATF was badly in need of a visible success to restore its reputation after an earlier botched raid that killed the wife and son of a person they sought. Its future funding was also in jeopardy. But it appears they had good reason to believe there were illegal firearms at Mount Carmel and after the raid numerous fully automatic weapons were found in their compound.

The ATF decided on a heavily armed approach to the Mount Carmel compound, which was a large two-story structure with multiple rooms. On February 28, 1993, armed ATF agents appeared at the front door, which was opened by David Koresh. He spoke with them briefly indicating there were children in their compound, then slammed the door, and shooting began. It is unclear who began the shooting, but the firing from both sides was intense and several agents and Branch Davidians were killed or wounded. Shooting lasted for about two hours when a cease fire was called to allow the ATF to evacuate its dead and wounded. Koresh had been hit twice, in the hand and torso, but was able to continue functioning as their leader. Soon after the cease fire, the Federal Bureau of Investigation (FBI) took charge and a 51-day siege began with the FBI having surrounded the compound. During this siege, Koresh talked extensively with government negotiators and a local radio station, explaining his scriptural message and his mission with the Branch Davidians. The FBI appeared uninterested in his theology, even though several consultants advised them that it was likely the key to achieving a peaceful end to the siege. The FBI had electricity to the compound turned off. They apparently assumed that the Davidians would eventually tire of the siege and the mothers would place their children's physical welfare as their first priority and give up. This was a mistake since it underestimated many of the Davidians' devotion to Koresh and his mission. Apparently Koresh did not require members to stay in the compound, and about 35 people did surrender during the siege, several with children. Surrendering adults were apparently separated from their children and jailed. Many of the mothers remaining in the compound learned this and decided not to give up. Eventually, the FBI escalated its tactics by installing large bright lights and loud speakers directed at the compound 24 hours a day to prevent the occupants from sleeping. A local sheriff who was friendly with Koresh tried unsuccessfully to broker a surrender.

During the siege, the Davidians watched as Koresh seemed to suffer physically and spiritually, yet he stuck to his vision that the attack represented Babylon coming to destroy them just before the new Kingdom of God was to be established. He described himself as the lamb at the end of days and told them only a little more time would pass until his believers would be redeemed to join the new Kingdom. At one point, he told them they had arranged to surrender and many were relieved. But he changed his mind at the last moment, telling them God had told him to wait. On April 19, after 51 days, the FBI decided on a final assault that included masses of tear gas injected into the compound to pressure the Davidians to leave. After the gas was injected into the building, a fire started. The residue of this gas, perhaps combined with spilled kerosene from damaged lanterns and a flash grenade used by the FBI, may have been the cause. Others believe the Davidians started the fire themselves. The fire spread quickly resulting in several large explosions when propane tanks were heated. All were killed in the compound except nine who escaped the fire. After the fire, Koresh was found with a bullet hole in his forehead, apparently administered by another Davidian. Many women and children died of smoke inhalation and their bodies were terribly burned in the fire.

Over 80 Branch Davidians died in the ATF attack, FBI siege, and fire including two stillborn babies born during the fire. Four ATF agents were killed. It seems clear that the government agencies involved made several poor decisions that contributed to the disaster. It is also apparent that David Koresh possessed much of the blame for the horrible tragedy experienced by his faithful followers.

David Koresh exhibited many of the characteristics of a *charismatic* leader. He truly *inspired* his followers with his knowledge and zealous interpretation of Biblical scripture, his *vision* of their role in a future Kingdom of God on earth, and his *mission* to unlock the mysteries of God from the Book of Revelation. He *stimulated their thinking* about what was necessary to follow God's word and qualify for redemption from their sinful ways. His extreme *self-confidence* and apparent *need for power* are also consistent with most theories of Charismatic Leadership. Although these properties are also characteristic of transformational leaders, Koresh was lacking in a single characteristic of Transformational Leadership in his apparent lack of true consideration for many of his followers. He was also an *authoritarian directive leader* who allowed no variation from his rules and regulations that governed Mount Carmel. Recall that directive leadership is not necessarily authoritarian, but Koresh's style allowed for no exceptions. He did not solicit *participation* from other Branch Davidians in making decisions, preferring to justify his directives with his own interpretations of Biblical scripture. These leader behaviors are described in Path-Goal Theory, Situational Leadership Theory, Fiedler's Contingency Theory, and the Leadership Grid models of leadership. He offered followers the *contingent reward* of salvation and a primary place in the new Kingdom of God if they were faithful to his teachings and directives. He also used *contingent punishment behavior* in expelling some followers who refused to follow certain of his rules. These leader behaviors are described in the Reformulated Path-Goal Theory and the Multiple Linkage Model of leadership. Although Koresh made an effort to represent his message, mission, and group to outsiders, he appeared to be ineffective at resolving conflicts and satisfying authorities who were investigating and besieging Mount Carmel. His *boundary spanning* behavior was not effective and is also described in the Multiple Linkage Model and Reformulated Path-Goal Theory. Much of Koresh's behavior and zealous preaching apparently fit a traditional Implicit Leadership Theory of evangelistic religious leaders. Although his *determination* and *self-confidence* are described in Trait Theories of leadership, his personal traits of *narcissism, visions of grandeur* and *sexual perversion* prevented him from being truly considerate and supportive of his followers. Koresh is an excellent example of the danger that accompanies charismatic leaders who are self-oriented and narcissistic.

Discussion Questions

1. Why do you think David Koresh had such strong influence over the Branch Davidians?
2. How can individuals protect themselves from the potential dangers of charismatic leaders like Koresh?
3. Can you think of any leadership neutralizers or substitutes that might be used to counter the influence of leaders like Koresh?
4. Can you think of other charismatic leaders like Koresh who are not affiliated with religious movements?

References

Bailey, B. & Darden, B. (1993). *Mad man in Waco*. Waco, TX: WRS Publishing.

Newport, K. G. C. (2006). *The Branch Davidians of Waco: The history and beliefs of an apocalyptic sect*. New York: Oxford University Press.

Thibodeau, D. (1999). *A place called Waco: A survivor's story*. New York: Public Affairs.

Chapter 31

Kenneth Lay
CEO of Enron Corporation

Kenneth Lay was an American business executive best known for his position as CEO of the infamous Enron Corporation until it declared bankruptcy and he resigned in 2002. Lay's leadership and Enron's practices were the focus of one of the largest corporate scandals in United States history. The charges included accounting fraud, bank fraud, securities fraud, and providing false and misleading statements to numerous stakeholders. In 2006 Lay was convicted on 10 counts of fraud and other charges and he died from a heart attack several weeks later.

Ken Lay was born in 1942 in Tyrone, Missouri. His family was poor and they lived on small farms without inside plumbing until he was 11 years old. His father had several jobs over the years including serving as a lay minister for his church. Ken began working at a young age on paper routes, raising chickens, and driving tractors—while dreaming of a business career. The family finally settled in Columbia, Missouri, where all three of their children attended the University of Missouri. Ken excelled in college where he was strongly influenced by a popular economics professor. He was both intelligent and popular and served as president of a large fraternity. His professor convinced him to stay to complete a master's degree in economics, and Lay built relationships that he would use throughout his life.

He was married in 1966 to a college sweetheart and began working for Humble Oil as an economist and speechwriter for the company CEO. He worked there for several years and began taking classes toward a PhD in economics. He then joined the Navy and obtained a posting to the Pentagon, thanks to the influence of his former economics professor. He worked in military procurement, which became the topic for his doctoral dissertation. After leaving the service and obtaining the PhD, his former professor, who was working for the Federal Power Commission, hired Lay as his top aide. The professor left his post after 18 months, and President Nixon appointed Lay as Undersecretary of Energy in the Department of the Interior, where he obtained an unusually high salary and became a key spokesman for the president's energy policy.

In 1973 the United States suffered an energy crisis that included high gasoline prices, as well as electrical and natural gas shortages. Lay concluded the crisis meant big changes for the energy business and decided to return to the business world.

He used a contact from an earlier conference to obtain a position as vice president for corporate planning with Florida Gas. He was promoted to head of the pipeline division the next year and became company president the following year (1979) when the previous president resigned. He began an affair with his secretary, divorced his wife in 1981, and called his previous boss to obtain a position in Houston as president of Transco Energy Company. Transco owned 10,000 miles of pipeline and provided gas for most of New York City and other eastern states. The federal government controlled gas prices, and producers claimed the price did not support new exploration. Pipeline companies were having problems with "take or pay" contracts they had signed with producers to take a certain amount of gas whether they needed it or not. Lay used his folksy style speaking skills effectively and became a vocal advocate and national spokesman for government deregulation of natural gas. He also set up a spot market for natural gas to allow producers (who were willing to cancel their "take or pay" contracts with Transco) to sell directly to end users with Transco transporting the gas. In 1984 Lay was recruited by Houston Natural Gas (HNG) to become its CEO and Chairman of the Board of Directors.

Lay anticipated federal deregulation of natural gas prices and began divesting HNG of non-pipeline divisions and acquiring more extensive pipeline networks. He reasoned that the company with the largest network would dominate the industry. In the following year he was contacted by InterNorth Inc., a very large pipeline company in Nebraska, who wanted to buy HNG. Lay and his staff conducted intense negotiations with InterNorth over the next two weeks, resulting in the acquisition of HNG and the astonishing agreement that Lay would be made CEO and board chairman in 18 months. The current CEO was soon forced out and Lay became CEO in less than 18 months. Lay made $3 million profit on his HNG stock with this acquisition and now controlled the largest gas distribution system in the United States—almost 40,000 miles of pipeline. He asserted his new power by moving the company headquarters to Houston and slowly forced out old InterNorth directors, replacing them with his own directors. They renamed the combined company Enron, and it showed a $14 million loss its first year of existence. Lay needed a new profit center for the company.

InterNorth had a small division in New York City they renamed Enron Oil. This group bought and sold contracts to deliver oil at a certain price in the future. The New York Mercantile Exchange had begun trading standardized oil contracts in 1983. The market for these contracts grew quickly, and speculation by Enron Oil earned millions for Enron in 1985 and 1986. Enron Oil also established phony companies and unrecorded bank accounts that were used to manipulate profits from quarter to quarter to show steady increases in earnings. This was helpful to Enron because it resulted in steady increases in Enron stock prices and avoided triggering short-term Enron loans whose stock was posted as collateral. This accounting chicanery was illegal, but Enron took no action to change it. Lay and his executives also ignored the fact that the two top people at Enron Oil siphoned off almost $4 million from the company to their personal accounts. One Enron executive warned Lay that Enron Oil was not operating above board, but Lay did nothing as long as they made money for the corporation. This was apparently the beginning of many accounting frauds used to manipulate reported profits at Enron.

Then Enron Oil took too many short positions on oil as the prices climbed and created potential losses of over $1 billion—an amount that could ruin the company. Suddenly Enron executives appeared shocked at the illegal dealing of the Enron Oil speculators. Lay claimed in front of Enron employees, bankers, and stock analysts that he knew nothing about the violations. Other Enron executives knew Lay was lying, but said nothing. The executive who had warned Lay about Enron Oil, took over their oil trading operation and used shrewd trading to cut their losses while Lay played dumb about the earlier deceptions. In 1988 Enron showed a book profit of $108 million, mostly from the sale of assets they claimed were recurring earnings. This was another accounting sham that no-one seemed to notice. Stock analysts and investors were high on Enron stock and they bought the story Lay gave them about Enron being a new kind of energy company for the future.

Also in 1988, a consultant from McKinsey and Company who had worked with Enron proposed that Enron start a gas bank. Enron would contract to buy gas from producers and to sell it to users at a specific price in the future—similar to the contracts by Enron Oil. They would make money on the price spread and eliminate user uncertainty by assuring adequate supply during cold snaps. They could often contract to sell gas before they bought it, because they knew the prices around the country and could move the gas at will on their own pipelines. They thus frequently knew their profit before they signed the contracts. The consultant was named Jeff Skilling, and he was hired him to run the gas bank. Once the gas bank was started, Skilling had his staff begin trading the buy and sell agreements just like commodity futures and Enron became a different company. It had the assets to move gas, and knowledge of the industry that no other company possessed. They created derivative securities that allowed someone to buy or sell gas in the future at a certain price. They used "mark to market" accounting procedures to value their contracts at the time they were signed. This allowed Enron to record the estimated profits based on unrealistic future sales price estimates and to inflate current earnings, long before any cash was received from the contracts. Enron traders obtained huge cash bonuses when the contracts were signed. These "paper profits" became the drivers behind Enron's steady increases in reported earnings that drove up its stock price. These "profits" were exploited and made millions for its executives and traders, who were given generous stock options based on Enron's reported earnings and increases in its stock price. Amazingly, accountants assigned to Enron from the prestigious Arthur Anderson firm did not object to these accounting methods nor did the Securities and Exchange Commission (SEC). Lay approved of these "profits" and bonuses for executives and traders and benefitted incredibly from the stock options and bonuses he continued to receive.

Enron established another division for international operations that included natural gas companies, electric power plants and water utilities. They also started a domestic electric power division and a broadband division. All these operations absorbed tremendous capital, created huge bonuses when deals were signed, helped increase the stock price and executive wealth, but brought in very little cash. Lay represented Enron to foreign dignitaries such as Prince Charles and Margaret Thatcher, regularly played golf with Bill Clinton, raised money for political candidates who were favorable toward Enron's activities, and was given the nick name "Kenny Boy" by George W. Bush. He made sure Enron executives were well rewarded financially while the company stock soared. But there appears to have been no overall control from Lay on Enron's operations. He became divorced from operations when Skilling was promoted to chief operating officer. Divisions operated independently within the Enron culture of moving fast, signing deals, collecting huge bonuses, and moving to the next deal. No one seemed concerned about managing these contracted projects once they were signed. Enron policies were violated with impunity as long as people made "bookable profits." When Enron did manage a project, such as providing electricity to California, they apparently abused their power over distribution systems to hike prices, which created horrible publicity for the company. Their billing systems were inaccurate and not timely. It appears that no one within Enron was directing operations to assure their contracts were carried out in a timely and efficient manner.

Enron's debt was growing fast to provide the cash to fund the trading, bonuses and other operations. They began creating special purpose entities (SPEs), which were often limited partnerships created to shield Enron's financial statements from the huge debt they needed when cash income was far below reported income. These SPEs were supposedly independent business organizations with outside investors and were not shown on Enron's balance sheet. But they were often started by Enron executives who made tremendous profits from their fees and deals with Enron using insider information. The SPEs would own Enron stock and use it to borrow money they then allowed Enron to use for its operations. Technically, the loans were owed by the SPEs but Enron was also responsible for their payment, even though these obligations were not shown on Enron financial statements.

Throughout the 1990s, stock analysts and investors were blind to these financial and accounting deceptions—they loved this new type of energy company. *Fortune* magazine applauded Enron's creativity, Harvard University faculty prepared cases for class discussion that commended Enron's success and its business model, and the dean of the Stanford Business School served on Enron's Board of Directors and chaired the audit committee. What could be wrong with this company? Its stock continued to climb, and Lay got the credit. He developed his image as a community leader, an advocate of continued energy deregulation, and a visionary leader of the top energy company in the world. But his colleagues at Enron found him easy to manipulate. When things were going well, almost anyone who threatened to leave got a big raise. He threw money at problems, ignored conflicts, and allowed Skilling and his Chief Financial Officer (Andrew Fastow) to operate uncontrolled—as long as they booked increasing profits and the stock price continued to climb. Lay and the board even waived adherence to Enron's conflict of interest rules for key executives involved in the SPEs. Lay loved to say that Enron provided energy to people who needed it and frequently cited Enron's vision and values—respect, integrity, honesty with accurate communication, and excellence. In truth, the only value that really characterized Enron was excellence in making deals and money for its executives and large investors. Lay was called on when Enron needed a speech or meeting to obtain cooperation from a state, federal or foreign governments, Wall Street analysts, banks or investors. In 2000 he changed Enron's vision from the World's Leading Energy Company to the World's Leading Company. At its peak, Enron was the seventh largest company in the United States with the market value of its stock reaching $70 billion.

For several months in 2001, Skilling replaced Lay as CEO with Lay remaining as Chairman of the Board of Directors. But by this time Enron's web of mark-to-market energy contracts that produced little cash, SPEs that hid huge debts, and poor management in the electrical, broadband and international divisions were creating problems. The company was having trouble meeting debt obligations and generating enough cash for operations. The bull market on Wall Street ended in early 2000, stocks started to decline, and analysts and investors started asking questions about highly valued companies like Enron. Articles began appearing that questioned mark-to-market accounting procedures and analysts and fund managers started investigating. Lay defended these methods, referring to Arthur Anderson's approval of their accounting methods, and insisted to employees and investors that Enron was healthy and thriving. Meanwhile, Lay, Skilling, and other Enron executives were quietly selling their Enron stock. Enron was also selling assets and recording the profits on the sales as recurring earnings from operations. This was a deception to disguise losses in several divisions. When investors and Wall Street analysts became suspicious, the company's stock began to decline, which threatened to trigger payoffs on loans in SPEs that used Enron stock as collateral. Enron was also obligated on these loans if the SPEs could not repay them, which was usually the case. As the Enron stock price fell, debts became due, cash was drying up, and more questions were asked. Lay was occupied selecting the interior decor for the new $45 million corporate jet he had ordered for Enron.

Skilling resigned a few months after becoming CEO and Lay resumed his position. He immediately announced that there were no problems with Enron. At that moment, the company had a negative cash flow of over $1 billion for the preceding 6 months and other executives were leaving Enron. Employees greeted Lay at an employee meeting with continued applause as their hero who would save the company after Skilling had created so many problems. He announced a grant of stock options to all employees for 5% of their base pay—assuring them the stock price would bounce back soon. The next day he flew to New York to assure analysts that Enron was healthy.

Sherron Watkins was an Enron vice president and previously an Arthur Anderson accountant. She had investigated Enron's SPEs and approached Lay with the news that SPE loans would soon be triggered for payoff and Enron could not pay them. She pointed out the accounting deceptions, conflicts of interests by Enron executives, and violations of security laws, and Lay said he would investigate them. He immediately called the law firm that set up the SPEs to have them investigate, which resulted in a whitewash. Lay also consulted another law firm to determine if he had grounds for firing Watkins, but was advised against it. More investigative articles appeared on SPEs and Enron was forced to report losses from eliminating some SPEs that lowered Enron's stated income. The SEC began investigating Enron, and Arthur Anderson began shredding documents related to their business with Enron. Lay began calling friends in Washington to ask for help—including Treasury Secretary Paul O'Neill, former Treasury Secretary Robert Rubin who was then at Citigroup, Alan Greenspan, and others. No help was offered. Lay then tried to sell Enron to another energy company but the deal fell through when the other executives learned about the hidden debt and accounting chicanery at Enron. Enron's credit rating was lowered, which triggered more loans. Numerous lawsuits appeared against Enron, including suits by employees who had lost their retirement savings and personal capital when the stock price fell by 99% from its highest value—while Lay was assuring them the company was healthy. The stock price fell to under $1, and the company declared bankruptcy on December 2, 2001. This became the largest bankruptcy in United States history. Lay had authorized paying out $55 million in bonuses to high level Enron executives just days before the bankruptcy.

Lay was subpoenaed to appear before the Senate Commerce Committee but refused to answer questions, claiming protection under the Fifth Amendment of the Constitution. He was eventually charged with 11 counts of conspiracy, fraud, and making false and misleading statements and was convicted on 10 of the charges. He died from a heart attack a few weeks after the conviction. Numerous Enron executives pled guilty to similar charges and others were tried and convicted. Thousands of Enron employees lost their jobs and many lost their retirement savings that they had invested in Enron stock at Lay's recommendation. The prestigious accounting firm of Arthur Anderson was found guilty of destroying evidence and eventually ceased operation after many clients moved on to other accounting firms. Much of Enron's apparent financial performance had been fictitious, the result of accounting and financial duplicity, and thousands of lives were damaged while Enron executives made scores of millions in personal income and lived in luxury.

Enron employees, investors, stock analysts, bankers, and academics viewed Ken Lay as a *charismatic/transformational* leader during most of his career at Enron. He emphasized the *vision* of Enron as the world's leading energy company and eventually the world's leading company. He stressed Enron's espoused *values* of respect, integrity, honesty, and excellence. He used *intellectual stimulation* and *inspirational rhetoric* by describing Enron as a new model for business organizations and a stimulating environment for employees to create new value for the company and themselves while bringing energy to those who needed it. He projected his own image of an ethical, religious, socially responsible leader. And he appeared to be *considerate* of his subordinates by serving them drinks when aboard the company jet, listening attentively with apparent interest, and lavishing them with expense accounts, bonuses and huge stock options. Lay clearly had a high *need for power* from a high position in business throughout his career. These leader attributes are described in most theories of Charismatic/Transformational leadership. Yet Lay's rhetoric was deceitful and Enron was filled with internal competition, political maneuvering, and self-promoting behavior by executives who modeled Lay's behavior of basking in luxury and compiling personal fortunes at the expense of employees, investors and customers. Enron's declared values were farthest from the minds of most of its executives. Lay also used extensive *leader reward behavior* to buy and maintain employee loyalty throughout Enron's 16-year life. Lay also relied heavily on *boundary spanning* behavior, as he represented Enron to employees, investors, analysts, officials, banks and other firms that affected Enron's operations. He was a skilled negotiator during most of his career. These behaviors are described in the Multiple Linkage Model and Reformulated Path-Goal Theories of leadership. Over time, Lay developed an *in-group* at Enron composed of Skilling and a few other key executives, demonstrating the dynamics described in the Leader Member Exchange Theory. He possessed *self-confidence, cognitive capacity,* and was very *sociable,* but his *integrity* and *honesty* left much to be desired. These personal traits are described in the Trait Theories of leadership.

Discussion Questions

1. During the 1990s, Lay was celebrated as a charismatic/transformational leader by academics and Wall Street alike. Do you think his celebrity status harmed Enron? If so, how and why? Does this mean that charismatic/transformational leadership is dangerous?
2. How important were Lay's extensive activities in boundary spanning for Enron? That is, did his many meetings and social engagements with government officials, foreign dignitaries, politicians, and speeches at conferences and to employees, help Enron significantly? Why or why not?
3. What were the major factors that contributed to Enron's unethical and illegal activities?
4. Early in his career, Ken Lay was known as a workaholic and highly involved in the operations of his organizations. Why do you think he became

divorced from operations as Enron grew and allowed Skilling, Fastow, and others to run Enron's operations until the company was ruined?

5. Do you think large organizations need two leaders—one for internal operations and one for external boundary spanning? Why or why not?

References

Bradley, W. (2002, January). Enron's end. *The American Prospect*, Retrieved June 23, 2011, from http://www.thirdworldtraveler.com/Corporations/Enron's_End.html

Kenneth Lay. (n.d.). In *Wikipedia*. Retrieved June 6, 2011, from http://en.wikipedia.org/wiki/Kenneth_Lay

Lease, D. R. (2006). *From great to ghastly: How toxic organizational cultures poison companies—the rise and fall of Enron, WorldCom, HealthSouth, and Tyco International* [Working paper]. Norwich, England: Norwich University.

McLean, B. & Elkind, P. (2003). *The smartest guys in the room: The amazing rise and scandalous fall of Enron*. London: Penguin Books.

Tourish, D. (2005). Charismatic leadership and corporate cultism at Enron: The elimination of dissent, the promotion of conformity and organizational collapse. *Leadership, 1*(4), 455–480.

Index